BREAD MACHINE BAKING—

PERFECT EVERY TIME

Also by Lora Brody

BREAD MACHINE BAKING—

PERFECT EVERY TIME

75 FOOLPROOF RECIPES FOR EVERY BREAD MACHINE ON THE MARKET —INCLUDING YOURS

Lora Brody *and* **Millie Apter**

William Morrow and Company, Inc.

New York

Grateful acknowledgment to Zojirushi for the loan of a bread machine.

Library of Congress Cataloging-in-Publication Data

Brody, Lora, 1945–
    Bread machine baking—perfect every time : 75 foolproof recipes for every bread machine on the market—including yours / Lora Brody and Millie Apter.
    —Rev. ed.   p.   cm.
      ISBN 0-688-14565-5
      Includes index.
      1. Bread.   2. Automatic bread machines.   I. Apter, Millie.
    II. Title.
    TX769.B79   1996
    641.8′15—dc20   95-487
                                                                     CIP

Printed in the United States of America

First Revised Edition

   2 3 4 5 6 7 8 9 10

BOOK DESIGN BY MICHAEL MENDELSOHN/MM DESIGN 2000

To all friends—especially
mothers and daughters—who
cook together

CONTENTS

ACKNOWLEDGMENTS

I wanted to do something really special to thank my mom, Millie Apter, for writing this book with me, and for working so hard to make it a big success. Her eightieth birthday last January presented me with the perfect opportunity. I took her to Club Med in the Bahamas, where she won first prize in the costumed lip-sync contest doing Madonna's "Like a Virgin."

"Mom," I said with amazement, "I didn't realize you knew the words to that song."

"I made up my own words," she said. "Moving my fanny around like that reminded me of something we know so well, so I was singing 'Like a Bread Machine . . . like a bread machine.' " Good old Mom, never a dull moment. Thank God.

Two other people helped not only to make this book possible but to make the recipes transcend the ordinary and reach the level of the extraordinary. Karen Slater and Lynne Bail in addition to testing every recipe (sometimes three and four times) added many brilliant creations of their own. Their combined hard work, enthusiasm, patience, wisdom, support, and friendship made working on this project very special for me. The other person who kept my life sane when I realized this was not going to be a book of 75 recipes, but of 504, was Deb Stanton, typist and organizer par excellence.

A great big hug of thanks goes to my friend Rita Fried of Brookline, Massachusetts, who, some years ago, put the bug in my ear about bread machines. Rita, if you hadn't proved their magic by force-feeding me a slice, this book would never have seen the light of day.

Endless thanks to P. J. Hamel and Ellen Davies at *The King Arthur Flour Baker's Catalogue,* who were always at the other end of the phone when we needed their sage advice. The King Arthur flours were a joy to use; we tested all the recipes with them. To order King Arthur products by mail, see page 339. Thanks as well to Susan Kennedy, who furnished us with a generous supply of the Kenyon Corn Meal Company's fine stone-ground products, as well as dozens of great baking tips.

In addition, I'd like to thank Elinor Nelson, who worked on this second edition. Elinor tested recipes and proofread and organized material. Her skill, endless patience, and good humor made this awesome job a lot easier.

I am so very grateful to the following people who sent me bread machines as well as offering me technical support and information: Mark Balsama at Panasonic, Tatsu Yamasaki at Zojirushi, Linda Griffen at Williams-Sonoma, Cheree Vons and Joanne Turchany at West Bend, Barbara Westfield at Breadman, Pat Boehm at Betty Crocker, Marilyn Wise at Toastmaster, Ken Normura at Pillsbury, Ann Hanson at Black & Decker, Chris Lazlo at Oster and Sunbeam, Adeline Halfman at Regal, Robert Sisco at Hitachi, Eilene Finneran at Sanyo, and Tom Lacalamita formerly at Welbilt.

I am grateful to Ada Lai, who writes *The Magic Bread Machine Letter*, for sharing her vast knowledge of baking and bread machines.

Thank you, David Strymish, at Jessica's Biscuit, who planted the idea (I hope you sell a million), and to my wonderful editor, Harriet Bell, who was quick to buy it. Hats off to my beloved agent, Susan Ginsburg, who promptly cranked up her trusty bread machine and tried out the recipes. A special thank you goes to copy editor Kathy Antrim, who turned chaos into calm; another goes to my dear friend Debbie Jacobs for her proofreading expertise.

Thank you to all the people who offered us ideas, recipes, and encouragement. Special thanks to my family, who sampled, critiqued, advised, and never complained when yet one more night I served bread—and only bread—for dinner.

Finally, a special thank-you to Mary Manning who single-handedly has sold more books than anyone. Keep up the good work!

Lora Brody

....

When Lora approached me with the idea of sharing in the magic of baking bread with bread machines my immediate reaction was one of joy. Lora chose me! Surely she felt that we could plan and work well together, and that our combined love of baking could meld into an even higher esteem of each other, and it has.

Along the way it became one great adventure. More times than not, the results were rewarding despite the repeated attempts and the few failures. Most of all what I treasure is the fun we had cooking together.

Millie Apter

INTRODUCTION

WELCOME TO YOUR BREAD MACHINE

Either you got it as a gift or you inherited it from someone who didn't use it, or you went out and bought it yourself. No matter how that bread machine made its way into your life, congratulate yourself and get ready for a treat. When bread machines first appeared ten years ago, they were bought by folks who didn't know a lot about baking bread but who craved the idea of waking up to the smell of a freshly baked loaf. "Throw in the flour, water, yeast, press a button, and bingo! fresh bread is yours" promised the manuals. This was true . . . sometimes. For every perfect loaf, one had to deal with the hockey pucks, the spongy raw messes, the overflows, the inedible crusts, the sunken, fallen and otherwise disastrous products of the bread machine gone awry. Some folks gave up, but most figured out that this machine is like any other kitchen tool: You have to make it work for you. The success rate increased when people stopped thinking the bread machine had a brain (although it does have a nifty computer chip) and started bossing it around a bit.

I got my first bread machine as a lark: I love gadgets and, honestly, most get used and then stashed away. I quickly discovered, however, the enormous creative and nutritional potential of this marvelous machine. My bread maker never leaves the counter. I use it every single day to make bread for my family, pizza for a quick supper, scones for my husband's breakfast, or biscotti to bring as a gift.

Once you've gotten the hang of your bread machine, start looking in your grocery store, gourmet shop, and health food store for ingredients to go into it. The possibilities are vast and varied.

Discover and use the dough cycle to make dough that you take out, form by hand, and bake in the oven. Any of the recipes in this book can be done this way. The rule of thumb is to allow the formed dough to rise on a baking sheet or in a bread pan until almost doubled in size, then to bake it at 375°F for 40 to 50 minutes, or until the bottom sounds hollow when lightly tapped with your fingertips, or until a thermometer inserted into the bread reads an internal temperature of 190° to 200°F.

I hope you will redefine your idea of a failed loaf. Just because it doesn't look

1

like something you would find at your local bakery doesn't mean it won't taste good. When it's sliced, who will know? If the bread doesn't rise at all, then remove the dough before the bake cycle goes on. Roll it out very thin and make flatbread or crackers. Not all breads rise to the top of the pan; the Swedish Rye (page 98), for example, is a very low, dense bread. Take care to read the description in the headnote before labeling that short, squat loaf a disaster.

While testing recipes for this new edition and my other bread machine books, I got to know the machines (I own them *all*) inside and out. Take the time to read all the information in this section of the book. Here you will find helpful hints, time-saving tips, and important information that will help you bake bread that is perfect every time.

WHAT WE LEARNED

Millie and I have always shared recipes, and bread machine recipes were no exception. She sent me hers from her Panasonic and I sent her mine from my DAK. Her recipes were my first failures and to my astonishment mine didn't work in her machine. There were other problems; the generic bread machine cookbooks gave one standard set of ingredients and instructions for "large" machines and another for "small" machines; many books required you to be able to read a recipe backward to fit the needs of your machine; all the recipes needed fine-tuning to really work. What was going on here? Weren't all those bread machines alike enough to use the same recipes? The answer was a big *no*.

All bread machines are built on the same principle. A nonstick pan with a paddle on the bottom is snapped into a white metal box that becomes through the commands of a computer microchip a proofing box (to get the ingredients up to a temperature at which yeast begins to feed on the carbohydrates and sugars), a mixing and kneading machine, and finally an oven. These functions can be modified and adjusted somewhat by selecting a function on the pad on the front of the machine. Some machines come with a basic set of functions; and others come with a host of options.

At first Millie and I assumed we could come up with a great recipe for, say, whole wheat bread and use it in any machine that called for three cups of flour. If that had been true, then writing this book would have been a piece of cake. We quickly discovered that while the different brands of machines are subtly different from one another, it was enough to make it impossible to give a generic recipe that would be successful in every machine. To ensure success, we created a version of each recipe for each machine on the market. Nine hundred recipes later we present you with a book full of recipes that will work for you and your bread machine. We have tried, in this new edition, to include every machine on the market. If you don't find yours, or have bread machine questions, you can write me at P.O. Box 831, Newton Centre, MA 02159, or e-mail me at Blanche007@aol.com.

You won't find recipes for plain white bread in these pages. What you will find is a truly unique and innovative collection of breads made with a worldwide buffet of ingredients from goat cheese and sun-dried cherries to sweet marsala and pepper vodka. These one-of-a-kind recipes with their diverse and exciting ingredients will make stunning loaves that will please your taste buds and enrich your appreciation for bread as an art form.

You can jump right in and make bread in your machine; but if you want guaranteed success every time, I suggest you read the information about flours and grains in this chapter. This step will make you as smart as your machine and help you develop your own recipes and be able to trouble-shoot with impunity should things run amok.

At the end of many recipes we've offered variations and tips. Don't forget to check for these notes—they'll make your life easier and your bread more successful.

WHICH BREAD MACHINE SHOULD I BUY?

Small? Large? One-pound? One-and-a-half pound? Two-pound? Basic one-two-three model or multifunctional? Single loaf, double loaf with a rice and jam-making capability, window, wheat cycle—the choices are overwhelming! Should you go for the least expensive model or splurge on the most expensive? Buy it from a catalog, department store, cookware specialty shop, or discount chain? Okay, here's what we think: Small (1-pound) machine: If you are not terribly adventurous (i.e., won't be using the machine for anything beyond making bread) and you are baking for just one or two people, then consider one of the small (1-pound) machines. We have to warn you, though, many people start out with a small machine only to upgrade to a larger version once the bread-baking bug bites them.

Large machine: So far, we have found loaves from the 2-pound machines to be of inconsistent quality, which is why the recipes in this book are not specifically geared to those machines. However, *and this is very important*, many of the machines in these pages make a loaf of bread that weighs in excess of two pounds. Confused? So were we until we figured out that when the manufacturers started talking about 2-pound loaves, they were talking volume, not weight. If you have a machine that calls for three to three and a half cups of flour, then that machine has the capacity to make a loaf of bread that weighs two pounds. To confuse the issue, there are now machines on the market that can make different-size loaves. Read on.

Basic vs. multifunctional model: Does the idea of programming your VCR send you into a state of high anxiety? Do you find comfort in the theory that more is less? If so, then you can certainly make do with a basic machine. Our only advice is to make sure that the one you choose has a dough or manual cycle which allows you to have the option of making free-form loaves, pastries, or pizza and baking them in the oven. If your basic machine lacks a raisin bread cycle, you can simply set the timer to ring in the last five minutes of the final knead cycle and add the raisins, nuts, or whatever when the timer goes off.

As for the machines with all the bells and whistles—we love them. While we've never made jam or cooked rice in a machine (and probably never will), we do like having the option of extending our knead, rise, and bake time. Sometimes we stop the dough after the first knead, give it a long slow rise in the refrigerator, and then return it to the bread machine for another knead and rise before it bakes.

All the machines have a timer setting that can be programmed so you can place the ingredients in a pan and program it to be finished close to the time you want to eat the bread. Most of the recipes in this book can be done this way. *Do not, under any circumstances, use the timer setting with perishable ingredients, particularly eggs, milk, and meat.* Holding these items in an unrefrigerated pan can easily result in food poisoning. And in warm weather, avoid using ingredients such as cottage cheese, cream cheese, sour cream, and yogurt.

If you want to make whole wheat bread, buy a heavy-duty machine with either a whole wheat cycle or one that can be programmed for a longer knead and rise cycle. A window in the machine is important only if you are hesitant to open the lid to check the progress of the dough (see page 17).

The single most important consideration in picking a machine is the follow-up support that you will get from the place you bought it and from the company that manufactures it. Chances are very good that no one at the local warehouse store is going to know anything about operating a bread machine. Buy one there and you're on your own. Department stores sometimes have product demonstrators who know the ins and outs of bread machines. Gourmet specialty shops are fine only if the staff actually uses the machines. While all the companies have a toll-free number, some are more helpful than others. (Who wants to be on terminal hold while baking bread?) Below, you will find a list of manufacturers and their numbers for the companies whose bread machines appear in this book. Call them and judge for yourself.

A well-written, understandable manual is another important plus. Ask to see the manual before you buy a machine. If you can't make heads or tails out of what it says, chances are you're in for even greater frustration when you get the machine home.

THE BREAD MACHINES WE USE IN THIS BOOK

Following is a list of machines that can be used for the recipes in this book along with the companies' phone numbers and toll-free numbers. In an attempt to keep things simple, machines that call for two cups of flour we refer to as small machines, and those that call for three or more cups of flour as large machines. Some bread machines, such as the Pillsbury and Toastmaster models, can make both large and small loaves: the difference is simply in the programming.

If you have a machine that is not listed, try the recipes given for the Hitachi for the large loaves and the Sanyo for the small loaves. You might have to make minor adjustments as suggested in the troubleshooting section on page 20.

We found that the Toastmaster, Breadman/Trillium (500), and Black & Decker bread machines have such strong kneading action that their recipes called for much less yeast than other machines. We also found, however, that the Breadman 600 did not have this same strong knead cycle and used the same amount of yeast as other machines. If you have a Breadman 600 and find the loaves are not rising high enough, disregard the reduced-yeast instructions.

Betty Crocker (large) (800) 688-8782
Black & Decker (large) (800) 231-9786
Breadman/Trillium (large) (800) 231-9786
DAK (large) No longer in business, no 800 number

Hitachi (large) (800) 241-6558, ext 22; (404) 279-5600
Maxim (small) (800) 233-9054; (708) 803-4600
Oster (large and small) (800) 526-2832; (708) 995-8900
Panasonic/National (large and small) (800) 922-0028; (201) 348-7000
Pillsbury (large and small) (800) 858-3277
Regal (large) (800) 998-8809; (414) 626-2121
Sanyo (small) East Coast (201) 641-3000; South (404) 925-8900; Midwest
    (708) 775-1414; West (310) 537-5830
Sunbeam (small) (800) 526-2832; (708) 995-8900
Toastmaster (large and small) (800) 947-3744; (314) 445-8666
Welbilt (large) (516) 365-5040
West Bend (large) (414) 334-2311
Williams-Sonoma (large) (800) 858-3277
Zojirushi (large and small) (800) 733-6270; (213) 264-6270

INGREDIENTS

You need only three things to make bread: flour, yeast (or a starter, page 10), and liquid. Of course, you can add lots of other things to make thousands of varieties of breads, each with its own texture and flavor. The more you know about the role ingredients play in bread making, the more expert you will be in creating your own variations, and even your own recipes.

Many of these recipes were invented as we walked through supermarkets, health food stores, ethnic markets, and gourmet shops, perusing the shelves for inspiration. Who would have dreamed you could make a fabulous loaf of bread with a tablespoonful of green peppercorns or a box of Toblerone chocolate? Keep your eyes open as you push that cart!

FLOUR

Many of the recipes in this book call for unbleached white flour. While we used King Arthur Flour in testing all the recipes, you can substitute any unbleached white flour made from hard wheat. Hard wheat yields the highest amount of protein. Another name for this protein is gluten. Gluten, when brought into contact with liquid and processed or kneaded, is an elastic material that gives bread that special "chewy" texture. The higher the level of gluten, the better the texture and the more liquid the bread will absorb, which results in a loaf that stays fresher longer.

Some flours are labeled "bread flour." Unfortunately, this sometimes means that potassium bromate or ascorbic acid has been added to the flour to give it more oomph. We recommend, if you possibly can, using flours without any chemical additives. Thankfully, there are some high-quality bread flours that are not chemically treated. You can tell by reading the label—it is essential to read the package label. It isn't necessary to use flour specifically labeled "bread flour." Ellen Davies, regional sales manager at King Arthur, showed us a fail-safe way to select high-gluten flour: Choose a flour that is ground from hard wheat (the package will say this), then look on the package label under the nutritional information or content. There will be a listing for the number of grams of protein. You are looking for the number 13 or higher—preferably 14 or 15 per cup. Remember, the higher the amount of protein, the better the bread.

When you use flour without chemical additives and preservatives, that's good news for your body. The only bad news is that pesticides and preservatives discourage meal moths and other unwelcome pests that are longing to make your bread ingredients their happy homes. Try to store as much as you can in the freezer in airtight plastic containers or plastic freezer bags. Store all stone-ground flours in the freezer or refrigerator as well. Unbleached white flour can be stored in a cool dry place. We store ours in ten-gallon snap-on lidded pails (we make a lot of bread), placed away from heat vents and direct sunlight. A bay leaf added to your canister is a good way to discourage pests.

Flours differ not only from the wheat from which they are grown but as a result of the growing conditions, how soon the wheat was ground after it was harvested, and the humidity level where it was stored. So a recipe that works splendidly with one brand of flour may have different results with another.

WHOLE WHEAT FLOUR: Ground from the whole wheat kernel, this flour is full-flavored and offers a big nutritional bonus since it retains both the germ (rich in vitamins) and the bran (loaded with fiber). Whole wheat flour also adds a delicious yet delicate sweetness to bread. The major drawback in using only whole wheat flour in recipes is that the bran reduces the effectiveness of gluten, which makes rising more of a challenge. Whole wheat loaves will not rise nearly as high as those made with white flour. These loaves will be moister and heavier in texture.

The trick is to combine white unbleached flour and whole wheat flour in a ratio of generally 1 cup whole wheat to 1 cup white. On the advice of the test kitchens of Regal, we tried using only whole wheat flour and running the machine through two complete kneading and rising processes, and then baking it. The result was fairly successful, but certainly time-consuming. Another trick is to set the machine to Manual or Dough, remove the dough at the end of the cycle and let it rise out of the machine for as long as it needs, then bake it in a conventional oven. Bread machines of the new generation have far more powerful kneading capabilities than the original models. This is great for the whole wheat bread, but can be problematic for other loaves. If your bread is rising too high (hitting the lid of the machine), try reducing the yeast by ½ to 1 teaspoon.

White whole wheat flour is a new product available from King Arthur Flour (page 339). Milled from a different strain of red wheat than most flour, it has a sweeter, lighter taste than regular whole wheat flour. White whole wheat flour has the same nutritive value of whole wheat flour, but without the slight bitter taste. A loaf made with this flour will resemble bread made with half whole wheat and half all-purpose white flour.

HIGH-GLUTEN FLOUR OR GLUTEN: This is simply hard wheat flour with some extra gluten or protein added. Use this when you have a bread made from mostly low-gluten grains, such as rye or whole wheat, to give an extra boost to the rising process. Instead of calling for gluten flour in these recipes, we recommend that you try Lora Brody's Bread Dough Enhancer™, a mix of all-natural ingredients (vital wheat gluten with two yeast foods, ascorbic acid, and diastatic malt). It was developed to solve the problem of those low-rising wheat loaves. It also helps attain the best possible rise out of bread with heavy ingredients such as cheese, fruit, and nuts. You can purchase Lora Brody's Bread Dough Enhancer™ in stores or by mail order (page 337).

GRAHAM FLOUR: Graham flour is coarsely milled, unsifted whole wheat flour which is hard to find but available by mail order (page 337).

RYE FLOUR: Found in most supermarkets and health food stores, rye flour is made from rye berries and is one of the magic ingredients in pumpernickel bread and chewy, crusty peasant-style rye breads. Rye flour is very low in gluten, too low to be used by itself, so care must be taken not to use more than the recommended amount given in a recipe, as the bread won't rise properly.

CORNMEAL: A great ingredient if ever there was one. Nutritious, tasty, and loaded with personality, a little cornmeal goes a long way in helping to create a loaf with a wonderful crunchy crumb (texture) and delightful flavor.

YEAST

Yeast makes bread rise, turning the solid, heavy quality of dough into an air-filled spongy mass that when baked will be fit to eat. It also adds flavor and the wondrously intoxicating hot alcohol aroma that fills your kitchen as the bread bakes.

Yeast, as you've no doubt heard a thousand times before, is a living organism, which is why you have to take care when using it. Too much heat at the wrong time, too much sugar, or an overdose of salt can kill it.

Yeast is activated by liquid but feeds on starch (from the flour) and sugar (which is why most recipes call for at least a little sugar, honey, or molasses). Yeast gives off carbon dioxide and alcohol, which are then trapped in the fabric created by the flour and liquid. This forms air bubbles, which leaven the bread—much like the way bubbles in the beaten egg whites of a hot soufflé expand when heated. The major difference between a loaf of bread and a soufflé is that the starch in the bread maintains this air-filled form long after it has cooled off, while a soufflé goes flat within minutes after exiting the oven.

Since machines cannot make judgment calls about amounts of ingredients, you must be precise when measuring. You will find a wide variation of yeast measurements from machine to machine.

The yeast we used in these recipes was "instant" active dry yeast. This is not to be confused with "rapid rise." Instant yeast is specially formulated to dissolve in the dough without having first to be proofed (mixed with warm liquid and a small amount of sweetener). Bread Machine Yeast is similar to rapid rise in that they both contain ascorbic acid to jump-start the yeast. Do not use compressed cake or fresh yeast in your bread machine. The recipes in this book were developed and tested with Red Star instant active and Saf-Instant yeast, both fine products that we highly recommend. Use whichever brand you prefer, but we strongly recommend against using yeast that comes packaged in individual envelopes. We found far too many variances, both at the production end and the consumer end (that last bit not emptying out). It is much better to buy a pound or two of active dry yeast (page 9) and keep it in a tightly sealed container in the refrigerator. We ordered granulated yeast (several pounds at one time) from King Arthur along with the handy glass container they sell for storing it in the refrigerator. (Remember, always use a clean, dry spoon when dipping into the container to measure.)

The new quick-rising yeasts are not used in these recipes since we found that regular yeast, which requires a longer rising time, allows the flavors to develop more fully. We are sure that with a minor amount of experimentation plus information from your machine's manual, you won't have any trouble adapting the recipes if you wish to do so.

When kept under ideal conditions, yeast will stay alive and healthy for many months. If you have doubts about whether your yeast is still active (alive), place 1 cup of warm (110°F) water in a bowl. Add 2 teaspoons of sugar, stir to dissolve, and then sprinkle 1 teaspoon of yeast on top. Let it sit there for a few minutes and then stir it until it dissolves. Cover the bowl with plastic wrap and set it in a warm, draft-free place (inside your turned-off oven, for instance). Within 5 to 10 minutes the top of the mixture should have turned foamy, which means the yeast is working. If there is no activity, then throw the yeast away and buy a new supply.

Sourdough Starters

Although the explanation about sourdough starters (sponges) may be long and seem a bit technical, making sourdough bread is *easy* and the delicious results are well worth the one extra step that is necessary in the making.

Before yeast was available in granulated form and packaged in jars or handy foil containers, housewives used sourdough starters to make bread. These starters were made from wild yeast, which is airborne—floating around right in your own house. These mixtures of yeast, flour, and water or other liquids, some generations old, were treasures passed from generation to generation. If the starter wasn't well tended, there would be no bread for the table.

The term *sourdough* comes from the fact that the action of the yeast on the starch gives off a fermented aroma, the personality of which depends on the strain of yeast. The famous California sourdough comes from a special variety of wild yeast found in that region. Each part of the country has its own strains.

You can make, borrow, or buy a starter (see page 341). The key here is to *plan ahead*. We give a recipe here for a rye sourdough starter which involves adding some active dry yeast to a mixture of flour and liquid and then setting the bowl out, uncovered, for a period of time to "catch" some wild yeast. You must make this starter—or any starter—at least twenty-four hours ahead of time, although the longer it can sit and develop, the stronger the flavor will be. And you get *much better* results when you use a starter that is at room temperature.

LIQUIDS

Beer, stout, wine, liqueurs, and liquors with even higher proof such as vodka can be used to make bread. In some cases, as with beer, ale, or stout, the alcohol or fermentation even acts as a yeast stimulant. Remember, though, that too much liquor with a high sugar content, such as sweet marsala or most dessert wines, can kill the yeast. When we call for beer we do not specify a certain kind (light, dry, etc.). We tended to use whatever was on hand and suggest you do the same, but you'll get more beer taste with dark beer than with light. When the recipe calls for flat beer and you don't want to wait around for it to become flat on its own, pour the beer into a small saucepan and heat it to a simmer. By the time it cools down, it will be flat.

No matter which of these liquids you use, it speeds the bread-making process to have them at room temperature when you add them to the machine. Even if your machine has a heating cycle, it's easier to warm the liquids in a microwave than use the bread machine to do it for you. Too much liquid will cause the bread to collapse when it is baking. It is essential to check the dough during the kneading process to make sure you have a firm, smooth ball of dough that does not stick to the sides or bottom of the pan (see page 17).

FATS: In bread baking, fats keep bread fresh longer and make for a finer, softer crumb, a more delicate flavor, and a richer, more substantial texture. Fats, and especially butter, are responsible for the golden, crispy crust everyone loves so dearly.

Fats such as butter, margarine, and vegetable oils can be substituted for one another in like amounts. Naturally the more flavorful the fat, the more flavor in the bread. Olive oil is great, especially when flavored with garlic or chili, in savory breads, and sweet (unsalted) butter is preferable in the more delicate sweet breads and coffee cakes. Canola oil, like olive oil, is cholesterol-free, so if you're watching your diet, then use one of these.

The amount of liquid in low-fat margarines makes them tricky to use in the bread machine. If your loaves are caving in, then reduce the liquid in the recipe.

To substitute oil for a solid fat (such as butter), reduce the amount of liquid in the recipe by 1 tablespoon. Check the dough during the first few minutes of the first knead cycle to make any necessary adjustments (see page 17).

DAIRY PRODUCTS: Milk, buttermilk, and goat's milk add flavor to bread and make a much tenderer delicate crumb than water or water-based liquids such as broth make. Milk products also extend the freshness of bread and give a calcuim boost as well. Because of the fat content it is more difficult to dissolve yeast in milk, so we like to use nonfat dry milk and powdered buttermilk. Both are sold in most grocery stores and powdered buttermilk (as well as powdered goat's milk) can be found in health food stores. When you have these ingredients on hand, you don't have to worry about having a bottle of milk in the refrigerator. Other dairy products such as sour cream, yogurt, soft or "wet" cheeses, including cottage cheese, ricotta, and goat's milk cheese, and even hard cheeses are considered "liquids" in these bread recipes. Remember that a bread with cheese as an ingredient will not rise as high as one without it; in fact, it may sink in the middle slightly, which will not affect its taste at all.

If you wish to amend a recipe to omit the dairy products, use an equal amount of water for the milk, cream, or yogurt measurement and an equal amount of vegetable oil for the butter. You may simply omit powered milk from a recipe without adversely affecting it.

EGGS: Think of egg yolks as a sort of flavorful fat, but one that is very high in cholesterol. Egg yolks add the very same things that any other fat does, along with a lovely golden color. Egg whites add liquid and body. You can leave out the egg yolks in a recipe, but remember to add an equal volume of liquid, about ¼ cup.

Always use the recommended egg size specified in each recipe, since the success of the bread very much depends on the volume of liquid.

When you're using the DAK and Welbilt machines it is important to have all the ingredients at room temperature. Because of potential egg-related health and safety problems, it is inadvisable to store eggs at room temperature. The easiest way to warm an egg is to place the whole (unopened) egg in a cup of hot tap water and in five minutes or less the egg will be room temperature. Discard any eggs that have cracked and, as we mentioned before, never use a recipe calling for eggs in programmed-ahead bread.

If you don't want to give up the flavor of eggs but are watching your fat and cholesterol intake, try experimenting with Nature's Choice, Egg Beaters, or other egg substitutes. Read the instructions on the package to make the substitutions in the recipes.

To reduce the amount of fat and cholesterol in the breads, use two egg whites instead of one whole egg.

OTHER INGREDIENTS

OTHER DRY INGREDIENTS: Along with flour, other dry ingredients used in making bread are buckwheat flour, which gives a mellow, earthy flavor, bran, oatmeal, cracked wheat, wheat germ, millet, wheat berries, cereals, seeds, and nuts. All of these make for gutsy, wholesome breads that burst with flavor and texture. You'll never eat boring white bread again!

As with flour, use grains, seeds, and nuts without chemical additives and preservatives, and store as much as you can in the freezer in airtight plastic containers or freezer bags.

HERBS AND SPICES: We have included many recipes calling for herbs and spices. While fresh herbs give you the most potent flavor, it's not always possible to get them. Our second choice would be dried, followed by ground. Dried or ground herbs and spices that have sat on cabinet shelves for a long time will be stale and not have much taste. If you see a recipe in this book that appeals to you with the exception of some herb or spice, then leave it out or substitute in like amounts one you prefer in its place.

Thanks to Joanne Turchany of the West Bend Company I finally learned why so many people (including me) were having problems with both cinnamon raisin and garlic bread. Cinnamon can break down the structure of the dough, affecting its size and texture, and garlic (especially fresh garlic) inhibits the activity of the yeast. So be judicious in your use of both! Fresh onion sometimes has the same effect on yeast.

Fresh basil leaves and fresh coriander (cilantro) get mushy and turn bitter as a result of the action of the kneading blade. Use dried instead. This does, however, not include pesto—made with fresh basil.

SALT: "Light" salt can be used in place of regular table salt only if it contains equal amounts of potassium chloride and sodium. While it is possible to make bread without salt, the resulting loaves tend to overrise and lack a well-rounded taste and good texture. Salt keeps the yeast working over the life span of the dough. This adds to the complexity and character of the bread.

SUGAR AND OTHER SWEETENERS: In addition to providing flavor, sweeteners act to stimulate the action of the yeast, give it a jump-start, as it were. This can backfire if you add too much sugar, which will kill the yeast. We learned this the hard way when, determined to make bread with chutney (a sweet conserve with mangoes and ginger), we couldn't get the bread to rise. Many expensive doughs were tossed into the garbage before we called P. J. Hamel at King Arthur Flour in desperation. She figured out that the high content of sugar in the chutney was doing in the yeast. We solved the problem by using the chutney as a glaze on top of the bread.

We've used white sugar, brown sugar, maple syrup, honey, and molasses as sweeteners in these recipes. You can easily substitute white and brown sugar for each other and the liquid sweeteners for each other, both in like amounts. If you want to substitute dry sweeteners for liquid sweeteners, you have to adjust the amount of liquid you are adding or subtracting. Even a tablespoon of liquid more or less can make a difference. Be careful when choosing molasses; blackstrap is much stronger-tasting than the regular kind. (Both provide lots of iron.)

DRIED FRUITS: Dried fruits, such as raisins, apricots, prunes, pears, apples, figs, and dates (not to mention blueberries, cherries, cranberries, and strawberries) are a delicious addition to breads. They add texture and have great nutritional value as well. Since dried fruits are very high in sugar, you have to take care not to shock the yeast when adding these ingredients. The best time to add dried fruit is during the very last few minutes of the final knead cycle. Set a timer (after referring to your manual to check the length of the cycles) and add them when it goes off. Or you can wait until the final knead cycle is finished, remove the dough, knead the fruit in by hand, and place the dough back in the machine to finish rising and baking. Study the chart in your manual that gives the length of times for the various cycles to know when your machine goes into its final knead cycle.

FOR PERFECT LOAVES EVERY TIME

KNOW YOUR DOUGH

OPEN THE MACHINE AND CHECK THE DOUGH DURING THE FIRST 5 TO 10 MINUTES OF THE FIRST KNEADING CYCLE even if your manual says not to do it. Flour acts as a sponge, absorbing moisture on wet days and becoming dehydrated during dry weather. You'll have to adjust for fluctuating humidity and barometric pressure by adding small amounts of flour or liquid to the dough.

So, you've never made bread before. How do you know how much to add? If the dough looks wet and is sticking to the bottom and sides of the pan, then sprinkle in a tablespoon of flour at a time (you may need up to an extra ½ cup) while the machine is kneading until you have a smooth, firm ball of dough. If the mixture is dry and corrugated-looking or the dough won't hold together, then sprinkle in additional liquid, a little at a time, until the dough is smooth and pliable and forms a cohesive ball. If you've wandered away from your machine only to return to find a wet messy glob or a dry desert thumping around in the machine, press Stop (you can do this at any time—except if the machine has gone into the bake cycle), add a small amount of flour or liquid, and press Start. Stick around and make additional adjustments, if necessary, until the dough looks right.

ADAPTING YOUR OWN RECIPES TO THE BREAD MACHINE

Once you see how easy it is to make bread in your machine, try adapting some of your own recipes to the machine. While it may take more than one attempt, keep at it. The following formula developed by Joanne Turchany of the West Bend Company will get you on your way.

For **each** cup of flour in the original recipe use:

3 ounces liquid
½ tablespoon fat
Scant ½ teaspoon salt
½ tablespoon sweetener
½ teaspoon active dry yeast

Do not use more than 3½ cups flour for the 1½-pound machine,
   or 2½ cups for the small (1-pound) machine.

MAKING SUBSTITUTIONS

As you become more and more experienced with your machine, you will be able to substitute ingredients and adapt these recipes. Our advice is to stick to the recipes, seeing what works well, what you like the taste and texture of, and what you don't like. Start slowly, substituting one kind of flour for another, then one liquid for another, then one dry ingredient for another. Remember to treat cheese as a wet ingredient: Even though that block of Cheddar looks hard while you slice it, it will melt into a liquid state as soon as the heat goes on.

ORDER OF INGREDIENTS

Pay attention to the order in which the ingredients are placed in the machine; it does make a difference. In some machines the dry ingredients go in first, starting with the yeast; in others the wet ingredients go in, then the dry, and finally the yeast. In the Panasonic and National models, the yeast is placed in its own separate dispenser. This ensures that the yeast does not come in contact with the wet ingredients (and become activated) until the machine is ready to start kneading the bread.

When you are programming to bake bread at a later time, pay close attention to the order in which the ingredients are to be placed in the machine. Follow the manufacturer's directions. We have found that when you are either making dough or placing the ingredients in the machine to make bread at that time, you can add either the liquids first or the dry ingredients first. The major exception to this is the old DAK (no longer manufactured), where the yeast must be placed in the bread pan first in a position farthest away from the kneading blade. When programming ahead, make sure to place any dried fruits away from any contact with wet ingredients as they will absorb those liquids and throw off the recipe.

TEMPERATURE OF INGREDIENTS

Some machines specify that all ingredients must be at room temperature. Those machines do not have preheating cycles. In others, ingredients taken from the refrigerator can be added; but with the exception of yeast, we don't recommend it. All loaves benefit from using room temperature ingredients. To bring eggs to room temperature quickly, place them in a pan of hot water for several minutes. Cut butter or margarine into small pieces before adding it to the machine.

MEASURING INGREDIENTS

Think of baking as chemistry. The proportions and amounts of the ingredients exist in relationship to one another. You need so much yeast and so much liquid to make so much flour rise into a digestible loaf instead of a soggy, leaden mass. You use certain things in certain amounts of flavorings to make things taste right.

In order for your bread to turn out, you must take the time to measure correctly. If you're new to the baking game that means throwing away all the dented measuring cups and cracked measuring spoons you've been using and investing in a new set. It also means, at least for the recipes in this book, putting away those cute little measuring gadgets that came with your bread machine.

Liquid measures should be made of heat-resistant glass or plastic. Buy a 1-cup and a 2-cup measure. Get a full set of dry measures, either metal or plastic. Make sure they can go in the dishwasher without melting. We love our Tupperware sets because they have unusual measurements such as ⅔ and ¾ cup that are frequently called for in these recipes. Invest in two sets of sturdy measuring spoons so you won't have to use the same teaspoon to measure water and then yeast. (You never want to get water, or any other stray ingredient, mixed in with your yeast.)

To measure wet ingredients, pour the liquid into the measuring cup and then bend over until you are at eye level with the red line. Add or subtract liquid as necessary. Don't be offhand about this—even a teaspoon can make a difference.

To measure dry ingredients, use a clean dry measuring spoon or cup to scoop into the container or bag, then level off the top with the flat side of a knife.

Never measure over the pan. In other words, don't pour from the container of salt into the tiny teaspoon held over the other ingredients.

You've never baked before; how can you tell if the dough looks right? Go to the store. Buy frozen dough and let it defrost according to the package directions. Place it on a lightly floured surface and play with it until you are familiar with the consistency. This is what you're aiming for from the bread machine.

Extras

Extra kneads and extra rise times all contribute to the depth of flavor, character of the crumb, and general personality of a loaf of bread. One of the reasons we dislike rapid rise yeast and rapid cycles on bread machines is that the dough really requires the entire life span of the yeast to become the amazing miracle that is bread. If you are partial to whole-grain breads and are winding up with lower loaves than you wish, then try a double knead cycle: Place the ingredients in the machine and program for Dough or Manual. At the end of the final knead, reprogram the machine for Bread (or Whole Wheat) and press Start. You've given the dough an extra workout to develop the gluten, which will result in a higher loaf. For an even higher loaf, you can (if your machine permits) program for a longer rise time, or simply remove the dough from the pan after the final rise cycle (but before baking), transfer it to a bread pan, and allow it to rise in a warm place until doubled in bulk. Then bake it in the oven.

Sweet doughs with lots of butter and eggs also respond well to a second long rise in a cool place. I remove my brioche from the machine after the dough cycle is completed. I place it in a large freezer-strength plastic bag and refrigerate it overnight. Then I place it back in the machine (my Zojirushi has flexible programming) and program for second rise and bake. If you can't program your machine this way, you can place the dough in a bread pan after you remove it from the machine, give it a long, refrigerated rise, and then bake it in the oven. Even nonwheat and nonsweet doughs can benefit from this. When you are using the dough setting and the dough has not yet completed its final rise but is up over the top of the pan (and threatening to overflow), pull it out before the beeper sounds.

Refrigerating and Freezing Dough

My freezer is well stocked with large freezer-strength resealable plastic bags filled with doughs of every imaginable kind. Doughs that contain butter and eggs can be frozen up to three months, other doughs up to six months. They can be defrosted in the refrigerator or at room temperature, although defrosted dough containing perishable ingredients should not sit at room temperature for more than two hours. Take care to label the bags carefully—pizza dough and maple buttermilk dough look alike when frozen. When the doughs are defrosted, you can form them into loaves, pizza, etc., allow them to rise per the recipe, and bake away. **Every recipe in this book can be removed from the machine at the dough stage, hand-formed, and then baked in the oven.** You can refrigerate doughs without perishable ingredients up to five days, and those with butter, eggs, milk, etc., for forty-eight hours. Again, use large resealable plastic bags; they're great for this purpose.

Rising Dough Outside the Machine

If you are rising bread outside the machine, you can tell if the rise is completed by poking the dough very gently with your finger. The hole should slowly disappear as the poke mark fills outs. Another way is to remove a small (pea-sized) bit of dough before you form the bread. Place the little piece in a glass of water. If it rises to the top, then the bread is ready to bake.

Baking Dough Outside the Machine

When baking doughs that contain 3 cups of flour (large machines), form the loaf and let it rise, covered, until doubled in bulk. Bake in a preheated 375°F oven for 35 to 40 minutes. At the end of that time, turn the bread out of the pan and allow it to bake an additional 10 minutes right on the oven rack. Cover it with foil if the top turns too brown. For loaves with 2 cups of flour, bake for 25 to 30 minutes. Test for doneness by tapping the underside with your fingertips—there should be a hollow sound insert an instant-read thermometer into the center of the bread. When it reads 190° to 200°F, then the inside is cooked and the bread is ready to come out of the oven.

Even though the temptation to dig into that loaf of bread hot from the machine is irresistible, try to hold off for 10 to 15 minutes. The bread is still baking inside, so it will be wet and difficult to slice. The action of the knife (no matter how sharp) will mash the slices. And speaking of knives, use a sharp serrated knife, one that's used only for cutting bread.

STORING BAKED LOAVES

Now that you can have great bread baked fresh every day, your only problem might be how to store leftovers. At room temperature, in a plastic bag (only after the bread is completely cooled off) is the best place. In the refrigerator is the worst place because the bread becomes dehydrated. Bread freezes very well if it is completely cooled off first, then put in a plastic freezer bag. Bread stored in the freezer is good for up to six months, although it is important to remember to label the loaves since you won't be able to tell rye from whole wheat after they are frozen. You can defrost bread by letting the loaf sit at room temperature still in its plastic bag, so any moisture will accumulate on the bag, and not on the bread. You can also use the microwave set on defrost. Keep the bread in the bag during the defrosting as well. If you are planning to use the bread for sandwiches, it is a good idea to slice it before you freeze it, as this will expedite thawing.

TROUBLESHOOTING—OR WHY DOES MY RYE BREAD LOOK LIKE A HOCKEY PUCK?

Bread machines are great, but they are not foolproof. They don't know if the weather has been dry as a desert for the past three weeks, or if your flour is dehydrated. The machine won't take into account that your sourdough starter needed to be fed before you used it, or that you used sweet coconut instead of unsweetened and the extra sugar stirred your yeast into a feeding frenzy and killed it. Aside from erupting sticky wet dough over the top of the pan and into the bottom of the machine, it has no way of warning you that you accidentally added too much yeast.

In some of our recipes we recommend that you add an additional amount of dry or wet ingredients to the dough once it has gone through the initial mixing process. That way if the dough is too sticky you can moisten it, and conversely, if it's much too wet you can add additional flour. In this way you can compensate for the effect weather (actually humidity or the lack of it) has on flour. When a recipe says add more flour, up to ¼ cup, 1 tablespoon at a time, you'll know why and when.

Remember, the more you use your machine, the more you'll know what the dough should look like to make a great loaf of bread. If, however, these following symptoms appear, here are some of the reasons and how to correct them.

THE BREAD HAS A CAVED-IN TOP OR SIDES: Too much liquid, too much cheese. Try reducing the amount of liquid or cheese by ¼ cup. Some loaves with cheese will have a caved-in or flat top no matter what, but it won't affect the taste.

THE BREAD IS RAW IN THE CENTER: The bread didn't rise enough because there wasn't enough yeast, or the rising time was too short. One solution is to make the dough in the machine, give it a final long rise in a bowl, then bake it in a conventional oven. Another is to program the machine for Manual or Dough and at the end of the process, reset the machine back to Start so that the dough has two complete kneading cycles before it is baked in the machine. This technique works very well for loaves made completely with all whole-grain flour.

THE BREAD IS RAW ON TOP: Too much yeast caused the bread to rise so high that it hit the top of the machine, prohibiting the circulation of hot air over and around the top of the bread. Try using ¼ to ½ teaspoon less yeast, or add a little "heavy" flour such as whole wheat or rye.

THE BREAD ROSE TO THE TOP OF THE MACHINE OR OVERFLOWED THE PAN: Too much yeast made the dough rise too high, or there was too much "light" flour such as white and not enough "heavy" flour such as whole wheat.

THE BREAD DIDN'T RISE AT ALL: You either forgot to add the yeast, or something killed it such as an overdose of salt or sugar, or the ratio of yeast to low-gluten flour was too low.

THE TOP OF THE LOAF IS PUCKERED OR SHRIVELED: Moisture condensed on the top of the bread while it was cooling. Remove the bread from the machine at the completion of the baking cycle.

THE TOP SANK IN: Too much liquid. This also happens when there is a lot of cheese in the bread. A bread that rises too fast and then doesn't have enough gluten to support it will also cave in when it bakes. Sometimes this happens when the bread has risen too long. Try cutting the amount of yeast, or the amount of liquid.

THE BREAD IS FULL OF LARGE HOLES: Too much yeast or too much liquid.

THE BREAD IS MISSHAPEN AND LUMPY: Not enough moisture in the dough. Watch the dough during the kneading process to make sure there is enough moisture to form a ball.

THE BREAD BURNED OR IS UNDERDONE: Try adjusting the temperature control. Breads with a high sugar content will brown faster than those without.

THE DOUGH IS VERY STICKY AND DOESN'T FORM A BALL WHEN KNEADED: Not enough flour. Try adding additional flour, a teaspoon at a time, waiting for each spoonful to be absorbed before adding the next.

THE DOUGH IS CRUMBLY AND DRY AND DOESN'T FORM A BALL WHEN KNEADED: Not enough liquid. Add small amounts of liquid, a teaspoon at a time, until the dough forms a ball.

ADDED INGREDIENTS SUCH AS RAISINS AND NUTS WERE PULVER-IZED: They were added too soon and ground into tiny pieces by the kneading blade. Try leaving things such as nuts and bits of dried fruit in larger pieces and adding them later in the kneading cycle.

ADDED INGREDIENTS SUCH AS RAISINS AND NUTS DIDN'T GET MIXED IN: They were added too late in the kneading cycle. Try adding them sooner and cut into smaller pieces.

THERE ARE DEPOSITS OF FLOUR ON THE SIDES OF THE LOAF: The flour and other dry ingredients were not mixing in during the kneading process and stuck in the sides of the bread pan. When the bread rose, the flour stuck to the sides. Try using a rubber scraper to push down any ingredients stuck to the sides of the pan during kneading.

THE BREAD WOULDN'T SLIDE OUT OF THE PAN: Did you happen to scratch the nonstick coating? Try turning the pan upside down on top of a towel placed on the work surface. Bang the pan down to release the bread. Never use anything abrasive to wash the pan. A sponge dipped in warm soapy water should do the trick. Use a small hand-held vacuum to suck up any large crumbs and other debris, then clean the inside of the machine with a wet paper towel.

YOU HAD TROUBLE REMOVING THE KNEADING BLADE FROM THE BOTTOM OF THE LOAF: Insert the end of a chopstick into the hole in the blade and pry it out.

 Speaking of the kneading blade, make sure you remove it from the loaf before you give the bread away to an unsuspecting friend or neighbor. Also, watch that it doesn't make that one-way journey down the garbage disposal.

THERE WAS SMOKE COMING FROM MY MACHINE WHEN THE BAKING CYCLE STARTED: You spilled ingredients on the heating element. Don't measure the ingredients into the bread pan while it is in the machine. Wipe out the machine with a damp paper towel after each use.

I CAN'T MAKE HEADS OR TAILS OUT OF THIS MANUAL AND OTHER FRUSTRATING PROBLEMS: You are not alone. Call the manufacturer's toll-free telephone number and hope you get a kind, patient person who will talk you through the problem. You can also take the manual back to the place where you bought the machine and ask a salesperson to spend some time showing you the ropes. On the Internet, there are thousands of bread machine users (including me) who will be happy to share their knowledge and experience.

Finally, an invaluable source is *The Magic Bread Letter*, a bimonthly publication for bread machine owners. The address is P.O. Box 337, Moss Beach, CA 94038–0337, or call (415)728-3502.

WHITE BREADS

LOAVES, PIZZA, BUNS,
AND BREADSTICKS

MAPLE BUTTERMILK BREAD

This is our idea of basic white bread, fresh and sweet as a summer morning. Serve this special loaf with unsalted butter and blackberry jam. It makes great French toast.

....

DAK/WELBILT

2½ teaspoons yeast

3 cups unbleached white flour

4 tablespoons powdered buttermilk

1 teaspoon salt

1 tablespoon butter

3 tablespoons plus 1 teaspoon pure
  maple syrup

1 cup water

Have all the ingredients at room temperature. Place all the ingredients in the machine, program for White Bread, and press Start.

....

BLACK & DECKER, BETTY CROCKER, BREADMAN/TRILLIUM, HITACHI, LARGE TOASTMASTER, AND WILLIAMS-SONOMA

1 tablespoon butter

3 tablespoons plus 1 teaspoon pure
  maple syrup

1 cup water

3 cups unbleached white flour

4 tablespoons powdered buttermilk

1 teaspoon salt

2 teaspoons yeast

Place all the ingredients in the machine, program for Bread, Basic Bread, Basic Wheat, Basic White, or White/Whole Grain, and press Start.

....

27

PANASONIC/NATIONAL

3 cups unbleached white flour

4 tablespoons powdered buttermilk

1 teaspoon salt

1 tablespoon butter

3 tablespoons plus 1 teaspoon pure
   maple syrup

1 cup water

2½ teaspoons yeast

Place all the ingredients except the yeast in the machine. Place the yeast in the dispenser. Program for Basic Bread and press Start.

REGAL, LARGE OSTER, WEST BEND, LARGE PILLSBURY, AND LARGE ZOJIRUSHI

1 tablespoon butter

3 tablespoons plus 1 teaspoon pure
   maple syrup

1 cup water

3 cups unbleached white flour

4 tablespoons powdered buttermilk

1 teaspoon salt

2½ teaspoons yeast

Place all the ingredients in the machine, program for Bread, Basic Bread, Basic White, Basic Wheat, or White/Whole Grain, and press Start or On.

MAPLE BUTTERMILK BREAD

MAXIM, SMALL OSTER, SANYO, SUNBEAM, SMALL PILLSBURY, SMALL TOASTMASTER, AND SMALL ZOJIRUSHI

1 tablespoon butter

2½ tablespoons pure maple syrup

½ cup plus 2 tablespoons water

2 cups unbleached white flour

3 tablespoons powdered buttermilk

1 teaspoon salt

1½ teaspoons yeast

Place all the ingredients in the machine, program for Standard, Basic, White, Basic Bread, or Bread, and press Start.

Small Welbilt

1½ teaspoons yeast

2 cups unbleached white flour

3 tablespoons powdered buttermilk

1 teaspoon salt

1 tablespoon butter

2½ tablespoons pure maple syrup

½ cup plus 2 tablespoons water

Have all the ingredients at room temperature. Place all the ingredients in the machine, program for Medium, and press Start.

Small Panasonic/National

2 cups unbleached white flour

3 tablespoons powdered buttermilk

1 teaspoon salt

1 tablespoon butter

2½ tablespoons pure maple syrup

½ cup plus 2 tablespoons water

1½ teaspoons yeast

Place all the ingredients except the yeast in the machine. Place the yeast in the dispenser. Program for Basic Bread and press Start.

PAIN DE CHAMPAGNE

Now for something new and different! We had some leftover champagne and thought it might make an interesting bread—little did we suspect how interesting. This is the quintessential elegant white loaf. It is very important to use a champagne labeled "brut," which means dry, because the sweet kind will kill the yeast. It is necessary to begin this recipe the night before when you make a sponge (a starter) and let it sit in a warm place for 12 hours.

DAK/Welbilt

For the Sponge

1 cup brut champagne

2 teaspoons yeast

1 cup unbleached white flour

Pour the champagne into a medium-size glass or plastic mixing bowl. Sprinkle on the yeast and stir to dissolve. Add the flour and mix well. Cover with plastic wrap and set in a warm place for at least 12 hours.

To Complete the Bread

1½ teaspoons yeast

1 teaspoon salt

4 tablespoons nonfat dry milk

2¼ cups unbleached white flour

2 tablespoons butter

1 extra-large egg

Sponge

Have all the ingredients at room temperature. Place all the ingredients in the machine, program for White Bread, and press Start.

BLACK & DECKER, BETTY CROCKER, BREADMAN/TRILLIUM, HITACHI, LARGE TOASTMASTER, AND WILLIAMS-SONOMA

FOR THE SPONGE

1 cup brut champagne

2 teaspoons yeast

1 cup unbleached white flour

Pour the champagne into a medium-size glass or plastic mixing bowl. Sprinkle on the yeast and stir to dissolve. Add the flour and mix well. Cover with plastic wrap and set in a warm place for at least 12 hours.

TO COMPLETE THE BREAD

Sponge

2 tablespoons butter

1 extra-large egg

1 teaspoon salt

3 tablespoons nonfat dry milk

2 cups unbleached white flour

1½ teaspoons yeast

Place all the ingredients in the machine, program for Bread, Basic Bread, Basic Wheat, Basic White, or White/Whole Grain, and press Start.

....

PANASONIC/NATIONAL

FOR THE SPONGE

1 cup brut champagne

2 teaspoons yeast

1 cup unbleached white flour

Pour the champagne into a medium-size glass or plastic mixing bowl. Sprinkle on the yeast and stir to dissolve. Add the flour and mix well. Cover with plastic wrap and set in a warm place for at least 12 hours.

Continued

To Complete the Bread

1 teaspoon salt

3 tablespoons nonfat dry milk

2 cups unbleached white flour

Sponge

2 tablespoons butter

1 extra-large egg

1½ teaspoons yeast

Place all the ingredients except the yeast in the machine. Place the yeast in the dispenser. Program for Basic Bread and press Start.

REGAL

For the Sponge

1 cup brut champagne

2 teaspoons yeast

1 cup unbleached white flour

Pour the champagne into a medium-size glass or plastic mixing bowl. Sprinkle on the yeast and stir to dissolve. Add the flour and mix well. Cover with plastic wrap and set in a warm place for at least 12 hours.

To Complete the Bread

Sponge

2 tablespoons butter

1 extra-large egg

1 teaspoon salt

3 tablespoons nonfat dry milk

2 cups unbleached white flour

1½ teaspoons yeast

Place all the ingredients in the machine, program for Bread, and press Start.

Large Oster, West Bend, Large Pillsbury, and Large Zojirushi

For the Sponge

1 cup brut champagne

2 teaspoons yeast

1 cup unbleached white flour

Pour the champagne into a medium-size glass or plastic mixing bowl. Sprinkle on the yeast and stir to dissolve. Add the flour and mix well. Cover with plastic wrap and set in a warm place for at least 12 hours.

To Complete the Bread

Sponge

2 tablespoons butter

1 extra-large egg

1 teaspoon salt

4 tablespoons nonfat dry milk

2¼ cups unbleached white flour

1½ teaspoons yeast

Place all the ingredients in the machine, program for Basic White Bread, Basic Bread, Basic Wheat, Basic White, or White/Whole Grain, and press Start or On.

Maxim, Small Oster, Sanyo, Sunbeam, Small Pillsbury, Small Toastmaster, and Small Zojirushi

For the Sponge

⅔ cup brut champagne

1 teaspoon yeast

⅔ cup unbleached white flour

Pour the champagne into a medium-size glass or plastic mixing bowl. Sprinkle on the yeast and stir to dissolve. Add the flour and mix well. Cover with plastic wrap and set in a warm place for at least 12 hours.

Continued

33

To Complete the Bread

Sponge
1 tablespoon butter
1 extra-large egg
½ teaspoon salt

2 tablespoons nonfat dry milk
1 cup plus 2 tablespoons unbleached
    white flour
1 teaspoon yeast

Have all the ingredients at room temperature. Place all the ingredients in the machine, program for Standard, Bread, Basic, White, or Basic Bread, and press Start.

....

SMALL WELBILT

FOR THE SPONGE

⅔ cup brut champagne
1 teaspoon yeast

⅔ cup unbleached white flour

Pour the champagne into a medium-size glass or plastic mixing bowl. Sprinkle on the yeast and stir to dissolve. Add the flour and mix well. Cover with plastic wrap and set in a warm place for at least 12 hours.

To Complete the Bread

1 teaspoon yeast
½ teaspoon salt
2 tablespoons nonfat dry milk
1 cup plus 2 tablespoons unbleached
    white flour

1 tablespoon butter
1 extra-large egg
Sponge

Have all the ingredients at room temperature. Place all the ingredients in the machine, program for Medium, and press Start.

....

SMALL PANASONIC/NATIONAL

FOR THE SPONGE

⅔ cup brut champagne

⅔ cup unbleached white flour

1 teaspoon yeast

Pour the champagne into a medium-size glass or plastic mixing bowl. Sprinkle on the yeast and stir to dissolve. Add the flour and mix well. Cover with plastic wrap and set in a warm place for at least 12 hours.

TO COMPLETE THE BREAD

2 tablespoons nonfat dry milk

1 cup plus 2 tablespoons unbleached
   white flour

1 tablespoon butter

1 extra-large egg

½ teaspoon salt

1 teaspoon yeast

Sponge

Place all the ingredients except the yeast in the machine. Place the yeast in the dispenser. Program for Basic Bread and press Start.

GARLIC FRENCH BREAD

Here the garlic is baked right into the bread.

DAK/WELBILT

1 tablespoon yeast

3 cups unbleached white flour (plus an additional ¼ cup if the dough looks very wet after the first 10 minutes of kneading)

2 teaspoons sugar

1 teaspoon salt

1½ to 2 teaspoons chopped garlic

2 tablespoons butter

1 cup warm water

2 egg whites, stiffly beaten

Have all the ingredients at room temperature. Place all the ingredients except the egg whites in the machine. Program for French Bread or if you want to form a baguette (the traditional-looking long loaf), then program for Manual. Press Start. Follow the Baking Instructions on page 39.

BLACK & DECKER, BETTY CROCKER, BREADMAN/TRILLIUM, HITACHI, LARGE TOASTMASTER, AND WILLIAMS-SONOMA

1½ teaspoons chopped garlic

2 tablespoons butter

1 cup warm water

2 teaspoons sugar

1 teaspoon salt

3 cups unbleached white flour (plus an additional ¼ cup if the dough looks very wet after the first 10 minutes of kneading)

2 teaspoons yeast

2 egg whites, stiffly beaten

Have all the ingredients at room temperature. Place all the ingredients except the egg whites in the machine. Program for French Bread or European or if you want to form a baguette (the traditional-looking long loaf), then program for Knead and First Rise or Dough. Press Start. Follow the Baking Instructions on page 39.

Panasonic/National

2 teaspoons sugar

1 teaspoon salt

3 cups unbleached white flour (plus an additional ¼ cup if the dough looks very wet after the first 10 minutes of kneading)

1½ teaspoons chopped garlic

2 tablespoons butter, at room temperature

1 cup warm water

2¾ teaspoons yeast

2 egg whites, stiffly beaten

Place all the ingredients except the egg whites and yeast in the machine. Place the yeast in the dispenser. Program for French Bread, and if you want to form a baguette (the traditional-looking long loaf), then also program for Dough or Manual. Press Start. Follow the Baking Instructions on page 39.

Regal, Large Oster, West Bend, Large Pillsbury, and Large Zojirushi

1½ teaspoons chopped garlic

2 tablespoons butter

1 cup warm water

2 teaspoons sugar

1 teaspoon salt

3 cups unbleached white flour (plus an additional ¼ cup if the dough looks very wet after the first 10 minutes of kneading)

1 tablespoon yeast

2 egg whites, stiffly beaten

Have all the ingredients at room temperature. Place all the ingredients except the egg whites in the machine. Program for French Bread or if you want to form a baguette (the traditional-looking long loaf), then program for Dough or Manual. Press Start or On. Follow the Baking Instructions on page 39.

Garlic French Bread

Maxim, Small Oster, Sunbeam, Small Pillsbury, Small Toastmaster, and Small Zojirushi

1½ teaspoons chopped garlic

1 tablespoon butter, at room
temperature

½ cup warm water

1 teaspoon sugar

½ teaspoon salt

2 cups unbleached white flour (plus an
additional 3 tablespoons if the dough
looks very wet after the first 10
minutes of kneading)

2 teaspoons yeast

1 egg white, stiffly beaten

Place all the ingredients except the egg white in the machine. Program for French
Bread or if you want to form a baguette (the traditional-looking long loaf), then
program for Dough or Manual. Press Start. Follow the Baking Instructions on
page 39.

....

Sanyo

1½ teaspoons chopped garlic

1 tablespoon butter

½ cup warm water

1 teaspoon sugar

½ teaspoon salt

1¾ cups unbleached white flour (plus
an additional 3 to 4 tablespoons if
the dough looks very wet after the
first 10 minutes of kneading)

1½ teaspoons yeast

1 egg white, stiffly beaten

Have all the ingredients at room temperature. Place all the ingredients except the
egg white in the machine. Program for Bread or if you want to form a baguette (the
traditional-looking long loaf), then program for Dough or Manual. Press Start.
Follow the Baking Instructions on page 39.

Small Welbilt

1½ teaspoons yeast

1½ cups unbleached white flour (plus an additional 3 to 4 tablespoons if the dough looks very wet after the first 10 minutes of kneading)

1 teaspoon sugar

½ teaspoon salt

1 teaspoon chopped garlic

1 tablespoon butter

½ cup warm water

1 egg white, stiffly beaten

Have all the ingredients at room temperature. Place all the ingredients except the egg white in the machine. Program for Medium or if you want to form a baguette (the traditional-looking long loaf), then program for Dough or Manual. Press Start. Follow the Baking Instructions below.

Small Panasonic/National

1 teaspoon sugar

½ teaspoon salt

2 cups unbleached white flour (plus an additional 3 tablespoons if the dough looks very wet after the first 10 minutes of kneading)

1½ teaspoons chopped garlic

1 tablespoon butter, at room temperature

½ cup warm water

2 teaspoons yeast

1 egg white, stiffly beaten

Place all the ingredients except the egg white and yeast in the machine. Place the yeast in the dispenser. Program for French Bread or if you want to form a baguette (the traditional-looking long loaf), then program for Dough or Manual. Press Start. Follow the Baking Instructions below.

Baking Instructions

1 egg white beaten together with 1 tablespoon water, for brushing

Continued

After all the ingredients are incorporated by the kneading blade, add the beaten egg white(s).

Either bake the bread in the machine, or if it is programmed for Manual, remove the dough at the end of the processing. Lightly grease a baking sheet and sprinkle it with cornmeal. Shape the dough into a baguette, approximately 10 to 12 inches long. Place the baguette on the prepared baking sheet, cover it with a clean dish towel, and set someplace warm and draft-free to rise until doubled in bulk.

Preheat the oven to 425°F. Place the rack on the center shelf. Brush the top of the baguette with the egg glaze. Bake in the center of the oven for 10 minutes at 425°F, then lower the temperature to 350°F for another 10 to 15 minutes. Bake until the top is light brown and the bottom sounds hollow when tapped.

HAMBURGER BUNS

Just right for holding juicy burgers, these are plump, golden buns with a substantial, but not too heavy, crumb.

Makes 10 (large machines) or 5 (small machines) buns

....

DAK/WELBILT

1 tablespoon yeast

3 cups unbleached white flour

¼ cup whole wheat flour

3 tablespoons nonfat dry milk

1 tablespoon sugar

1½ teaspoons salt

1 cup water

2 tablespoons butter OR margarine

Have all the ingredients at room temperature. Place all the ingredients in the machine, program for Dough or Manual, and press Start. When the cycle is completed, remove the dough, punch it down, and either let it rise for 20 additional minutes in the machine (set to Manual) or let it sit, covered with a clean dish towel, on a work surface in a warm, draft-free spot for 20 minutes. Follow the Baking Instructions on page 44.

....

BLACK & DECKER, BETTY CROCKER, BREADMAN/TRILLIUM, HITACHI, LARGE TOASTMASTER, AND WILLIAMS-SONOMA

1 cup water

2 tablespoons butter OR margarine, softened

3 cups unbleached white flour

¼ cup whole wheat flour

3 tablespoons nonfat dry milk

1 tablespoon sugar

1½ teaspoons salt

2½ teaspoons yeast (2 teaspoons for the Black & Decker, the Breadman/Trillium, and the Toastmaster)

Continued

41

Place all the ingredients in the machine, program for Dough or Knead and First Rise, and press Start. After the final knead cycle, remove the dough, punch it down, and let it sit, covered with a clean dish towel, on a work surface in a warm, draft-free spot for 20 minutes. Follow the Baking Instructions on page 44.

PANASONIC/NATIONAL

2¾ cups unbleached white flour
¼ cup whole wheat flour
3 tablespoons nonfat dry milk
1 tablespoon sugar
1½ teaspoons salt

1 cup water
2 tablespoons butter OR margarine, softened
1 tablespoon yeast

Place all the ingredients except the yeast in the machine. Place the yeast in the dispenser. Program for Dough and press Start. When the cycle is completed, remove the dough, punch it down, and either let it rise for 20 additional minutes in the machine (set to Manual) or let it sit, covered with a clean dish towel, on a work surface in a warm, draft-free spot for 20 minutes. Follow the Baking Instructions on page 44.

REGAL, LARGE OSTER, WEST BEND, LARGE PILLSBURY, AND LARGE ZOJIRUSHI

1 cup water
2 tablespoons butter OR margarine, softened
2¾ cups unbleached white flour
¼ cup whole wheat flour

2¾ tablespoons nonfat dry milk
1 tablespoon sugar
1½ teaspoons salt
1 tablespoon yeast

Place all the ingredients in the machine, program for Dough, and press Start or On. When the cycle is completed, remove the dough, punch it down, and let it sit, covered with a clean dish towel, on a work surface in a warm, draft-free spot for 20 minutes. Follow the Baking Instructions on page 44.

HAMBURGER - BUNS
MAXIM, SMALL OSTER, SANYO, SUNBEAM, SMALL PILLSBURY, SMALL TOASTMASTER, AND SMALL ZOJIRUSHI

¾ cup water

1½ tablespoons butter OR margarine, softened

2 cups unbleached white flour

3 tablespoons whole wheat flour

2 tablespoons nonfat dry milk

2 teaspoons sugar

1 teaspoon salt

2 teaspoons yeast

Place all the ingredients in the machine, program for Dough or Manual, and press Start. When the cycle is completed, remove the dough, punch it down, and either let it rise for 20 additional minutes in the machine (set to Manual) or let it sit, covered with a clean dish towel, on a work surface in a warm, draft-free spot for 20 minutes. Follow the Baking Instructions on page 44.

SMALL WELBILT

2 teaspoons yeast

2 cups unbleached white flour

3 tablespoons whole wheat flour

2 tablespoons nonfat dry milk

2 teaspoons sugar

1 teaspoon salt

¾ cup water

1½ tablespoons butter OR margarine

Have all the ingredients at room temperature. Place all the ingredients in the machine, program for Manual, and press Start. When the cycle is completed, remove the dough, punch it down, and either let it rise for 20 additional minutes in the machine (set to Manual) or let it sit, covered with a clean dish towel, on a work surface in a warm, draft-free spot for 20 minutes. Follow the Baking Instructions on page 44.

Small Panasonic/National

2 cups unbleached white flour

3 tablespoons whole wheat flour

2 tablespoons nonfat dry milk

2 teaspoons sugar

1 teaspoon salt

¾ cup water

1½ tablespoons butter OR margarine, softened

2 teaspoons yeast

Place all the ingredients except the yeast in the machine. Place the yeast in the dispenser. Program for Dough or Manual, and press Start. When the cycle is completed, remove the dough, punch it down, and either let it rise for 20 additional minutes in the machine (set to Manual) or let it sit, covered with a clean dish towel, on a work surface in a warm, draft-free spot for 20 minutes. Follow the Baking Instructions below.

Baking Instructions

Large machines: Divide the dough into 10 equal pieces. Small machines: Divide the dough into 5 equal pieces. Form each piece into a smooth round ball. Place the balls on a greased baking sheet about 2 inches apart and press them lightly with the palm of your hand to flatten slightly. Cover them with the same clean dish towel and let rise in a warm, draft-free place until doubled in bulk, about 1 hour.

Bake at 375°F on a rack set in the center of the oven for 15 to 20 minutes, or until the buns are well browned. Remove from the baking sheet (separating, if necessary) and cool on wire racks.

Variations: Just before baking, brush the tops of the buns with 1 egg white beaten together with 1 tablespoon of water. Sprinkle sesame or caraway seeds on top of each bun. Add 1 tablespoon of dried dill to the dry ingredients.

PIZZA CRUST

This recipe is an adaptation of one created by George Germain and JoAnn Kileen, who own Al Forno, our very favorite restaurant in Providence, Rhode Island. The pizza that they serve is grilled over a wood fire. The only way to get the real thing is to visit Al Forno; you can eat this while you pack your bags.

....

DAK/WELBILT

1 tablespoon yeast

1 teaspoon sugar

2 teaspoons salt

¼ cup cornmeal

3 tablespoons whole wheat flour

3 cups unbleached white flour

1¼ cups water (plus an additional 1 or 2 tablespoons if the mixture looks dry and crumbly after the first 10 minutes of kneading)

2 tablespoons olive oil

Have all the ingredients at room temperature. Place all the ingredients in the machine, program for Dough or Manual, and press Start. Remove the dough from the machine and let it rest for 10 minutes at room temperature. Follow the Baking Instructions on page 47.

....

BLACK & DECKER, BETTY CROCKER, BREADMAN/TRILLIUM, HITACHI, LARGE TOASTMASTER, WILLIAMS-SONOMA, REGAL, LARGE OSTER, WEST BEND, LARGE PILLSBURY, AND LARGE ZOJIRUSHI

1¼ cups water (plus an additional 1 or 2 tablespoons if the mixture looks dry and crumbly after the first 10 minutes of kneading)

2 tablespoons olive oil

1 teaspoon sugar

2 teaspoons salt

¼ cup cornmeal

3 tablespoons whole wheat flour

3 cups unbleached white flour

1 tablespoon yeast (2 teaspoons for the Black & Decker, the Toastmaster, and the Breadman/Trillium)

Continued

Place all the ingredients in the machine, program for Knead and First Rise, Dough, or Manual, and press Start or On. Remove the dough from the machine and let it rest for 10 minutes at room temperature. Follow the Baking Instructions on page 47.

PANASONIC/NATIONAL

1 teaspoon sugar

2 teaspoons salt

¼ cup cornmeal

3 tablespoons whole wheat flour

3 cups unbleached white flour

1¼ cups water (plus an additional 1 or 2 tablespoons if the mixture looks dry and crumbly after the first 10 minutes of kneading)

2 tablespoons olive oil

1 tablespoon yeast

Place all the ingredients except the yeast in the machine. Place the yeast in the dispenser. Program for Dough or Manual, and press Start. Remove the dough from the machine and let it rest for 10 minutes at room temperature. Follow the Baking Instructions on page 47.

PIZZA CRUST

MAXIM, SMALL OSTER, SANYO, SUNBEAM, SMALL PILLSBURY, SMALL TOASTMASTER, AND SMALL ZOJIRUSHI

¾ cup water (plus an additional 1 or 2 tablespoons if the mixture looks dry and crumbly after the first 10 minutes of kneading)

2 tablespoons olive oil

½ teaspoon sugar

1 teaspoon salt

3 tablespoons cornmeal

2 tablespoons whole wheat flour

2 cups unbleached white flour

2 teaspoons yeast

Place all the ingredients in the machine, program for Dough or Manual, and press Start. Remove the dough from the machine and let it rest for 10 minutes at room temperature. Follow the Baking Instructions on page 47.

SMALL WELBILT

2 teaspoons yeast
½ teaspoon sugar
1 teaspoon salt
3 tablespoons cornmeal
2 tablespoons whole wheat flour
2 cups unbleached white flour

¾ cup water (plus an additional 1 or 2 tablespoons if the mixture looks dry and crumbly after the first 10 minutes of kneading)
2 tablespoons olive oil

Have all the ingredients at room temperature. Place all the ingredients in the machine, program for Manual, and press Start. Remove the dough from the machine and let it rest for 10 minutes at room temperature. Follow the Baking Instructions below.

SMALL PANASONIC/NATIONAL

½ teaspoon sugar
1 teaspoon salt
3 tablespoons cornmeal
2 tablespoons whole wheat flour
2 cups unbleached white flour

¾ cup water (plus an additional 1 or 2 tablespoons if the mixture looks dry and crumbly after the first 10 minutes of kneading)
2 tablespoons olive oil
2 teaspoons yeast

Place all the ingredients except the yeast in the machine. Place the yeast in the dispenser. Program for Dough or Manual and press Start. Remove the dough from the machine and let it rest for 10 minutes at room temperature. Follow the Baking Instructions below.

BAKING INSTRUCTIONS

If you have a pizza stone or tiles, place them on the middle rack of the oven. Preheat the oven to 450°F. Sprinkle either a wooden pizza paddle or a heavy-duty cookie sheet with cornmeal. Divide the dough into 2 pieces. Use your hands or a floured rolling pin to form 1 piece into a flat 10- to 12-inch disk (large machines) or a 6- to 8-inch disk (small machines). Add the toppings of your choice (suggestions follow) and either slide the pizza onto the hot stone or tiles or slide the cookie sheet into the oven.

Bake for 12 to 15 minutes (large machines) or 10 to 12 minutes (small machines), depending how thick you made the crust, or until the pizza is cooked all the way through (test the center with the point of a sharp knife). Repeat with the remaining disk.

Serve hot.

Tip: We find it much easier to work with chilled pizza dough. Oil a large bowl and place the dough in it after it is finished in the machine. Cover tightly with plastic wrap and refrigerate for 2 hours to overnight. Punch the dough down and proceed as above.

Hints: Remember to leave at least a 1-inch unsauced border around the outer raised edge of the pizza so the sauce doesn't flow off when you remove it from the oven. If the top seems to be burning and the crust isn't done, lower the oven temperature to 375°F and lay a sheet of foil, shiny side down, over the burned area. Make mini-pizzas by dividing the dough into 4 pieces rather than 2.

Make 2 batches of dough if you want to make more than 2 pizzas. Store the first one in the refrigerator while you make the second.

Substitute garlic oil for the olive oil.

Assemble all the toppings ahead of time and have them at room temperature.

Variation: Add 1 teaspoon of a dried herb such as thyme, basil, or oregano with the ingredients.

PIZZA TOPPINGS

As you will see from this list, we are fans of easy yet nontraditional pizza toppings. After you get the hang of this, you can easily make up your own toppings. Check the refrigerator for leftovers, too. You can use either high-quality store-bought tomato sauce or your own, and top the pizza with grated cheese. Count on about ½ cup tomato sauce for each pizza.

Crumbled goat cheese, sun-dried tomatoes, and capers

Crumbled Roquefort or Stilton cheese, bacon, and thinly sliced red (Bermuda) onion

Brie or Camembert cheese and walnuts that have been quickly sautéed in butter

Sautéed mushroom slices and grated Cheddar cheese

Salsa and grated Monterey Jack or Cheddar cheese

Canned Italian tuna, slightly drained of its oil and crumbled, capers, lemon juice, sliced black olives, and anchovies (optional)

Cooked sausage, crumbled, sautéed green and red peppers, and onions

Thinly sliced cooked potatoes, Dijon mustard, and grated Swiss cheese

Pesto sauce (homemade or commercially prepared), pine nuts, and grated Parmesan cheese

Leftover cooked boneless chicken and the cheese of your choice

Cooked shrimp, crumbled feta cheese, and black olives

ROSEMARY FOCACCIA

What's hotter than pizza and trendier than dried tomatoes? Focaccia. This rustic Italian yeast flatbread is so simple to make that you'll never buy one again. The bread machine makes the dough, which is similar to pizza dough, and you form it, then bake it in the oven. You can use either fresh or dried rosemary in this recipe. If you use dry, then make sure it's leaves and not powdered (ground).

Focaccia can be served hot from the oven or at room temperature. Cut into wedges or slice it horizontally to make the world's best sandwiches.

Since you are making dough, you won't be using the timer. Ingredients can go into the machine in any order, except with DAK, which requires that the yeast go in first.

FOR ALL LARGE MACHINES

2½ teaspoons yeast

3 cups unbleached white flour

½ cup cornmeal

2 teaspoons salt

⅓ cup plus ¼ cup olive oil (use
   flavored garlic- rosemary- or basil-
   oils if you wish)

1⅓ cups water

2 tablespoons fresh rosemary leaves OR
   1 tablespoon dried rosemary leaves

2 teaspoons coarse salt

Place all the ingredients except the coarse salt and the ¼ cup olive oil in the machine. Program for Knead, Basic Dough, or Manual and press Start or On. Check the dough after the first 5 to 7 minutes of the first knead cycle and add additional water, a tablespoon at a time, if necessary, to make a smooth, soft ball of dough. See page 51 to form and bake the focaccia.

For All Small Machines

1½ teaspoons yeast

2 cups unbleached white flour

⅓ cup cornmeal

1½ teaspoons salt

¼ cup plus 2 tablespoons olive oil (use
   flavored garlic- rosemary- or basil-
   oils if you wish)

¾ cups water

1 tablespoon fresh rosemary leaves OR 2
   teaspoons dried rosemary leaves

1½ teaspoons coarse salt

Place all the ingredients except the coarse salt and the 2 tablespoons olive oil in the machine. Program for Knead, Dough, or Manual and press Start. Check the dough after the first 5 to 7 minutes of the first knead cycle and add additional water, a tablespoon at a time, if necessary, to make a smooth, soft ball of dough.

Shaping and Baking the Focaccia

Sprinkle a heavy baking sheet with cornmeal. At the end of the final cycle, remove the dough from the machine to a lightly floured work surface. Pat it into a 1-inch-thick disk (12 inches in diameter for large machines, 9 inches for small). Place the disk on the prepared baking sheet and cover with a clean towel or plastic wrap and allow it to rise for about 30 minutes, or until almost doubled in height and puffy. Preheat the oven to 425°F with the rack in the center position. Using your finger-tips, poke dimples all over the surface of the dough. Sprinkle with the coarse salt and drizzle with the oil. Bake the focaccia for 10 minutes at 425°F, then reduce the heat to 350°F and bake for an additional 12 to 15 minutes, or until the top is golden brown. Serve it hot or at room temperature by cutting it into wedges.

BREADSTICKS

This great recipe came from Lynne Bail, one of our recipe testers. These breadsticks are far superior to any you'll find in a store.

Makes 32 breadsticks

....

1 recipe Pizza Crust (page 45)
1 egg lightly beaten with 1 tablespoon
  water

3 tablespoons sesame seeds OR caraway
  seeds

Preheat the oven to 425°F. Place the rack in the center position. Grease 2 heavy-duty baking sheets or line them with foil, shiny side up.

Divide the dough into 12 pieces (large machines) or 8 pieces (small machines). On a lightly floured board, roll each piece to a 4 x 2½-inch rectangle. Cut each rectangle lengthwise into four 4-inch sticks. Transfer the sticks to the prepared sheets, leaving ½ inch between the sticks.

Brush the top of each stick with the egg glaze and sprinkle with sesame seeds. Bake for 10 minutes, or until golden brown. When the breadsticks are completely cool, store them in an airtight container.

PITA BREAD

These are authentic and so deliciously fresh-tasting. They can be eaten as is, or split in half and toasted with sprinkled Parmesan cheese.

DAK/WELBILT

2½ teaspoons yeast
3¼ cups unbleached white flour
1 tablespoon sugar

1 teaspoon salt
1 cup plus 2 tablespoons warm water
2 tablespoons olive oil

Have all the ingredients at room temperature. Place all the ingredients in the machine, program for Dough or Manual, and press Start. At the end of the final cycle, remove the dough. Cover it with a clean dish towel and let it rest for 15 minutes. Follow the Baking Instructions on page 55.

BLACK & DECKER, BETTY CROCKER, BREADMAN/TRILLIUM, HITACHI, LARGE TOASTMASTER, WILLIAMS-SONOMA, REGAL, LARGE OSTER, WEST BEND, LARGE PILLSBURY, AND LARGE ZOJIRUSHI

2 tablespoons olive oil
1 cup plus 2 tablespoons warm water
3¼ cups unbleached white flour
1 tablespoon sugar

1 teaspoon salt
2½ teaspoons yeast (2 teaspoons for
    the Black & Decker, Toastmaster,
    and Breadman/Trillium)

Place all the ingredients in the machine, program for Dough or Manual, and press Start or On. At the end of the final cycle, turn the dough onto a lightly floured board set in a warm, draft-free place and cover it with a clean dish towel for 30 minutes. Follow the Baking Instructions on page 55.

Panasonic/National

2 tablespoons olive oil

1 tablespoon sugar

1 cup plus 2 tablespoons warm water

1 teaspoon salt

3¼ cups unbleached white flour

2½ teaspoons yeast

Place all the ingredients except the yeast in the machine. Place the yeast in the dispenser. Program for Dough or Manual and press Start. When the beeper sounds, remove the dough. Cover it with a clean dish towel and let it rest for 15 minutes. Follow the Baking Instructions on page 55.

PITA BREAD

Maxim, Small Oster, Sanyo, Sunbeam, Small Pillsbury, Small Toastmaster, and Small Zojirushi

1 tablespoon olive oil

2 teaspoons sugar

¾ cup plus 1 tablespoon warm water

¾ teaspoon salt

2 cups unbleached white flour

1½ teaspoons yeast

Place all the ingredients in the machine, program for Dough or Manual, and press Start. When the beeper sounds, remove the dough. Follow the Baking Instructions on page 55.

Small Welbilt

1½ teaspoons yeast

¾ teaspoon salt

2 cups unbleached white flour

1 tablespoon olive oil

2 teaspoons sugar

¾ cup plus 1 tablespoon warm water

Have all the ingredients at room temperature. Place all the ingredients in the machine, program for Manual, and press Start. When the beeper sounds, remove the dough. Cover it with a clean dish towel and let it rest for 15 minutes. Follow the Baking Instructions on page 55.

Small Panasonic/National

2 cups unbleached white flour

2 teaspoons sugar

¾ teaspoon salt

1 tablespoon olive oil

¾ cup plus 1 tablespoon warm water

1½ teaspoons yeast

Place all the ingredients except the yeast in the machine. Place the yeast in the dispenser. Program for Dough or Manual, and press Start. When the beeper sounds, remove the dough. Cover it with a clean dish towel and let it rest for 15 minutes. Follow the Baking Instructions below.

Baking Instructions

While the dough is resting, preheat the oven to 450°F with the rack on the lowest position. Set a pizza stone, or bread tiles, or a very heavy-duty cookie sheet (one that won't warp under high heat), or a flat ovenproof metal skillet on the rack to let it preheat.

Divide the dough into 6 equal pieces and shape each into a ball. Use a rolling pin to flatten each ball into an 8-inch circle (large machines) or a 5-inch circle (small machines). Use a wide spatula to slide the pitas onto the heated stone, tiles, cookie sheet, or skillet and bake for 5 minutes. The tops will not be brown. If you wish to brown the tops, set them under the broiler for 30 to 40 seconds. Watch them carefully because they burn easily.

WHOLE WHEAT PITA

The addition of whole wheat flour gives these loaves a nutty, sweet taste. You have the option to add dried herbs (leaves, not ground), which makes for a more complex taste. Try rosemary, dill, or thyme by themselves or in combination.

Makes 6 (large machines) or 4 (small machines) pitas

FOR ALL LARGE MACHINES

2½ teaspoons yeast

2 cups whole wheat flour

1¼ cups unbleached white flour

1 teaspoon salt

1 teaspoon dried herbs of your choice
 (optional)

1 cup plus 2 tablespoons water

2 tablespoons vegetable oil

Place all the ingredients in the machine, program for Dough, Manual, or Knead, and press Start. Check the dough after the first 5 minutes of kneading, adding additional water or flour to make a smooth, supple ball of dough that is not sticky to the touch. At the end of the final cycle, remove the dough to a lightly floured work surface, cover it with a clean towel, and allow it to rest for 30 minutes. Follow the Baking Instructions on page 57.

FOR ALL SMALL MACHINES

1½ teaspoons yeast

1⅓ cups whole wheat flour

⅔ cup unbleached white flour

¾ teaspoon salt

¾ teaspoon dried herbs of your choice
 (optional)

¾ cup plus 1 tablespoon water

1 tablespoon vegetable oil

Place all the ingredients in the machine, program for Dough, Manual, or Knead, and press Start. Check the dough after the first 5 minutes of kneading, adding additional water or flour to make a smooth, supple ball of dough that is not sticky to the touch. At the end of the final cycle, remove the dough to a lightly floured work surface, cover it with a clean towel, and allow it to rest for 15 minutes. Follow the Baking Instructions below.

BAKING INSTRUCTIONS

Preheat the oven to 450°F with the rack in the lowest position. Set a pizza stone, bread tiles, or a very heavy-duty baking sheet on the rack to allow it to preheat.

Divide the dough into 6 (large machines) or 4 (small machines) equal pieces. Use a rolling pin to roll each piece to a 6-inch circle, making the dough as thin as you can. The dough does not rise after it is rolled out. Use a wide metal spatula to slide each circle onto the heated stone, tiles, or pan, and bake for 5 to 7 minutes. Cool on a rack and serve warm or at room temperature.

WHOLE WHEAT AND MULTIGRAIN BREADS

BASIC WHOLE WHEAT BREAD

The addition of gluten to this recipe helps the bread rise higher than it normally would. This is a nutty, dense loaf with a fine crumb and a great crust that can be thinly sliced for sandwiches.

DAK/Welbilt

1 tablespoon yeast

1½ teaspoons salt

3 cups whole wheat flour

½ cup unbleached white flour

⅓ cup cornmeal

3 teaspoons Lora Brody's Bread Dough
   Enhancer™ OR 2 tablespoons gluten

3 tablespoons nonfat dry milk

⅓ cup honey

1⅓ cups water

2 tablespoons vegetable oil OR butter

Have all the ingredients at room temperature. Place all the ingredients in the machine, program for White Bread, and press Start.

Black & Decker, Betty Crocker, Breadman/Trillium, Hitachi, Large Oster, Regal, Large Toastmaster, and Williams-Sonoma

⅓ cup honey

1⅓ cups water

2 tablespoons vegetable oil OR butter, at
   room temperature

1½ teaspoons salt

3 tablespoons nonfat dry milk

3 cups whole wheat flour

½ cup unbleached white flour

⅓ cup cornmeal

3 teaspoons Lora Brody's Bread Dough
   Enhancer™ OR 2 tablespoons gluten

2 teaspoons yeast

Place all the ingredients in the machine, program for Bread, Whole Wheat, Basic Wheat, Whole Wheat/Multigrain, White/Whole Grain, or Wheat, and press Start.

PANASONIC/NATIONAL

1½ teaspoons salt

3 cups whole wheat flour

½ cup unbleached white flour

⅓ cup cornmeal

3 teaspoons Lora Brody's Bread Dough
Enhancer™ OR 2 tablespoons gluten

3 tablespoons nonfat dry milk

⅓ cup honey

1⅓ cups water

2 tablespoons vegetable oil OR butter, at
room temperature

1 tablespoon yeast

Place all the ingredients except the yeast in the machine. Place the yeast in the dispenser. Program for Basic Bread and press Start.

WEST BEND, LARGE PILLSBURY, AND LARGE ZOJIRUSHI

⅓ cup honey

1⅓ cups water

2 tablespoons vegetable oil OR butter, at
room temperature

1½ teaspoons salt

3 tablespoons nonfat dry milk

3 cups whole wheat flour

½ cup unbleached white flour

⅓ cup cornmeal

3 teaspoons Lora Brody's Bread Dough
Enhancer™ OR 2 tablespoons gluten

1 tablespoon yeast

Place all the ingredients in the machine, program for Basic White Bread, Whole Wheat, Basic Wheat, Whole Wheat/Multigrain, White/Whole Grain, or Wheat, and press Start or On.

BASIC WHOLE WHEAT BREAD

MAXIM, SMALL OSTER, SANYO, SUNBEAM, SMALL PILLSBURY, SMALL TOASTMASTER, AND SMALL ZOJIRUSHI

¼ cup honey

¾ cup plus 3 tablespoons water

1½ tablespoons vegetable oil OR butter,
at room temperature

1 teaspoon salt

1¾ cups whole wheat flour

¼ cup unbleached white flour

¼ cup cornmeal

2 teaspoons Lora Brody's Bread Dough
Enhancer™ OR 1 tablespoon gluten

2 tablespoons nonfat dry milk

2 teaspoons yeast

Continued

Place all the ingredients in the machine, program for Whole Wheat, Whole Grain, Standard, or Bread, and press Start.

SMALL WELBILT

2 teaspoons yeast

1 teaspoon salt

1¾ cups whole wheat flour

¼ cup unbleached white flour

¼ cup cornmeal

2 teaspoons Lora Brody's Bread Dough Enhancer™ OR 1 tablespoon gluten

2 tablespoons nonfat dry milk

¼ cup honey

¾ cup plus 3 tablespoons water

1½ tablespoons vegetable oil OR butter

Have all the ingredients at room temperature. Place all the ingredients in the machine, program for Medium, and press Start.

SMALL PANASONIC/NATIONAL

1¾ cups whole wheat flour

¼ cup unbleached white flour

¼ cup cornmeal

2 teaspoons Lora Brody's Bread Dough Enhancer™ OR 1 tablespoon gluten

2 tablespoons nonfat dry milk

¼ cup honey

¾ cup plus 3 tablespoons water

1½ tablespoons vegetable oil OR butter, at room temperature

1 teaspoon salt

2 teaspoons yeast

Place all the ingredients except the yeast in the machine. Place the yeast in the dispenser. Program for Basic Bread and press Start.

MILLIE'S BASIC WHOLE WHEAT BREAD

This is a nutty, slightly sweet, fine-grained compact loaf that slices beautifully. Millie recommends toasting it and slathering it with crunchy peanut butter. It also can be sliced paper-thin and served with sweet butter and smoked salmon.

DAK/WELBILT

1 tablespoon yeast

2 cups whole wheat flour

1 cup unbleached white flour

1½ tablespoons powdered skim milk

½ cup cornmeal

1½ teaspoons salt

2 tablespoons gluten OR 3 teaspoons Lora Brody's Bread Dough Enhancer™ (optional for a higher loaf)

1 extra-large egg, placed in a 1-cup measure, plus enough warm water to measure 1 cup liquid total

2 tablespoons butter OR margarine

¼ cup molasses

2 tablespoons honey

Have all the ingredients at room temperature. Place all the ingredients in the machine, program for White Bread, and press Start. Check the dough after the first 10 minutes of kneading, adding several tablespoons more unbleached white flour if the dough appears very moist.

Black & Decker, Betty Crocker, Breadman/Trillium, Hitachi, Large Toastmaster, Williams-Sonoma, Regal, Large Oster, West Bend, Large Pillsbury, and Large Zojirushi

1 extra-large egg, placed in a 1-cup measure, plus enough warm water to measure 1 cup liquid total

2 tablespoons butter OR margarine, at room temperature

¼ cup molasses

2 tablespoons honey

½ cup cornmeal

2 cups whole wheat flour

1 cup unbleached white flour

1½ tablespoons powdered skim milk

1½ teaspoons salt

2 tablespoons gluten OR 3 teaspoons Lora Brody's Bread Dough Enhancer™ (optional for a higher loaf)

2½ teaspoons yeast

Place all the ingredients in the machine, program for Bread, Basic White Bread, Whole Wheat, Basic Wheat, Whole Wheat/Multigrain, White/Whole Grain, or Wheat, and press Start or On. Check the dough after the first 10 minutes of kneading, adding several tablespoons more unbleached white flour if the dough appears very moist.

Panasonic/National

2 cups whole wheat flour

1 cup unbleached white flour

1½ tablespoons powdered skim milk

½ cup cornmeal

1½ teaspoons salt

2 tablespoons gluten OR 3 teaspoons Lora Brody's Bread Dough Enhancer™ (optional for a higher loaf)

1 extra-large egg, placed in a 1-cup measure, plus enough warm water to measure 1 cup liquid total

2 tablespoons butter OR margarine, at room temperature

¼ cup molasses

2 tablespoons honey

2½ teaspoons yeast

Place all the ingredients except the yeast in the machine. Place the yeast in the dispenser. Program for Basic Bread and press Start. Check the dough after the first

10 minutes of kneading, adding several tablespoons more unbleached white flour if the dough appears very moist.

Maxim, Small Oster, Sanyo, Sunbeam, Small Pillsbury, Small Toastmaster, and Small Zojirushi

1 extra-large egg, placed in a 1-cup measure, plus enough warm water to measure ¾ cup liquid total

1½ tablespoons butter OR margarine, at room temperature

3 tablespoons molasses

1½ tablespoons honey

1½ cups whole wheat flour

⅓ cup cornmeal

½ cup unbleached white flour

1 tablespoon powdered skim milk

1 teaspoon salt

1½ tablespoons gluten OR 2 teaspoons Lora Brody's Bread Dough Enhancer™ (optional for a higher loaf)

2 teaspoons yeast

Place all the ingredients in the machine, program for Whole Wheat, Whole Grain, Standard, or Bread, and press Start. Check the dough after the first 10 minutes of kneading, adding several tablespoons more unbleached white flour if the dough appears very moist.

Small Welbilt

2 teaspoons yeast

1½ cups whole wheat flour

½ cup unbleached white flour

⅓ cup cornmeal

1 tablespoon powdered skim milk

1 teaspoon salt

1½ tablespoons gluten OR 2 teaspoons Lora Brody's Bread Dough Enhancer™ (optional for a higher loaf)

1 extra-large egg, placed in a 1-cup measure, plus enough warm water to measure ¾ cup liquid total

1½ tablespoons butter OR margarine

3 tablespoons molasses

1½ tablespoons honey

Continued

Have all the ingredients at room temperature. Place all the ingredients in the machine, program for Medium, and press Start. Check the dough after the first 10 minutes of kneading, adding several tablespoons more unbleached white flour if the dough appears very moist.

SMALL PANASONIC/NATIONAL

1½ cups whole wheat flour

½ cup unbleached white flour

1 tablespoon powdered skim milk

⅓ cup cornmeal

1 teaspoon salt

1½ tablespoons gluten OR 2 teaspoons Lora Brody's Bread Dough Enhancer™ (optional for a higher loaf)

1 extra-large egg, placed in a 1-cup measure, plus enough warm water to measure ¾ cup liquid total

1½ tablespoons butter OR margarine, at room temperature

3 tablespoons molasses

1½ tablespoons honey

2 teaspoons yeast

Place all the ingredients except the yeast in the machine. Place the yeast in the dispenser. Program for Basic Bread and press Start. Check the dough after the first 10 minutes of kneading, adding several tablespoons more unbleached white flour if the dough appears very moist.

HAZELNUT BUCKWHEAT BREAD

This compact bread has a deep nut-brown crust into which the hazelnuts are embedded, making for a handsome loaf. It has the assertive taste of buckwheat infused with the flavor of hazelnuts. Serve this as an accompaniment to a cheese course along with a bunch of large, juicy purple grapes. Hazelnut and walnut oils are available at specialty food stores.

DAK/Welbilt

2½ teaspoons yeast

½ cup buckwheat flour

2½ cups unbleached white flour

1½ teaspoons salt

1 cup water

3 tablespoons hazelnut oil OR walnut oil

2 tablespoons molasses

1 cup hazelnuts, skinned, toasted, and coarsely chopped (see Note)

Have all the ingredients at room temperature. Place all the ingredients except the hazelnuts in the machine, program for White Bread, and press Start. Add the hazelnuts when the beeper sounds. Not all of the nuts will be incorporated into the inner part of the dough—some will remain as part of the outer crust, which is fine since it makes the bread even more beautiful to look at.

BLACK & DECKER, BETTY CROCKER, BREADMAN/TRILLIUM, HITACHI, LARGE OSTER, LARGE TOASTMASTER, AND WILLIAMS-SONOMA

1 cup water

3 tablespoons hazelnut oil OR walnut oil

2 tablespoons molasses

½ cup buckwheat flour

2½ cups unbleached white flour

1½ teaspoons salt

2 teaspoons yeast

1 cup hazelnuts, skinned, toasted, and coarsely chopped (see Note)

Continued

Place all the ingredients except the hazelnuts in the machine, program for Bread, Raisin Bread or Fruit and Nut, Whole Wheat, Basic Wheat, Whole Wheat/Multigrain, White/Whole Grain, or Wheat, and press Start. Add the hazelnuts when the beeper sounds or during the last 5 minutes of the final knead cycle. Not all of the nuts will be incorporated into the inner part of the dough—some will remain as part of the outer crust, which is fine since it makes the bread even more beautiful to look at.

PANASONIC/NATIONAL

½ cup buckwheat flour

2½ cups unbleached white flour

1½ teaspoons salt

1 cup water

3 tablespoons hazelnut oil OR walnut oil

2 tablespoons molasses

2½ teaspoons yeast

1 cup hazelnuts, skinned, toasted, and coarsely chopped (see Note)

Have all the ingredients at room temperature. Place all the ingredients except the hazelnuts in the machine. Program for Basic Bread and press Start. Add the hazelnuts after 20 minutes into the processing. Not all of the nuts will be incorporated into the inner part of the dough—some will remain as part of the outer crust, which is fine since it makes the bread even more beautiful to look at.

REGAL

1 cup water

3 tablespoons hazelnut oil OR walnut oil

2 tablespoons molasses

½ cup buckwheat flour

2½ cups unbleached white flour

1½ teaspoons salt

2½ teaspoons yeast

1 cup hazelnuts, skinned, toasted, and coarsely chopped (see Note)

Have all the ingredients at room temperature. Place all the ingredients except the hazelnuts in the machine, program for Raisin Bread, and press Start. Add the hazelnuts when the beeper sounds. Not all of the nuts will be incorporated into the inner part of the dough—some will remain as part of the outer crust, which is fine since it makes the bread even more beautiful to look at.

....

Large Pillsbury, Large Zojirushi, and West Bend

1 cup water

¼ cup hazelnut oil OR walnut oil

2 tablespoons molasses

2 teaspoons salt

⅔ cup buckwheat flour

3 cups unbleached white flour

1 tablespoon yeast

1 cup hazelnuts, skinned, toasted, and
   coarsely chopped (see Note)

Place all the ingredients except the hazelnuts in the machine, program for Raisin Bread, Whole Wheat, Basic Wheat, Whole Wheat/Multigrain, White/Whole Grain, or Wheat, and press Start or On. Add the hazelnuts when the beeper sounds or during the last 5 minutes of the final knead cycle. Not all of the nuts will be incorporated into the inner part of the dough—some will remain as part of the outer crust, which is fine since it makes the bread even more beautiful to look at.

....

Maxim, Small Oster, Small Pillsbury, Sanyo, Sunbeam, Small Toastmaster, and Small Zojirushi

⅔ cup water

2 tablespoons hazelnut oil OR walnut oil

1 tablespoon molasses

½ cup buckwheat flour

1½ cups unbleached white flour

1 teaspoon salt

2 teaspoons yeast

⅔ cup hazelnuts, skinned, toasted, and
   coarsely chopped (see Note)

Have all the ingredients at room temperature. Place all the ingredients except the hazelnuts in the machine, program for Whole Wheat, Whole Grain, Standard, or Bread, and press Start. Add the hazelnuts when the beeper sounds or 20 minutes into the kneading cycle. Not all of the nuts will be incorporated into the inner part of the dough—some will remain as part of the outer crust, which is fine since it makes the bread even more beautiful to look at.

SMALL WELBILT

2 teaspoons yeast
½ cup buckwheat flour
1½ cups unbleached white flour
1 teaspoon salt
⅔ cup water

2 tablespoons hazelnut oil OR walnut oil
1 tablespoon molasses
⅔ cup hazelnuts, skinned, toasted, and
   coarsely chopped (see Note)

Have all the ingredients at room temperature. Place all the ingredients except the hazelnuts in the machine, program for Medium, and press Start. Add the hazelnuts when the beeper sounds. Not all of the nuts will be incorporated into the inner part of the dough—some will remain as part of the outer crust, which is fine since it makes the bread even more beautiful to look at.

SMALL PANASONIC/NATIONAL

½ cup buckwheat flour
1½ cups unbleached white flour
1 teaspoon salt
⅔ cup water
2 tablespoons hazelnut oil OR walnut oil

1 tablespoon molasses
2 teaspoons yeast
⅔ cup hazelnuts, skinned, toasted, and
   coarsely chopped (see Note)

Have all the ingredients at room temperature. Place all the ingredients except the yeast and the hazelnuts in the machine. Place the yeast in the dispenser. Program for Basic Bread and press Start. Add the hazelnuts 20 minutes into the processing. Not all of the nuts will be incorporated into the inner part of the dough—some will remain as part of the outer crust, which is fine since it makes the bread even more beautiful to look at.

NOTE: Occasionally you can buy hazelnuts that have been shelled and the thin brown skin removed. In this case, simply place the hazelnuts in one layer on a rimmed baking sheet or pan in a 400°F oven for about 5 to 10 minutes. Every minute or so, reach in with a pot holder and shake the pan to rotate the nuts so they can cook evenly. When the nuts are a deep golden brown (don't make yourself crazy trying to get them uniformly brown), remove them from the oven and cool.

If you have bought unskinned hazelnuts, proceed as above, but when the skins have started to flake off and the nuts have turned golden brown, remove the sheet from the oven and spread a heavy towel over the nuts. Use both hands to roll the nuts under the towel to remove as much of the skin as possible. Pick out the nuts and discard the skin. Don't worry if there are pieces of skin still attached or if there are a few dark spots. Cool before using.

Since this is a time-consuming job, our advice is to make two or three times the amount you need for the recipe and freeze the rest for another time. Store the nuts in a plastic freezer bag.

RUSSIAN BLACK BREAD

We think this looks and tastes worlds better than the store-bought variety. The deep, dense, compact loaf *will not rise very high at all unless you add gluten or dough enhancer*; however, the hearty slices are filling and they make a perfect accompaniment, if not a whole meal, when served with soup.

DAK/Welbilt

2½ teaspoons yeast

1 cup rye flour

1½ cups unbleached white flour

½ cup oat bran

1 teaspoon sugar

1 teaspoon salt

2 tablespoons gluten OR 3 teaspoons Lora Brody's Bread Dough Enhancer™ (optional for a higher loaf)

1 teaspoon instant coffee (powder or granules)

1 teaspoon minced dried onion OR ½ small raw onion, finely chopped

1½ tablespoons unsweetened cocoa

1 tablespoon vinegar

2 tablespoons vegetable oil

1 cup water

2 tablespoons caraway seeds

Have all the ingredients at room temperature. Place all the ingredients in the machine, program for White Bread, and press Start.

Black & Decker, Betty Crocker, Breadman/Trillium, Hitachi, Large Oster, Large Toastmaster, and Williams-Sonoma

1 tablespoon vinegar

2 tablespoons vegetable oil

1 cup water

1 cup rye flour

1½ cups unbleached white flour

1 teaspoon salt

2 tablespoons gluten OR 3 teaspoons Lora Brody's Bread Dough Enhancer™ (optional for a higher loaf)

1 teaspoon sugar

½ cup oat bran

2 tablespoons caraway seeds

1 teaspoon instant coffee (powder or granules)

1 teaspoon minced dried onion OR ½ small raw onion, finely chopped

1½ tablespoons unsweetened cocoa

2½ teaspoons yeast

Place all the ingredients in the machine, program for Bread, Whole Wheat, Basic Wheat, Whole Wheat/Multigrain, White/Whole Grain, or Wheat, and press Start.

PANASONIC/NATIONAL

1 cup rye flour

1½ cups unbleached white flour

½ cup oat bran

2 tablespoons caraway seeds

1 teaspoon instant coffee (powder or granules)

1 teaspoon minced dried onion OR ½ small raw onion, finely chopped

1½ tablespoons unsweetened cocoa

1 teaspoon salt

2 tablespoons gluten OR 3 teaspoons Lora Brody's Bread Dough Enhancer™ (optional for a higher loaf)

1 teaspoon sugar

1 tablespoon vinegar

2 tablespoons vegetable oil

1 cup water

2½ teaspoons yeast

Place all the ingredients except the yeast in the machine. Place the yeast in the dispenser. Program for Basic Bread and press Start. Follow the Baking Instructions on page 75.

LARGE PILLSBURY, REGAL, LARGE ZOJIRUSHI, AND WEST BEND

1 tablespoon vinegar

2 tablespoons vegetable oil

1 cup water

1 teaspoon minced dried onion OR ½ small raw onion, finely chopped

1 teaspoon salt

2 tablespoons gluten OR 3 teaspoons Lora Brody's Bread Dough Enhancer™ (optional for a higher loaf)

1 teaspoon sugar

1 cup rye flour

1½ cups unbleached white flour

½ cup oat bran

2 tablespoons caraway seeds

1 teaspoon instant coffee (powder or granules)

1½ tablespoons unsweetened cocoa

2½ teaspoons yeast

Place all the ingredients in the machine, program for Bread, Basic White Bread, Whole Wheat, Basic Wheat, Whole Wheat/Multigrain, White/Whole Grain or Wheat, and press Start or On.

RUSSIAN BLACK BREAD

MAXIM, SMALL OSTER, SANYO, SUNBEAM, SMALL PILLSBURY, SMALL TOASTMASTER, AND SMALL ZOJIRUSHI

In these small models there is not enough rising time, so you must remove the dough and let it rise and bake out of the machine. Since you cannot delay this process (overnight) and must make the bread immediately, the order the ingredients go into the machine does not matter.

2 teaspoons vinegar

1½ tablespoons vegetable oil

⅔ cup water

¾ teaspoon salt

¾ teaspoon sugar

½ cup rye flour

1¼ cups unbleached white flour

¼ cup oat bran

1½ tablespoons gluten OR 2 teaspoons Lora Brody's Bread Dough Enhancer™ (optional for a higher loaf)

1½ tablespoons caraway seeds

¾ teaspoon instant coffee (powder or granules)

¾ teaspoon minced dried onion OR 3 tablespoons raw onion, finely chopped

1 tablespoon unsweetened cocoa

2 teaspoons yeast

Place all the ingredients in the machine, program for Dough or Manual, and press Start. Follow the Baking Instructions on page 75.

SMALL WELBILT

2 teaspoons yeast

¾ teaspoon salt

¾ teaspoon sugar

1½ tablespoons gluten OR 2 teaspoons Lora Brody's Bread Dough Enhancer™ (optional for a higher loaf)

½ cup rye flour

1¼ cups unbleached white flour

¼ cup oat bran

1½ tablespoons caraway seeds

¾ teaspoon instant coffee (powder or granules)

¾ teaspoon minced dried onion OR 3 tablespoons raw onion, finely chopped

1 tablespoon unsweetened cocoa

2 teaspoons vinegar

1½ tablespoons vegetable oil

⅔ cup water

Have all the ingredients at room temperature. Place all the ingredients in the machine, program for Manual, and press Start. Follow the Baking Instructions below.

SMALL PANASONIC/NATIONAL

½ cup rye flour

1¼ cups unbleached white flour

¼ cup oat bran

1½ tablespoons caraway seeds

¾ teaspoon instant coffee (powder or granules)

¾ teaspoon minced dried onion OR 3 tablespoons raw onion, finely chopped

1 tablespoon unsweetened cocoa

¾ teaspoon salt

1½ tablespoons gluten OR 2 teaspoons Lora Brody's Bread Dough Enhancer™ (optional for a higher loaf)

¾ teaspoon sugar

2 teaspoons vinegar

1½ tablespoons vegetable oil

⅔ cup water

2 teaspoons yeast

Place all the ingredients except the yeast in the machine. Place the yeast in the dispenser. Program for Dough or Manual and press Start. Follow the Baking Instructions below.

BAKING INSTRUCTIONS

1 egg white beaten together with 1 tablespoon of water

Sesame seeds or caraway seeds, for sprinkling

At the end of the cycle, remove the dough to an oiled bowl and cover with plastic wrap. Set the dough in a warm, draft-free place to rise until nearly doubled in bulk. This may take anywhere from 1 to 2 hours.

Lightly grease a baking sheet or sprinkle it with cornmeal. Punch down the dough and on a floured board, shape it into either a loaf or dome. Paint the top with the egg glaze. Sprinkle with sesame or caraway seeds and let the bread rise once again until almost doubled in bulk.

Preheat the oven to 375°F with the rack in the center position. Bake for 15 minutes at 375°F and then lower the oven to 350°F and bake an additional 30 minutes, or until the bottom sounds hollow when tapped.

CARAWAY RYE BREAD

Hearty and robust, this loaf is a meal in itself when spread with grated cheese and placed under the broiler for a minute until the cheese melts. Add a slice of tomato if you wish. This is not a high-rising loaf. If you wish, you can add some gluten or bread dough enhancer to give more lift. Take care not to overdo it, as too much makes the bread hard and dry.

DAK/Welbilt

1 tablespoon yeast

3 cups unbleached white flour

¾ cup plus 2 tablespoons rye flour

2 tablespoons caraway seeds

2 tablespoons sugar

4 tablespoons powdered skim milk

1½ teaspoons salt

1 tablespoon gluten OR 2 teaspoons Lora Brody's Bread Dough Enhancer™ (optional for a higher loaf)

1½ cups water

1½ tablespoons butter OR margarine

Have all the ingredients at room temperature. Place all the ingredients in the machine, program for White Bread, and press Start.

Black & Decker, Betty Crocker, Breadman/Trillium, Hitachi, Large Oster, Regal, Large Toastmaster, and Williams-Sonoma

1½ cups water

1½ tablespoons butter OR margarine

3 cups unbleached white flour

¾ cup plus 2 tablespoons rye flour

2 tablespoons caraway seeds

2 tablespoons sugar

1½ tablespoons powdered skim milk

1 tablespoon gluten OR 2 teaspoons Lora Brody's Bread Dough Enhancer™ (optional for a higher loaf)

1½ teaspoons salt

2½ teaspoons yeast

Place all the ingredients in the machine, program for Bread, Whole Wheat, Basic Wheat, Whole Wheat/Multigrain, White/Whole Grain, or Wheat, and press Start.

PANASONIC/NATIONAL

3 cups unbleached white flour

¾ cup plus 2 tablespoons rye flour

2 tablespoons caraway seeds

2 tablespoons sugar

4 tablespoons powdered skim milk

1½ teaspoons salt

1 tablespoon gluten OR 2 teaspoons Lora
   Brody's Bread Dough Enhancer™
   (optional for a higher loaf)

1½ cups water

1½ tablespoons butter OR margarine

1 tablespoon yeast

Place all the ingredients except the yeast in the machine. Place the yeast in the dispenser. Program for Basic Bread and press Start.

LARGE PILLSBURY, LARGE ZOJIRUSHI, AND WEST BEND

1½ cups water

1½ tablespoons butter OR margarine

3 cups unbleached white flour

¾ cup plus 2 tablespoons rye flour

2 tablespoons caraway seeds

2 tablespoons sugar

1½ teaspoons salt

1 tablespoon gluten OR 2 teaspoons Lora
   Brody's Bread Dough Enhancer™
   (optional for a higher loaf)

4 tablespoons powdered skim milk

1 tablespoon yeast

Place all the ingredients in the machine, program for Basic White Bread, Whole Wheat, Basic Wheat, Whole Wheat/Multigrain, White/Whole Grain, or Wheat, and press Start or On.

CARAWAY RYE BREAD

MAXIM, SMALL OSTER, SMALL PILLSBURY, SANYO, SUNBEAM, SMALL TOASTMASTER, AND SMALL ZOJIRUSHI

¾ cup water

1 tablespoon butter OR margarine

1½ cups unbleached white flour

½ cup plus 2 tablespoons rye flour

1 tablespoon plus 1 teaspoon caraway
   seeds

4 teaspoons sugar

1 teaspoon salt

2 teaspoons gluten OR 1 teaspoon Lora
   Brody's Bread Dough Enhancer™
   (optional for a higher loaf)

2 tablespoons powdered skim milk

2 teaspoons yeast

Continued

Place all the ingredients in the machine, program for Whole Wheat, Whole Grain, Standard, or Bread, and press Start.

Small Welbilt

2 teaspoons yeast
1½ cups unbleached white flour
½ cup rye flour
1 tablespoon plus 1 teaspoon caraway
seeds
4 teaspoons sugar
1 teaspoon salt

2 teaspoons gluten OR 1 teaspoon Lora
Brody's Bread Dough Enhancer™
(optional for a higher loaf)
2 tablespoons powdered skim milk
¾ cup water
1 tablespoon butter OR margarine

Have all the ingredients at room temperature. Place all the ingredients in the machine, program for Medium, and press Start.

Small Panasonic/National

1½ cups unbleached white flour
½ cup plus 2 tablespoons rye flour
1 tablespoon plus 1 teaspoon caraway
seeds
4 teaspoons sugar
1 teaspoon salt

2 teaspoons gluten OR 1 teaspoon Lora
Brody's Bread Dough Enhancer™
(optional for a higher loaf)
2 tablespoons powdered skim milk
¾ cup water
1 tablespoon butter OR margarine
2 teaspoons yeast

Place all the ingredients except the yeast in the machine. Place the yeast in the dispenser. Program for Basic Bread and press Start.

Variation: Add ½ cup dried onions soaked for 5 minutes in 1 cup hot water and then drained for a zesty flavor.

SIMPLE OATMEAL BREAD

This small, crusty, fragrant, uncomplicated loaf is a great way to start your day. It makes superb toast and terrific sandwich bread.

....

DAK/WELBILT

2½ teaspoons yeast
1 teaspoon salt
¾ cup quick-cooking oats
2½ cups unbleached white flour
¾ cup plus 3 tablespoons water

1 tablespoon butter, margarine, OR
   vegetable oil
1 tablespoon molasses
1 tablespoon brown sugar

Have all the ingredients at room temperature. Place all the ingredients in the machine, program for White Bread, and press Start.

....

BLACK & DECKER, BETTY CROCKER, BREADMAN/TRILLIUM, HITACHI, LARGE OSTER, REGAL, LARGE TOASTMASTER, AND WILLIAMS-SONOMA

¾ cup plus 3 tablespoons water
1 tablespoon butter, margarine, OR
   vegetable oil
1 tablespoon molasses
1 tablespoon brown sugar

1 teaspoon salt
¾ cup quick-cooking oats
2½ cups unbleached white flour
2 teaspoons yeast

Place all the ingredients in the machine, program for Bread, Whole Wheat, Basic Wheat, Whole Wheat/Multigrain, White/Whole Grain, or Wheat, and press Start.

....

PANASONIC/NATIONAL

1 teaspoon salt

¾ cup quick-cooking oats

2½ cups unbleached white flour

¾ cup plus 3 tablespoons water

1 tablespoon butter, margarine, OR
   vegetable oil

1 tablespoon molasses

1 tablespoon brown sugar

2½ teaspoons yeast

Place all the ingredients except the yeast in the machine. Place the yeast in the dispenser. Program for Basic Bread and press Start.

LARGE PILLSBURY, LARGE ZOJIRUSHI, AND WEST BEND

¾ cup plus 3 tablespoons water

1 tablespoon butter, margarine, OR
   vegetable oil

1 tablespoon molasses

1 tablespoon brown sugar

1 teaspoon salt

¾ cup quick-cooking oats

2½ cups unbleached white flour

2½ teaspoons yeast

Place all the ingredients in the machine, program for Basic White Bread, Whole Wheat, Basic Wheat, Whole Wheat/Multigrain, White/Whole Grain, or Wheat, and press Start or On.

Simple Oatmeal Bread

MAXIM, SMALL OSTER, SMALL PILLSBURY, SANYO, SUNBEAM, SMALL TOASTMASTER, AND SMALL ZOJIRUSHI

⅔ cup water

2 teaspoons butter, margarine, OR
   vegetable oil

2 teaspoons molasses

2 teaspoons brown sugar

½ teaspoon salt

½ cup quick-cooking oats

1½ cups unbleached white flour

1½ teaspoons yeast

Place all the ingredients in the machine, program for Whole Wheat, Whole Grain, Standard, or Bread, and press Start.

Small Welbilt

1½ teaspoons yeast
½ teaspoon salt
½ cup quick-cooking oats
1¾ cups unbleached white flour
⅔ cup water

2 teaspoons butter, margarine, OR
    vegetable oil
2 teaspoons molasses
2 teaspoons brown sugar

Have all the ingredients at room temperature. Place all the ingredients in the machine, program for Medium, and press Start.

Small Panasonic/National

2 teaspoons brown sugar
½ teaspoon salt
½ cup quick-cooking oats
1½ cups unbleached white flour
⅔ cup water

2 teaspoons butter, margarine, OR
    vegetable oil
2 teaspoons molasses
1½ teaspoons yeast

Place all the ingredients except the yeast in the machine. Place the yeast in the dispenser. Program for Basic Bread and press Start.

GUINNESS OATMEAL BREAD

The deep, complex flavor comes from Guinness stout. If you can't find Guinness, substitute another brand of stout. This recipe also calls for maple syrup. The best kind to use is the very dark amber kind, if you can find it. Make sure you use real maple syrup, no matter what color you choose.

A ploughman's lunch is traditional pub fare throughout England. You can serve your own at home. Arrange a thick slab of Cheddar cheese, pickles, chutney, and a slice or two of this bread on a plate. Wash it down with a pint of stout.

DAK/Welbilt

1 tablespoon yeast

2 cups unbleached white flour

½ cup whole wheat flour

1 cup quick-cooking oatmeal

½ cup cornmeal

1½ teaspoons salt

4 tablespoons powdered buttermilk

½ cup flat Guinness stout (see Note)

3 tablespoons pure maple syrup

1 extra-large egg

½ cup water

Have all the ingredients at room temperature. Place all the ingredients in the machine, program for White Bread, and press Start.

Black & Decker, Betty Crocker, Breadman/Trillium, Hitachi, Large Oster, Regal, Large Toastmaster, and Williams-Sonoma

½ cup flat Guinness stout, at room
    temperature (see Note)

3 tablespoons pure maple syrup

1 extra-large egg

½ cup water

4 tablespoons powdered buttermilk

2 cups unbleached white flour

½ cup whole wheat flour

1 cup quick-cooking oatmeal

½ cup cornmeal

1½ teaspoons salt

2 teaspoons yeast

Place all the ingredients in the machine, program for Bread, Whole Wheat, Basic Wheat, Whole Wheat/Multigrain, White/Whole Grain, or Wheat, and press Start.

PANASONIC/NATIONAL

2 cups unbleached white flour

½ cup whole wheat flour

1 cup quick-cooking oatmeal

½ cup cornmeal

1½ teaspoons salt

4 tablespoons powdered buttermilk

½ cup flat Guinness stout, at room temperature (see Note)

3 tablespoons pure maple syrup

1 extra-large egg

½ cup water

2½ teaspoons yeast

Place all the ingredients except the yeast in the machine. Place the yeast in the dispenser. Program for Basic Bread and press Start.

LARGE PILLSBURY, LARGE ZOJIRUSHI, AND WEST BEND

½ cup flat Guinness stout, at room temperature (see Note)

3 tablespoons pure maple syrup

1 extra-large egg

½ cup water

2 cups unbleached white flour

½ cup whole wheat flour

1 cup quick-cooking oatmeal

½ cup cornmeal

1½ teaspoons salt

4 tablespoons powdered buttermilk

1 tablespoon yeast

Place all the ingredients in the machine, program for Basic White Bread, Whole Wheat, Basic Wheat, Whole Wheat/Multigrain, White/Whole Grain, or Wheat, and press Start or On.

Maxim, Small Oster, Small Pillsbury, Sunbeam, and Small Toastmaster

⅓ cup flat Guinness stout, at room temperature (see Note)

2 tablespoons pure maple syrup

1 medium egg

¼ cup water

1 cup plus 2 tablespoons unbleached white flour

¼ cup whole wheat flour

½ cup quick-cooking oatmeal

¼ cup cornmeal

1 teaspoon salt

3 tablespoons powdered buttermilk

2 teaspoons yeast

Place all the ingredients in the machine, program for Standard, Whole Wheat, or Whole Grain, and press Start.

....

Small Pillsbury, Sanyo, and Small Zojirushi

⅓ cup flat Guinness stout, at room temperature (see Note)

2 tablespoons pure maple syrup

1 medium egg

¼ cup water

4 tablespoons powdered buttermilk

1 cup unbleached white flour

¼ cup whole wheat flour

½ cup quick-cooking oatmeal

¼ cup cornmeal

1 teaspoon salt

2 teaspoons yeast

Place all the ingredients in the machine, program for Bread, Whole Wheat, or Whole Grain, and press Start.

....

Small Welbilt

2 teaspoons yeast

1 cup unbleached white flour

¼ cup whole wheat flour

½ cup quick-cooking oatmeal

¼ cup cornmeal

1 teaspoon salt

3 tablespoons powdered buttermilk

⅓ cup flat Guinness stout (see Note)

2 tablespoons pure maple syrup

1 medium egg

¼ cup water

Have all the ingredients at room temperature. Place all the ingredients in the machine, program for Medium, and press Start.

Small Panasonic/National

1 cup plus 2 tablespoons unbleached white flour

¼ cup whole wheat flour

½ cup quick-cooking oatmeal

¼ cup cornmeal

1 teaspoon salt

3 tablespoons powdered buttermilk

⅓ cup flat Guinness stout, at room temperature (see Note)

2 tablespoons pure maple syrup

1 medium egg

¼ cup water

2 teaspoons yeast

Place all the ingredients except the yeast in the machine. Place the yeast in the dispenser. Program for Basic Bread and press Start.

Note: If you don't want to wait around for the stout to become flat on its own, pour it into a small saucepan and heat it to a simmer, then remove it from the heat. By the time the stout cools down, it will be flat.

Variation: Add 1 tablespoon sprouted wheat berries for more texture.

MILLIE'S WHOLE WHEAT CHALLAH

All the flavors and aroma of sweet tradition converge in this delicious loaf while the addition of whole wheat makes for a really satisfyingly nutty taste.

Millie discovered that it's better to use whole wheat pastry flour available in health food stores, which has less gluten. You can use regular whole wheat flour, but the bread's texture will not be as light.

DAK/Welbilt

2¾ teaspoons yeast

2 cups unbleached white flour

1 cup whole wheat pastry flour

1¼ teaspoons salt

1 tablespoon sugar

4 tablespoons vegetable oil

2 tablespoons honey

2 extra-large eggs

¾ cup water

Have all the ingredients at room temperature. Place all the ingredients in the machine, program for White Bread, and press Start. You can bake this in the machine for a high, domed loaf or do it by hand in the traditional braid (page 89).

Black & Decker, Betty Crocker, Breadman/Trillium, Hitachi, Large Oster, Large Toastmaster, and Williams-Sonoma

4 tablespoons vegetable oil

2 tablespoons honey

2 extra-large eggs

¾ cup water

2 cups unbleached white flour

1 cup whole wheat pastry flour

1¼ teaspoons salt

1 tablespoon sugar

2 teaspoons yeast

Place all the ingredients in the machine, program for Bread, Whole Wheat, Basic Wheat, Whole Wheat/Multigrain, White/Whole Grain, or Wheat, and press Start. You can bake this in the machine for a high, domed loaf or do it by hand in the traditional braid (page 89).

PANASONIC/NATIONAL

2 cups unbleached white flour

1 cup whole wheat pastry flour

1¼ teaspoons salt

1 tablespoon sugar

4 tablespoons vegetable oil

2 tablespoons honey

2 extra-large eggs

¾ cup water

2½ teaspoons yeast

Place all the ingredients except the yeast in the machine. Place the yeast in the dispenser. Program for Basic Bread and press Start. You can bake this in the machine for a high, domed loaf or do it by hand in the traditional braid (page 89).

REGAL, LARGE PILLSBURY, LARGE ZOJIRUSHI, AND WEST BEND

4 tablespoons vegetable oil

2 tablespoons honey

2 extra-large eggs

¾ cup water

2 cups unbleached white flour

1 cup whole wheat pastry flour

1¼ teaspoons salt

1 tablespoon sugar

2½ teaspoons yeast

Place all the ingredients in the machine, program for Bread, Basic White Bread, Whole Wheat, Basic Wheat, Whole Wheat/Multigrain, White/Whole Grain, or Wheat, and press Start or On. You can bake this in the machine for a high, domed loaf or do it by hand in the traditional braid (page 89).

Millies Whole Wheat Challah

MAXIM, SMALL OSTER, SMALL PILLSBURY, SANYO, SUNBEAM, SMALL TOASTMASTER, AND SMALL ZOJIRUSHI

3 tablespoons vegetable oil

1½ tablespoons honey

2 medium eggs

½ cup water

2 teaspoons yeast

1¼ cups unbleached white flour

¾ cup whole wheat pastry flour

1 teaspoon salt

2 teaspoons sugar

Continued

Place all the ingredients in the machine, program for Whole Wheat, Whole Grain, Standard, or Bread, and press Start. You can bake this in the machine for a high, domed loaf or do it by hand in the traditional braid (page 89).

Small Welbilt

2 teaspoons yeast

1¼ cups unbleached white flour

¾ cup whole wheat pastry flour

1 teaspoon salt

2 teaspoons sugar

3 tablespoons vegetable oil

1½ tablespoons honey

2 medium eggs

½ cup water

Have all the ingredients at room temperature. Place all the ingredients in the machine, program for Medium, and press Start. You can bake this in the machine for a high, domed loaf or do it by hand in the traditional braid (page 89).

Small Panasonic/National

1¼ cups unbleached white flour

¾ cup whole wheat pastry flour

1 teaspoon salt

2 teaspoons sugar

3 tablespoons vegetable oil

1½ tablespoons honey

2 medium eggs

½ cup water

2 teaspoons yeast

Place all the ingredients except the yeast in the machine. Place the yeast in the dispenser. Program for Basic Bread and press Start. You can bake this in the machine for a high, domed loaf or do it by hand in the traditional braid (page 89).

To Braid

1 egg beaten together with 1 tablespoon water

sesame seeds or poppy seeds, for sprinkling (optional)

When the cycle you have programmed is completed, remove the dough and let it rest, covered with a clean cloth, for 20 minutes on a lightly floured board.

Divide the dough into 3 equal pieces and form each piece into a 10-inch strip (large machines) or an 8-inch strip (small machines). Pinch the strips together at one end and loosely braid them to form the loaf. Pinch the other ends together.

Place the loaf on either a lightly greased baking sheet or one sprinkled with cornmeal. Cover once again with the cloth and let the bread rise in a warm, draft-free place until doubled in bulk, about 45 minutes to 1 hour.

Preheat the oven to 400°F with the rack in the center position. Brush the top of the bread with the egg glaze. Sprinkle with sesame or poppy seeds, if desired.

Bake the bread for 15 minutes at 400°F, then lower the temperature to 375°F and bake an additional 20 to 30 minutes, or until the bottom of the loaf sounds hollow when tapped.

WHOLE WHEAT CAJUN SPICE BREAD

This was one of the breads we just couldn't stop sampling. It is a gutsy, delicious, compact loaf with a fabulously crunchy crust. The texture is coarse and chewy and the bread is the color of golden oak. Spicy yet not overwhelming, certainly interesting, this is one of our favorites. Try it to make a turkey sandwich—the combination is terrific.

DAK/Welbilt

1 tablespoon yeast

1½ tablespoons Cajun spice, preferably unsalted

1 teaspoon salt (see Notes)

1 cup whole wheat flour

2 cups unbleached white flour

⅓ cup cornmeal

1 tablespoon molasses

1 tablespoon honey

1 medium-size red (Bermuda) onion, coarsely chopped

1 tablespoon chili oil OR vegetable oil

¾ cup flat beer (see Notes)

⅓ cup bacon bits (we used vegetarian bacon bits that we found in the health food market, but you may use real ones if you wish)

Have all the ingredients at room temperature. Place all the ingredients except the bacon bits in the machine and program for White Bread. Press Start. Add the bacon bits when the beeper sounds during the last 10 minutes of kneading.

BLACK & DECKER, BETTY CROCKER, BREADMAN/TRILLIUM, HITACHI, LARGE OSTER, REGAL, LARGE TOASTMASTER, AND WILLIAMS-SONOMA

1 tablespoon molasses

1 tablespoon honey

1 medium-size red (Bermuda) onion, coarsely chopped

1 tablespoon chili oil OR vegetable oil

¾ cup plus 2 tablespoons flat beer (see Notes)

1¼ tablespoons Cajun spice, preferably unsalted

1 teaspoon salt (see Notes)

¾ cup whole wheat flour

2 cups unbleached white flour

¼ cup cornmeal

2 teaspoons yeast

⅓ cup bacon bits (we used vegetarian bacon bits that we found in the health food market, but you may use real ones if you wish)

Place all the ingredients except the bacon bits in the machine and program for Mix Bread, Fruit and Nut, Raisin Bread, Whole Wheat, Basic Wheat, Whole Wheat/Multigrain, White/Whole Grain, or Wheat. Press Start. Add the bacon bits when the beeper sounds or during the last 5 minutes of the final knead cycle.

PANASONIC/NATIONAL

1 tablespoon molasses

1 tablespoon honey

1 medium-size red (Bermuda) onion, coarsely chopped

1 tablespoon chili oil OR vegetable oil

¾ cup plus 2 tablespoons flat beer (see Notes)

1¼ tablespoons Cajun spice, preferably unsalted

1 teaspoon salt (see Notes)

¾ cup whole wheat flour

2 cups unbleached white flour

¼ cup cornmeal

2½ teaspoons yeast

⅓ cup bacon bits (we used vegetarian bacon bits that we found in the health food market, but you may use real ones if you wish)

Place all the ingredients except the yeast and bacon bits in the machine. Place the yeast in the dispenser. Program for Basic Bread and press Start. Add the bacon bits after 20 minutes when prekneading is completed.

Large Pillsbury, Large Zojirushi, and West Bend

1 tablespoon molasses

1 tablespoon honey

1 medium-size red (Bermuda) onion, coarsely chopped

1 tablespoon chili oil OR vegetable oil

¾ cup plus 2 tablespoons flat beer (see Notes)

1½ tablespoons Cajun spice, preferably unsalted

1 teaspoon salt (see Notes)

1 cup whole wheat flour

2 cups unbleached white flour

⅓ cup cornmeal

1 tablespoon yeast

⅓ cup bacon bits (we used vegetarian bacon bits that we found in the health food market, but you may use real ones if you wish)

Place all the ingredients except the bacon bits in the machine and program for Raisin Bread, Whole Wheat, Basic Wheat, Whole Wheat/Multigrain, or White/Whole Grain, or Wheat. Press Start or On. Add the bacon bits when the beeper sounds or during the last five minutes of the final knead cycle.

Whole Wheat Cajun Spice Bread.

Maxim, Small Oster, Small Pillsbury, Sanyo, Sunbeam, Small Toastmaster, and Small Zojirushi

2 teaspoons molasses

2 teaspoons honey

1 small-size red (Bermuda) onion, coarsely chopped

2 teaspoons chili oil OR vegetable oil

¼ cup plus 2 tablespoons flat beer (see Notes)

1 tablespoon Cajun spice, preferably unsalted

½ teaspoon salt (see Notes)

½ cup whole wheat flour

1 cup unbleached white flour

2 tablespoons cornmeal

1½ teaspoons yeast

¼ cup bacon bits (we used vegetarian bacon bits that we found in the health food market, but you may use real ones if you wish)

Place all the ingredients except the bacon bits in the machine, program for Whole Wheat, Whole Grain, Standard, or Bread, and press Start. Add the bacon bits when the beeper sounds or during the last 5 minutes of the final knead cycle.

SMALL WELBILT

1½ teaspoons yeast

1 tablespoon Cajun spice, preferably unsalted

½ teaspoon salt (see Notes)

½ cup whole wheat flour

1 cup unbleached white flour

2 tablespoons cornmeal

2 teaspoons molasses

2 teaspoons honey

1 small-size red (Bermuda) onion, coarsely chopped

2 teaspoons chili oil OR vegetable oil

6 tablespoons flat beer (see Notes)

¼ cup bacon bits (we used vegetarian bacon bits that we found in the health food market, but you may use real ones if you wish)

Have all the ingredients at room temperature. Place all the ingredients except the bacon bits in the machine, program for Dark, and press Start. Add the bacon bits when the beeper sounds during the last 10 minutes of kneading.

SMALL PANASONIC/NATIONAL

2 teaspoons molasses

2 teaspoons honey

1 small-size red (Bermuda) onion, coarsely chopped

2 teaspoons chili oil OR vegetable oil

¼ cup plus 2 tablespoons flat beer (see Notes)

1 tablespoon Cajun spice, preferably unsalted

½ teaspoon salt (see Notes)

½ cup whole wheat flour

1 cup unbleached white flour

2 tablespoons cornmeal

1½ teaspoons yeast

¼ cup bacon bits (we used vegetarian bacon bits that we found in the health food market, but you may use real ones if you wish)

Continued

Place all the ingredients except the yeast and bacon bits in the machine. Place the yeast in the dispenser. Program for Basic Bread and press Start. Add the bacon bits during the last 10 minutes of kneading.

NOTES: If you cannot find unsalted Cajun spice (check the label for the list of ingredients), then omit the salt from the recipe.

If you don't want to wait around for the beer to become flat on its own, pour it into a small saucepan and heat it to a simmer. By the time the beer cools down, it will be flat.

MUSTARD WHEAT RYE SANDWICH BREAD

This zesty, wholesome loaf will make you look forward to lunch. It makes great grilled cheese or Reuben sandwiches.

DAK/WELBILT

1 tablespoon yeast

2 cups unbleached white flour

⅔ cup rye flour

⅔ cup whole wheat flour

1½ tablespoons gluten OR 3 teaspoons
  Lora Brody's Bread Dough
  Enhancer™

1 cup water

½ cup Dijon mustard

1½ tablespoons olive oil

1½ tablespoons molasses

Have all the ingredients at room temperature. Place all the ingredients in the machine, program for White Bread, and press Start.

BLACK & DECKER, BETTY CROCKER, BREADMAN/TRILLIUM, HITACHI, LARGE OSTER, REGAL, LARGE TOASTMASTER, WILLIAMS-SONOMA, LARGE PILLSBURY, LARGE ZOJIRUSHI, AND WEST BEND

1 cup water

½ cup Dijon mustard

2 tablespoons olive oil

1½ tablespoons molasses

2 cups unbleached white flour

⅔ cup rye flour

⅔ cup whole wheat flour

1½ tablespoons gluten OR 3 teaspoons
  Lora Brody's Bread Dough
  Enhancer™

2½ teaspoons yeast

Place all the ingredients in the machine, program for Bread, Basic White Bread, Whole Wheat, Basic Wheat, Whole Wheat/Multigrain, White/Whole Grain, or Wheat, and press Start or On.

PANASONIC/NATIONAL

2 cups unbleached white flour

⅔ cup rye flour

⅔ cup whole wheat flour

1½ tablespoons gluten OR 3 teaspoons
Lora Brody's Bread Dough Enhancer™

1 cup water

½ cup Dijon mustard

2 tablespoons olive oil

1½ tablespoons molasses

2½ teaspoons yeast

Place all the ingredients except the yeast in the machine. Place the yeast in the dispenser. Program for Basic Bread and press Start.

MAXIM, SMALL OSTER, SMALL PILLSBURY, SANYO, SUNBEAM, SMALL TOASTMASTER, AND SMALL ZOJIRUSHI

⅔ cup water

⅓ cup Dijon mustard

1 tablespoon olive oil

1 tablespoon molasses

1 cup unbleached white flour

½ cup rye flour

½ cup whole wheat flour

1 tablespoon gluten OR 2 teaspoons Lora
Brody's Bread Dough Enhancer™

2 teaspoons yeast

Place all the ingredients in the machine, program for Whole Wheat, Whole Grain, Standard, or Bread, and press Start.

SMALL WELBILT

2 teaspoons yeast

1 cup unbleached white flour

½ cup rye flour

½ cup whole wheat flour

1 tablespoon gluten OR 2 teaspoons Lora
Brody's Bread Dough Enhancer™

⅔ cup water

⅓ cup Dijon mustard

1 tablespoon olive oil

1½ tablespoons molasses

Have all the ingredients at room temperature. Place all the ingredients in the machine, program for Medium, and press Start.

Small Panasonic/National

1 cup unbleached white flour
½ cup rye flour
½ cup whole wheat flour
1 tablespoon gluten OR 2 teaspoons Lora Brody's Bread Dough Enhancer™

⅔ cup water
⅓ cup Dijon mustard
1 tablespoon olive oil
1 tablespoon molasses
2 teaspoons yeast

Place all the ingredients except the yeast in the machine. Place the yeast in the dispenser. Program for Basic Bread and press Start.

SWEDISH RYE BREAD

This loaf is very compact, low, and dense. It hardly rises at all. It's very much like the thinly sliced German cocktail bread that one might associate with open-faced smoked salmon canapés. You can add gluten or Lora Brody's Bread Dough Enhancer™ if you wish, but you'll end up with a different type of bread.

DAK/Welbilt

1 tablespoon yeast

1¼ cups rye flour

1½ cups white flour

⅓ cup cornmeal

1½ teaspoons salt

1¼ cups water

4 tablespoons honey

2 tablespoons butter OR vegetable oil

2 teaspoons caraway seeds

1½ teaspoons dried orange peel

Have all the ingredients at room temperature. Place all the ingredients in the machine, program for White Bread, and press Start.

Black & Decker, Betty Crocker, Breadman/Trillium, Hitachi, Large Oster, Large Toastmaster, and Williams-Sonoma

1¼ cups water

4 tablespoons honey

2 tablespoons butter OR vegetable oil

1½ teaspoons salt

1¼ cups rye flour

1½ cups white flour

⅓ cup cornmeal

2 teaspoons caraway seeds

1½ teaspoons dried orange peel

2½ teaspoons yeast

Place all the ingredients in the machine, program for Bread, Whole Wheat, Basic Wheat, Whole Wheat/Multigrain, White/Whole Grain, or Wheat, and press Start.

PANASONIC/NATIONAL

1¼ cups rye flour

1½ cups white flour

⅓ cup cornmeal

1½ teaspoons salt

1¼ cups water

4 tablespoons honey

2 tablespoons butter OR vegetable oil

2 teaspoons caraway seeds

1½ teaspoons dried orange peel

1 tablespoon yeast

Place all the ingredients except the yeast in the machine. Place the yeast in the dispenser. Program for Basic Bread and press Start.

REGAL, LARGE PILLSBURY, LARGE ZOJIRUSHI, AND WEST BEND

1¼ cups water

4 tablespoons honey

2 tablespoons butter OR vegetable oil

1½ teaspoons salt

1¼ cups rye flour

1½ cups white flour

⅓ cup cornmeal

2 teaspoons caraway seeds

1½ teaspoons dried orange peel

1 tablespoon yeast

Place all the ingredients in the machine, program for Bread, Basic White Bread, Whole Wheat, Basic Wheat, Whole Wheat/Multigrain, White/Whole Grain, or Wheat, and press Start or On.

Swedish Rye Bread

MAXIM, SMALL OSTER, SMALL PILLSBURY, SANYO, SUNBEAM, SMALL TOASTMASTER, AND SMALL ZOJIRUSHI

⅔ cup water

2½ tablespoons honey

1 tablespoon butter OR vegetable oil

1 teaspoon salt

⅔ cup rye flour

1 cup white flour

⅓ cup cornmeal

1½ teaspoons caraway seeds

1 teaspoon dried orange peel

2 teaspoons yeast

Place all the ingredients in the machine, program for Whole Wheat, Whole Grain, Standard, or Bread, and press Start.

Small Welbilt

2 teaspoons yeast

1 teaspoon salt

⅔ cup rye flour

1 cup white flour

⅓ cup cornmeal

1½ teaspoons caraway seeds

1 teaspoon dried orange peel

⅔ cup water

2½ tablespoons honey

1 tablespoon butter OR vegetable oil

Have all the ingredients at room temperature. Place all the ingredients in the machine, program for Medium, and press Start.

Small Panasonic/National

1 teaspoon salt

⅔ cup rye flour

1 cup white flour

⅓ cup cornmeal

1½ teaspoons caraway seeds

1 teaspoon dried orange peel

⅔ cup water

2½ tablespoons honey

1 tablespoon butter OR vegetable oil

2 teaspoons yeast

Place all the ingredients except the yeast in the machine. Place the yeast in the dispenser. Program for Basic Bread and press Start.

CORNMEAL WHEAT BREAD

Wait until you taste the fantastic crust on this loaf. It's a perfect match for the slightly sweet, moist, even crumb inside. If you plan to program this bread ahead, treat the cornmeal mixed with boiling water as a wet ingredient, keeping it away from the yeast.

DAK/Welbilt

⅓ cup cornmeal

¾ cup boiling water

¾ cup nonfat milk, heated to a simmer
    and then cooled to lukewarm

1 tablespoon yeast

2 cups unbleached white flour

1 cup whole wheat flour

1½ teaspoons salt

¼ cup brown sugar

Sprinkle the cornmeal on top of the boiling water. Off the heat, stir until smooth, then stir in the milk. Cool for 15 minutes. Have the other ingredients at room temperature. Place the yeast, flours, salt, sugar, and finally the cornmeal mixture in the machine, program for White Bread, and press Start.

Black & Decker, Betty Crocker, Breadman/Trillium, Hitachi, Large Oster, Regal, Large Toastmaster, and Williams-Sonoma

⅓ cup cornmeal

¾ cup boiling water

¾ cup nonfat milk, heated to a simmer
    and then cooled to lukewarm

2 cups unbleached white flour

1 cup whole wheat flour

1½ teaspoons salt

¼ cup brown sugar

2½ teaspoons yeast

Sprinkle the cornmeal on top of the boiling water. Off the heat, stir until smooth. Stir in the milk. Place the cornmeal mixture, flours, salt, sugar, and finally the yeast in the machine, program for White Bread, Standard, Whole Wheat, Basic Wheat, Whole Wheat/Multigrain, White/Whole Grain, or Wheat, and press Start.

PANASONIC/NATIONAL

⅓ cup cornmeal

¾ cup boiling water

¾ cup nonfat milk, heated to a simmer
and then cooled to lukewarm

2 cups unbleached white flour

1 cup whole wheat flour

1½ teaspoons salt

¼ cup brown sugar

1 tablespoon yeast

Sprinkle the cornmeal on top of the boiling water. Off the heat, stir until smooth. Stir in the milk. Place the flours, salt, sugar, and finally the cornmeal mixture in the machine. Place the yeast in the dispenser. Program for Basic Bread and press Start.

LARGE PILLSBURY, LARGE ZOJIRUSHI, AND WEST BEND

⅓ cup cornmeal

¾ cup boiling water

¾ cup nonfat milk, heated to a simmer
and then cooled to lukewarm

2 cups unbleached white flour

1 cup whole wheat flour

1½ teaspoons salt

¼ cup brown sugar

1 tablespoon yeast

Sprinkle the cornmeal on top of the boiling water. Off the heat, stir until smooth. Stir in the milk. Place the flours, salt, sugar, cornmeal mixture, and finally the yeast in the machine, program for Basic White Bread, Whole Wheat, Basic Wheat, Whole Wheat/Multigrain, White/Whole Grain, or Wheat, and press Start or On.

MAXIM, SMALL OSTER, SMALL PILLSBURY, SANYO, SUNBEAM, SMALL TOASTMASTER, AND SMALL ZOJIRUSHI

1½ cups unbleached white flour

½ cup whole wheat flour

½ teaspoon salt

2 tablespoons brown sugar

¼ cup cornmeal

⅓ cup boiling water

½ cup nonfat milk, heated to a simmer
and then cooled to lukewarm

2 teaspoons yeast

Sprinkle the cornmeal on top of the boiling water. Off the heat, stir until smooth. Stir in the milk. Place all the ingredients in the machine. Program for Whole Wheat, Whole Grain, Standard, or Bread, and press Start.

SMALL WELBILT

¼ cup cornmeal

⅓ cup boiling water

2 teaspoons yeast

1½ cups unbleached white flour

½ cup whole wheat flour

½ teaspoon salt

2 tablespoons brown sugar

½ cup nonfat milk, heated to a simmer and then cooled to lukewarm

Sprinkle the cornmeal on top of the boiling water. Off the heat, stir until smooth, then stir in the milk. Cool for 15 minutes. Have the other ingredients at room temperature. Place the yeast, flours, salt, sugar, and finally the cornmeal mixture in the machine, program for Medium, and press Start.

SMALL PANASONIC/NATIONAL

¼ cup cornmeal

⅓ cup boiling water

1½ cups unbleached white flour

½ cup whole wheat flour

½ teaspoon salt

2 tablespoons brown sugar

½ cup nonfat milk, heated to a simmer and then cooled to lukewarm

2 teaspoons yeast

Sprinkle the cornmeal on top of the boiling water. Off the heat, stir until smooth. Stir in the milk. Place the flours, salt, sugar, and finally the cornmeal mixture in the machine. Place the yeast in the dispenser. Program for Basic Bread and press Start.

WHOLE WHEAT–POTATO ROLLS

Pretty to look at with a hearty flavor and robust texture, these rolls are a very satisfying accompaniment to a fresh garden salad.

Potatoes act as a yeast food and give these rolls an extra boost while they rise.

Makes 12 (large machines) or 8 (small machines) rolls

DAK/WELBILT

2 teaspoons yeast

2 cups unbleached white flour

1 tablespoon oat bran

1 cup whole wheat flour

4 tablespoons powdered buttermilk

1 teaspoon salt

½ cup instant potato granules

2½ tablespoons butter

1 tablespoon honey OR molasses

1 extra-large egg

1 cup water

Have all the ingredients at room temperature. Place all the ingredients in the machine, program for Dough or Manual, and press Start. When the beeper sounds, remove the dough and let it rest for 10 minutes on a lightly floured board. Follow the Baking Instructions on page 107.

BLACK & DECKER, BETTY CROCKER, BREADMAN/TRILLIUM, HITACHI, LARGE OSTER, LARGE TOASTMASTER, AND WILLIAMS-SONOMA

2½ tablespoons butter

1 tablespoon honey OR molasses

1 extra-large egg

1 cup water

2 cups unbleached white flour

1 tablespoon oat bran

1 cup whole wheat flour

4 tablespoons powdered buttermilk

1 teaspoon salt

½ cup instant potato granules

2 teaspoons yeast

Place all the ingredients in the machine, program for Dough or Knead and First Rise, and press Start. When the beeper sounds, remove the dough and let it rest for 10 minutes on a lightly floured board. Follow the Baking Instructions on page 107.

Panasonic/National

2 cups unbleached white flour

1 tablespoon oat bran

1 cup whole wheat flour

4 tablespoons powdered buttermilk

1 teaspoon salt

½ cup instant potato granules

2½ tablespoons butter

1 tablespoon honey OR molasses

1 extra-large egg

1 cup water

2 teaspoons yeast

Place all the ingredients except the yeast in the machine. Place the yeast in the dispenser. Program for both Basic Bread and Dough and press Start. When the beeper sounds, remove the dough and let it rest for 10 minutes on a lightly floured board. Follow the Baking Instructions on page 107.

Regal

2½ tablespoons butter

1 tablespoon honey OR molasses

1 extra-large egg

1 cup water

2 cups unbleached white flour

1 tablespoon oat bran

1 cup whole wheat flour

4 tablespoons powdered buttermilk

1 teaspoon salt

½ cup instant potato granules

2 teaspoons yeast

Place all the ingredients in the machine, program for Dough or Manual, and press Start. When the beeper sounds, remove the dough and let it rest for 10 minutes on a lightly floured board. Follow the Baking Instructions on page 107.

Large Pillsbury, Large Zojirushi, and West Bend

2½ tablespoons butter

1 tablespoon honey OR molasses

1 extra-large egg

1 cup water

2 cups unbleached white flour

1 tablespoon oat bran

1 cup whole wheat flour

4 tablespoons powdered buttermilk

1 teaspoon salt

½ cup instant potato granules

2 teaspoons yeast

Place all the ingredients in the machine, program for Dough or Manual, and press Start or On. When the beeper sounds, remove the dough and let it rest for 10 minutes on a lightly floured board. Follow the Baking Instructions on page 107.

WHOLE WHEAT POTATO ROLLS

Maxim, Small Oster, Small Pillsbury, Sanyo, Sunbeam, Small Toastmaster, and Small Zojirushi

2 tablespoons butter

1 tablespoon honey OR molasses

1 medium egg

¾ cup water

1⅓ cups unbleached white flour

1 tablespoon oat bran

⅔ cup whole wheat flour

2 tablespoons powdered buttermilk

½ teaspoon salt

¼ cup instant potato granules

1½ teaspoons yeast

Place all the ingredients in the machine, program for Dough or Manual, and press Start. When the beeper sounds, remove the dough and let it rest for 10 minutes on a lightly floured board. Follow the Baking Instructions on page 108.

Small Welbilt

1½ teaspoons yeast

1⅓ cups unbleached white flour

1 tablespoon oat bran

⅔ cup whole wheat flour

2 tablespoons powdered buttermilk

½ teaspoon salt

¼ cup instant potato granules

2 tablespoons butter

1 tablespoon honey OR molasses

1 medium egg

¾ cup water

Have all the ingredients at room temperature. Place all the ingredients in the machine, program Manual, and press Start. When the beeper sounds, remove the dough and let it rest for 10 minutes on a lightly floured board. Follow the Baking Instructions on page 108.

SMALL PANASONIC/NATIONAL

1⅓ cups unbleached white flour

1 tablespoon oat bran

⅔ cup whole wheat flour

2 tablespoons powdered buttermilk

½ teaspoon salt

¼ cup instant potato granules

2 tablespoons butter

1 tablespoon honey OR molasses

1 medium egg

¾ cup water

1½ teaspoons yeast

Place all the ingredients except the yeast in the machine. Place the yeast in the dispenser. Program for Basic Bread and press Start. Remove the dough before the bake cycle and let it rest for 10 minutes on a lightly floured board. Follow the Baking Instructions on page 108.

BAKING INSTRUCTIONS (LARGE MACHINES)

1 egg combined with 1 tablespoon water   Sesame seeds, for sprinkling (optional)

Use scissors, a sharp knife, or your hands to divide the dough into 12 pieces. Form each piece into a ball. Lightly grease the bottom and sides of 2 round 8-inch or 9-inch cake pans. Place 6 balls in each pan and flatten the tops slightly with your hand. Brush the tops with the egg glaze. Sprinkle with sesame seeds, if desired. Set the pans in a warm, draft-free place and let rise until doubled in bulk, about 30 to 40 minutes.

Preheat the oven to 375°F with the rack in the center position and bake for 20 to 25 minutes until golden brown.

1 egg combined with 1 tablespoon water   Sesame seeds, for sprinkling (optional)

Use scissors, a sharp knife, or your hands to divide the dough into 8 pieces. Form each piece into a ball. Lightly grease the bottom and sides of one 9-inch square or round cake pan. Place the balls in the prepared pan and flatten the tops slightly with your hand. Brush the tops with the egg glaze. Sprinkle with sesame seeds, if desired. Set the pan in a warm, draft-free place and let rise until doubled in bulk, about 30 to 40 minutes.

Preheat the oven to 375°F with the rack in the center position and bake for 20 to 25 minutes until golden brown.

WHOLE WHEAT CORNMEAL BREAD

A hearty, satisfying loaf. You may use either fine- or coarse-ground cornmeal. The coarser the grind, the crunchier the bread.

DAK/WELBILT

2½ teaspoons yeast

⅓ cup cornmeal

1 cup whole wheat flour

1½ cups unbleached white flour

1½ teaspoons salt

2 tablespoons gluten OR 3 teaspoons Lora
   Brody's Bread Dough Enhancer™
   (optional for a higher loaf)

2½ tablespoons butter OR margarine

¼ cup honey

1¼ cups water (plus an additional 1 or
   2 tablespoons if the dough looks dry
   and crumbly after the first 10
   minutes of kneading)

Have all the ingredients at room temperature. Place all the ingredients in the machine, program for White Bread, and press Start.

BLACK & DECKER, BETTY CROCKER, BREADMAN/TRILLIUM, HITACHI, LARGE OSTER, REGAL, LARGE TOASTMASTER, AND WILLIAMS-SONOMA

1¼ cups water (plus an additional 1 or
   2 tablespoons if the dough looks dry
   and crumbly after the first 10
   minutes of kneading)

¼ cup honey

2½ tablespoons butter OR margarine, at
   room temperature

⅓ cup cornmeal

1 cup whole wheat flour

1½ cups unbleached white flour

1½ teaspoons salt

2 tablespoons gluten OR 3 teaspoons Lora
   Brody's Bread Dough Enhancer™
   (optional for a higher loaf)

2 teaspoons yeast

Place all the ingredients in the machine, program for Bread, Whole Wheat, Basic Wheat, Whole Wheat/Multigrain, White/Whole Grain, or Wheat, and press Start.

Panasonic/National

⅓ cup cornmeal

1 cup whole wheat flour

1½ cups unbleached white flour

1½ teaspoons salt

2 tablespoons gluten OR 3 teaspoons Lora Brody's Bread Dough Enhancer™ (optional for a higher loaf)

2½ tablespoons butter OR margarine, at room temperature

¼ cup honey

1¼ cups water (plus an additional 1 or 2 tablespoons if the dough looks dry and crumbly after the first 10 minutes of kneading)

2 teaspoons yeast

Place all the ingredients except the yeast in the machine. Place the yeast in the dispenser. Program for Basic Bread and press Start.

Large Pillsbury, Large Zojirushi, and West Bend

2½ tablespoons butter OR margarine, at room temperature

¼ cup honey

1¼ cups water (plus an additional 1 or 2 tablespoons if the dough looks dry and crumbly after the first 10 minutes of kneading)

⅓ cup cornmeal

1 cup whole wheat flour

1½ cups unbleached white flour

2 tablespoons gluten OR 3 teaspoons Lora Brody's Bread Dough Enhancer™ (optional for a higher loaf)

1½ teaspoons salt

2½ teaspoons yeast

Place all the ingredients in the machine, program for Basic White Bread, Whole Wheat, Basic Wheat, Whole Wheat/Multigrain, White/Whole Grain, or Wheat, and press Start or On.

Maxim, Small Oster, Small Pillsbury, Sanyo, Sunbeam, Small Toastmaster, and Small Zojirushi

1½ tablespoons butter OR margarine, at
    room temperature
3 tablespoons honey
⅔ cup water
¼ cup cornmeal
¾ cup whole wheat flour

1 cup unbleached white flour
1 teaspoon salt
1½ tablespoons gluten OR 2 teaspoons
    Lora Brody's Bread Dough Enhancer™
    (optional for a higher loaf)
1½ teaspoons yeast

Place all the ingredients in the machine, program for Whole Wheat, Whole Grain, Standard, or Bread, and press Start.

Small Welbilt

1½ teaspoons yeast
¼ cup cornmeal
¾ cup whole wheat flour
1 cup unbleached white flour
1½ tablespoons gluten OR 2 teaspoons
    Lora Brody's Bread Dough Enhancer™
    (optional for a higher loaf)

1 teaspoon salt
1½ tablespoons butter OR margarine
3 tablespoons honey
⅔ cup water

Have all the ingredients at room temperature. Place all the ingredients in the machine, program for Medium, and press Start.

SMALL PANASONIC/NATIONAL

¼ cup cornmeal

¾ cup whole wheat flour

1 cup unbleached white flour

1 teaspoon salt

1½ tablespoons gluten OR 2 teaspoons
Lora Brody's Bread Dough Enhancer™
(optional for a higher loaf)

1½ tablespoons butter OR margarine, at
room temperature

3 tablespoons honey

⅔ cup water

1½ teaspoons yeast

Place all the ingredients except the yeast in the machine. Place the yeast in the dispenser. Program for Basic Bread and press Start.

Variation: With the other ingredients, add 1 small carrot, grated.

OAT BRAN BREAD

This beautiful crusty brown loaf makes nutritious sandwiches and snacks and is great for toasted cheese sandwiches.

DAK/WELBILT

2½ teaspoons yeast

1½ cups unbleached white flour

1½ cups whole wheat flour

½ cup oat bran

¼ cup steel-cut oats

1½ tablespoons powdered skim milk

1½ teaspoons salt

2 tablespoons gluten OR 3 teaspoons Lora Brody's Bread Dough Enhancer™ (optional for a higher loaf)

1 tablespoon wheat germ

⅓ cup molasses

1 cup water (plus several more tablespoons, added one at a time, if the dough looks dry and crumbly after the first 10 minutes of kneading)

3½ tablespoons vegetable oil

2 tablespoons honey

1 extra-large egg

Have all the ingredients at room temperature. Place all the ingredients in the machine, program for White Bread, and press Start.

BLACK & DECKER, BETTY CROCKER, BREADMAN/TRILLIUM, HITACHI, LARGE OSTER, REGAL, LARGE TOASTMASTER, WILLIAMS-SONOMA, LARGE PILLSBURY, LARGE ZOJIRUSHI, AND WEST BEND

1 cup water (plus several more tablespoons, added one at a time, if the dough looks dry and crumbly after the first 10 minutes of kneading)

3½ tablespoons vegetable oil

2 tablespoons honey

⅓ cup molasses

1 extra-large egg

1½ cups unbleached white flour

1½ cups whole wheat flour

½ cup oat bran

¼ cup steel-cut oats

1½ tablespoons powdered skim milk

1½ teaspoons salt

2 tablespoons gluten OR 3 teaspoons Lora Brody's Bread Dough Enhancer™ (optional for a higher loaf)

1 tablespoon wheat germ

2½ teaspoons yeast

Continued

Place all the ingredients in the machine, program for Basic White Bread, Whole Wheat, Basic Wheat, Whole Wheat/Multigrain, White/Whole Grain, or Wheat, and press Start or On.

PANASONIC/NATIONAL

1½ cups unbleached white flour

1½ cups whole wheat flour

½ cup oat bran

¼ cup steel-cut oats

1 tablespoon wheat germ

1½ tablespoons powdered skim milk

1½ teaspoons salt

2 tablespoons gluten OR 3 teaspoons Lora Brody's Bread Dough Enhancer™ (optional for a higher loaf)

3½ tablespoons vegetable oil

1 cup water (plus several more tablespoons, added one at a time, if the dough looks dry and crumbly after the first 10 minutes of kneading)

2 tablespoons honey

⅓ cup molasses

1 extra-large egg

2½ teaspoons yeast

Place all the ingredients except the yeast in the machine. Place the yeast in the dispenser. Program for Basic Bread and press Start.

Oat Bran Bread

MAXIM, SMALL OSTER, SMALL PILLSBURY, SANYO, SUNBEAM, SMALL TOASTMASTER, AND SMALL ZOJIRUSHI

¼ cup molasses

½ cup plus 3 tablespoons water (plus an additional 1 or 2 tablespoons if the dough seems dry and crumbly after the first 10 minutes of kneading)

2 tablespoons vegetable oil

1 tablespoon honey

1 medium egg

1 cup unbleached white flour

1 cup whole wheat flour

¼ cup plus 2 tablespoons oat bran

3 tablespoons steel-cut oats

1 tablespoon powdered skim milk

1½ tablespoons gluten OR 2 teaspoons Lora Brody's Bread Dough Enhancer™ (optional for a higher loaf)

1 teaspoon salt

1 tablespoon wheat germ

2 teaspoons yeast

Place all the ingredients in the machine, program for Whole Wheat, Whole Grain, Standard, or Bread, and press Start.

SMALL WELBILT

2 teaspoons yeast

1 cup unbleached white flour

1 cup whole wheat flour

¼ cup plus 2 tablespoons oat bran

3 tablespoons steel-cut oats

1 tablespoon powdered skim milk

1 teaspoon salt

1½ tablespoons gluten OR 2 teaspoons
   Lora Brody's Bread Dough Enhancer™
   (optional for a higher loaf)

1 tablespoon wheat germ

¼ cup molasses

½ cup plus 3 tablespoons water (plus
   an additional 1 or 2 tablespoons if
   the dough seems dry and crumbly
   after the first 10 minutes of
   kneading)

2 tablespoons vegetable oil

1 tablespoon honey

1 medium egg

Have all the ingredients at room temperature. Place all the ingredients in the machine, program for Medium, and press Start.

SMALL PANASONIC/NATIONAL

1 cup unbleached white flour

1 cup whole wheat flour

¼ cup plus 2 tablespoons oat bran

3 tablespoons steel-cut oats

1 tablespoon powdered skim milk

1 teaspoon salt

1½ tablespoons gluten OR 2 teaspoons
   Lora Brody's Bread Dough Enhancer™
   (optional for a higher loaf)

1 tablespoon wheat germ

¼ cup molasses

½ cup plus 3 tablespoons water (plus
   an additional 1 or 2 tablespoons if the
   dough seems dry and crumbly after
   the first 10 minutes of kneading)

2 tablespoons vegetable oil

1 tablespoon honey

1 medium egg

2 teaspoons yeast

Place all the ingredients except the yeast in the machine. Place the yeast in the dispenser. Program for Basic Bread and press Start.

GRAINY MUSTARD WHOLE WHEAT BREAD

The addition of fresh sprouts gives this light, fine-grained bread a lovely moist, wholesome texture and a snappy, pleasing taste.

....

DAK/Welbilt

1 tablespoon yeast

2 tablespoons dark brown sugar

1 teaspoon salt

2 tablespoons gluten OR 3 teaspoons Lora Brody's Bread Dough Enhancer™ (optional for a higher loaf)

⅔ cup whole wheat flour

⅓ cup cornmeal

2 cups unbleached white flour

4 tablespoons nonfat dry milk

2 tablespoons vegetable oil

1 extra-large egg

⅓ cup grainy mustard

⅔ cup water

1 cup fresh alfalfa sprouts OR other sprouts, separated out of their clump

Have all the ingredients at room temperature. Place all the ingredients in the machine and program for White Bread. Set the Light-Dark control one third of the way past Medium toward Dark and press Start.

....

Black & Decker, Betty Crocker, Breadman/Trillium, Hitachi, Large Oster, Large Toastmaster, and Williams-Sonoma

1½ tablespoons vegetable oil

1 extra-large egg

¼ cup grainy mustard

⅔ cup water

2 tablespoons gluten OR 3 teaspoons Lora Brody's Bread Dough Enhancer™ (optional for a higher loaf)

1 teaspoon salt

⅔ cup whole wheat flour

⅓ cup cornmeal

2 cups unbleached white flour

4 tablespoons nonfat dry milk

2 tablespoons dark brown sugar

1 cup fresh alfalfa sprouts OR other sprouts, separated out of their clump

2½ teaspoons yeast

Place all the ingredients in the machine, program for Bread, Whole Wheat, Basic Wheat, Whole Wheat/Multigrain, White/Whole Grain, or Wheat, and press Start.

PANASONIC/NATIONAL

1 teaspoon salt

⅔ cup whole wheat flour

⅓ cup cornmeal

2 cups unbleached white flour

4 tablespoons nonfat dry milk

2 tablespoons dark brown sugar

2 tablespoons gluten OR 3 teaspoons Lora Brody's Bread Dough Enhancer™ (optional for a higher loaf)

1½ tablespoons vegetable oil

1 extra-large egg

¼ cup grainy mustard

⅔ cup water

1 cup fresh alfalfa sprouts OR other sprouts, separated out of their clump

1 tablespoon yeast

Place all the ingredients except the yeast in the machine. Place the yeast in the dispenser. Program for Basic Bread and press Start.

LARGE PILLSBURY, LARGE ZOJIRUSHI, AND WEST BEND

1½ tablespoons vegetable oil

1 extra-large egg

¼ cup grainy mustard

⅔ cup water

1 teaspoon salt

⅔ cup whole wheat flour

⅓ cup cornmeal

2 cups unbleached white flour

4 tablespoons nonfat dry milk

2 tablespoons gluten OR 3 teaspoons Lora Brody's Bread Dough Enhancer™ (optional for a higher loaf)

2 tablespoons dark brown sugar

1 cup fresh alfalfa sprouts OR other sprouts, separated out of their clump

1 tablespoon yeast

Place all the ingredients in the machine and program for Bread, Basic White Bread, Whole Wheat, Basic Wheat, Whole Wheat/Multigrain, White/Whole Grain, or Wheat, and press Start or On.

Maxim, Small Oster, Small Pillsbury, Sanyo, Sunbeam, Small Toastmaster, and Small Zojirushi

1½ tablespoons vegetable oil

1 medium egg

¼ cup grainy mustard

½ cup water

1 tablespoon plus 1 teaspoon dark brown sugar

½ teaspoon salt

½ cup whole wheat flour

¼ cup cornmeal

1¼ cups unbleached white flour

1½ tablespoons gluten OR 2 teaspoons Lora Brody's Bread Dough Enhancer™ (optional for a higher loaf)

3 tablespoons nonfat dry milk

⅔ cup fresh alfalfa sprouts OR other sprouts, separated out of their clump

2 teaspoons yeast

Place all the ingredients in the machine, program for Whole Wheat, Whole Grain, Standard, or Bread, and press Start.

....

Small Welbilt

2 teaspoons yeast

1 tablespoon plus 1 teaspoon dark brown sugar

½ teaspoon salt

½ cup whole wheat flour

1½ tablespoons gluten OR 2 teaspoons Lora Brody's Bread Dough Enhancer™ (optional for a higher loaf)

¼ cup cornmeal

1¼ cups unbleached white flour

3 tablespoons nonfat dry milk

1½ tablespoons vegetable oil

1 medium egg

¼ cup grainy mustard

½ cup water

1 cup fresh alfalfa sprouts OR other sprouts, separated out of their clump

Have all the ingredients at room temperature. Place all the ingredients in the machine, program for Dark, and press Start.

....

Small Panasonic/National

1 tablespoon plus 1 teaspoon dark
  brown sugar

½ teaspoon salt

½ cup whole wheat flour

1½ tablespoons gluten OR 2 teaspoons
  Lora Brody's Bread Dough Enhancer™
  (optional for a higher loaf)

¼ cup cornmeal

1¼ cups unbleached white flour

3 tablespoons nonfat dry milk

1½ tablespoons vegetable oil

1 medium egg

¼ cup grainy mustard

½ cup water

⅔ cup fresh alfalfa sprouts OR other
  sprouts, separated out of their clump

2 teaspoons yeast

Place all the ingredients except the yeast in the machine. Place the yeast in the dispenser. Program for Basic Bread and press Start.

HONEY WHOLE WHEAT BREAD

We like this hearty loaf with the optional addition of one-third cup hulled, roasted pumpkin seeds, which can be found in health food stores. Steel-cut oats are also found there.

DAK/WELBILT

2½ teaspoons yeast

1¼ cups whole wheat flour

2 cups unbleached white flour

1½ teaspoons salt

2 tablespoons gluten OR 3 teaspoons Lora Brody's Bread Dough Enhancer™ (optional for a higher loaf)

1 tablespoon steel-cut oats

2 tablespoons powdered buttermilk

3½ tablespoons butter OR margarine

3½ tablespoons honey

2 tablespoons wheat germ

1 cup water

1 extra-large egg

Have all the ingredients at room temperature. Place all the ingredients in the machine, program for White Bread, and press Start.

BLACK & DECKER, BETTY CROCKER, BREADMAN/TRILLIUM, HITACHI, LARGE OSTER, LARGE TOASTMASTER, AND WILLIAMS-SONOMA

3½ tablespoons butter OR margarine

3½ tablespoons honey

2 tablespoons wheat germ

1 cup water

1 extra-large egg

1¼ cups whole wheat flour

2 cups unbleached white flour

1½ teaspoons salt

1 tablespoon steel-cut oats

2 tablespoons powdered buttermilk

2 tablespoons gluten OR 3 teaspoons Lora Brody's Bread Dough Enhancer™ (optional for a higher loaf)

2 teaspoons yeast

Place all the ingredients in the machine, program for Bread, Whole Wheat, Basic Wheat, Whole Wheat/Multigrain, White/Whole Grain, or Wheat, and press Start.

PANASONIC/NATIONAL

1¼ cups whole wheat flour

2 cups unbleached white flour

1½ teaspoons salt

2 tablespoons gluten OR 3 teaspoons Lora
  Brody's Bread Dough Enhancer™
  (optional for a higher loaf)

1 tablespoon steel-cut oats

2 tablespoons powdered buttermilk

3½ tablespoons butter OR margarine

3½ tablespoons honey

2 tablespoons wheat germ

1 cup water

1 extra-large egg

2½ teaspoons yeast

Place all the ingredients except the yeast in the machine. Place the yeast in the dispenser. Program for Basic Bread and press Start.

REGAL, LARGE PILLSBURY, LARGE ZOJIRUSHI, AND WEST BEND

3½ tablespoons butter OR margarine

3½ tablespoons honey

2 tablespoons wheat germ

1 cup water

1 extra-large egg

1¼ cups whole wheat flour

2 cups unbleached white flour

1½ teaspoons salt

1 tablespoon steel-cut oats

2 tablespoons gluten OR 3 teaspoons Lora
  Brody's Bread Dough Enhancer™
  (optional for a higher loaf)

2 tablespoons powdered buttermilk

2½ teaspoons yeast

Place all the ingredients in the machine, program for Bread, Basic White Bread, Whole Wheat, Basic Wheat, Whole Wheat/Multigrain, White/Whole Grain, or Wheat, and press Start or On.

Honey Whole Wheat

MAXIM, SMALL OSTER, SMALL PILLSBURY, SANYO, SUNBEAM, SMALL TOASTMASTER, AND SMALL ZOJIRUSHI

2 tablespoons butter OR margarine

2 tablespoons honey

⅔ cup water

1 medium egg

1 cup whole wheat flour

1¼ cups unbleached white flour

1 teaspoon salt

1½ tablespoons gluten OR 2 teaspoons
  Lora Brody's Bread Dough Enhancer™
  (optional for a higher loaf)

1 tablespoon steel-cut oats

1½ tablespoons wheat germ

4 tablespoons powdered buttermilk

2 teaspoons yeast   *Continued*

121

Place all the ingredients in the machine, program for Whole Wheat, Whole Grain, Standard, or Bread, and press Start.

....

Small Welbilt

2 teaspoons yeast

1 cup whole wheat flour

1¼ cups unbleached white flour

1 teaspoon salt

1½ tablespoons gluten OR 2 teaspoons
    Lora Brody's Bread Dough Enhancer™
    (optional for a higher loaf)

1 tablespoon steel-cut oats

4 teaspoons powdered buttermilk

2 tablespoons butter OR margarine

2 tablespoons honey

1½ tablespoons wheat germ

⅔ cup water

1 medium egg

Have all the ingredients at room temperature. Place all the ingredients in the machine, program for Medium, and press Start.

....

Small Panasonic/National

2 tablespoons butter OR margarine

2 tablespoons honey

⅔ cup water

1 medium egg

1 cup whole wheat flour

1¼ cups unbleached white flour

1 teaspoon salt

1½ tablespoons gluten OR 2 teaspoons
    Lora Brody's Bread Dough Enhancer™
    (optional for a higher loaf)

1 tablespoon steel-cut oats

1½ tablespoons wheat germ

4 tablespoons powdered buttermilk

2 teaspoons yeast

Place all the ingredients except the yeast in the machine. Place the yeast in the dispenser. Program for Basic Bread and press Start.

LIGHT WHOLE WHEAT BREAD

If you use white wheat flour to make this loaf you'll end up with something so light and airy you'll need an extra layer of jam to hold it down. Look for white wheat in your supermarket or health food store, or order it from King Arthur Flour (see page 339).

DAK/Welbilt

1 tablespoon yeast

1¼ cups whole wheat flour OR white wheat flour

1¾ cups unbleached white flour

4 tablespoons powdered buttermilk plus 1 cup water OR 1 cup cultured buttermilk

2 teaspoons salt

¼ cup honey

1 extra-large egg

Have all the ingredients at room temperature. Place all the ingredients in the machine, program for White Bread, and press Start.

Black & Decker, Betty Crocker, Breadman/Trillium, Hitachi, Large Oster, Regal, Large Toastmaster, and Williams-Sonoma

1 extra-large egg

3 tablespoons honey

3 tablespoons powdered buttermilk plus ¾ cup water OR ¾ cup cultured buttermilk

1½ teaspoons salt

1 cup whole wheat flour

2 cups unbleached white flour OR white wheat flour

2 teaspoons yeast

Place all the ingredients in the machine, program for Bread, Whole Wheat, Basic Wheat, Whole Wheat/Multigrain, White/Whole Grain, or Wheat, and press Start.

PANASONIC/NATIONAL

1½ teaspoons salt

1½ cups whole wheat flour OR white
    wheat flour

2 cups unbleached white flour

1 extra-large egg

⅓ cup honey

4 tablespoons powdered buttermilk plus
    1 cup water OR 1 cup cultured
    buttermilk

1 tablespoon yeast

Place all the ingredients except the yeast in the machine. Place the yeast in the dispenser. Program for Basic Bread, or Whole Wheat if you have this setting, and press Start.

LARGE PILLSBURY, LARGE ZOJIRUSHI, AND WEST BEND

1 extra-large egg

⅓ cup honey

4 tablespoons powdered buttermilk plus
    1 cup water OR 1 cup cultured
    buttermilk

2 teaspoons salt

1½ cups whole wheat flour OR white
    wheat flour

2 cups unbleached white flour

1 tablespoon yeast

Place all the ingredients in the machine, program for Basic White Bread, Whole Wheat, Basic Wheat, Whole Wheat/Multigrain, White/Whole Grain, or Wheat, and press Start or On.

Light Whole Wheat Bread.

MAXIM, SMALL OSTER, SMALL PILLSBURY, SANYO, SUNBEAM, SMALL TOASTMASTER, AND SMALL ZOJIRUSHI

1 large egg

3 tablespoons honey

2 tablespoons powdered buttermilk plus
    ½ cup water OR ½ cup cultured
    buttermilk

1 teaspoon salt

1 cup whole wheat flour OR white
    wheat flour

1 cup plus 1 tablespoon unbleached
    white flour

2 teaspoons yeast

Place all the ingredients in the machine, program for Whole Wheat, Whole Grain, Standard, or Bread, and press Start.

SMALL WELBILT

1 large egg

3 tablespoons honey

3 tablespoons powdered buttermilk plus ½ cup plus 1 tablespoon water OR ½ cup plus 1 tablespoon cultured buttermilk

1½ teaspoons salt

¾ cup whole wheat flour OR white wheat flour

1 cup unbleached white flour

1½ teaspoons yeast

Have all the ingredients at room temperature. Place all the ingredients in the machine, program for Medium, and press Start.

SMALL PANASONIC/NATIONAL

1 teaspoon salt

1 cup whole wheat flour OR white wheat flour

1 cup plus 1 tablespoon unbleached white flour

2 tablespoons powdered buttermilk plus ½ cup water OR ½ cup cultured buttermilk

1 large egg

3 tablespoons honey

2 teaspoons yeast

Place all the ingredients except the yeast in the machine. Place the yeast in the dispenser. Program for Basic Bread and press Start.

Variations: Add 2 tablespoons sesame, sunflower, or caraway seeds to the ingredients.

If you're not looking to make a low-calorie bread, then add 2 tablespoons of butter or vegetable oil for a loaf that will stay fresher longer.

SUNFLOWER HEALTH LOAF

This extremely hearty (and healthy) loaf has a lovely thick crust and a complex and satisfying texture inside. It's wonderful for a vegetarian sandwich with lots of sprouts and avocado topped with a slice of Cheddar cheese.

DAK/Welbilt

1 tablespoon yeast

½ cup unprocessed bran flakes

1 teaspoon salt

2 cups unbleached white flour

½ cup plus 3 tablespoons whole wheat flour

2 tablespoons gluten OR 3 teaspoons Lora Brody's Bread Dough Enhancer™ (optional for a higher loaf)

2 tablespoons wheat germ

1 tablespoon blackstrap molasses

2 tablespoons honey

2 tablespoons vegetable oil

1 cup plus 2 tablespoons water

⅓ cup sunflower seeds

Have all the ingredients at room temperature. Place all the ingredients except the sunflower seeds in the machine, program for Raisin Bread, and press Start. When the beeper sounds at the end of the second kneading, add the sunflower seeds.

Black & Decker, Betty Crocker, Breadman/Trillium, Hitachi, Large Oster, Regal, Large Toastmaster, and Williams-Sonoma

1 tablespoon blackstrap molasses

2 tablespoons honey

2 tablespoons vegetable oil

1 cup water

¼ cup unprocessed bran flakes

1 teaspoon salt

2 cups unbleached white flour

½ cup whole wheat flour

2 tablespoons wheat germ

2 tablespoons gluten OR 3 teaspoons Lora Brody's Bread Dough Enhancer™ (optional for a higher loaf)

2 teaspoons yeast

⅓ cup sunflower seeds

Place all the ingredients except the sunflower seeds in the machine, program for Mix Bread, Bread, Raisin Bread, Fruit and Nut, Whole Wheat, Basic Wheat, Whole Wheat/Multigrain, White/Whole Grain, or Wheat, and press Start. Add the sunflower seeds when the beeper sounds or during the last 5 minutes of the final knead cycle.

PANASONIC/NATIONAL

2 cups unbleached white flour
½ cup whole wheat flour
2 tablespoons wheat germ
½ cup unprocessed bran flakes
1 teaspoon salt
2 tablespoons gluten OR 3 teaspoons Lora Brody's Bread Dough Enhancer™ (optional for a higher loaf)

1 tablespoon blackstrap molasses
2 tablespoons honey
2 tablespoons vegetable oil
1 cup plus 2 tablespoons water
2¾ teaspoons yeast
⅓ cup sunflower seeds

Place all the ingredients except the yeast and the sunflower seeds in the machine. Place the yeast in the dispenser. Program for Basic Bread and press Start. At the end of the prekneading cycle, add the sunflower seeds.

LARGE PILLSBURY, LARGE ZOJIRUSHI, AND WEST BEND

1 tablespoon blackstrap molasses
2 tablespoons honey
2 tablespoons vegetable oil
1 cup plus 2 tablespoons water
½ cup unprocessed bran flakes
1 teaspoon salt
2 cups unbleached white flour

½ cup plus 3 tablespoons whole wheat flour
2 tablespoons wheat germ
2 tablespoons gluten OR 3 teaspoons Lora Brody's Bread Dough Enhancer™ (optional for a higher loaf)
1 tablespoon yeast
⅓ cup sunflower seeds

Place all the ingredients except the sunflower seeds in the machine, program for Raisin Bread, Whole Wheat, Basic Wheat, Whole Wheat/Multigrain, White/Whole Grain, or Wheat, and press Start or On. Add the sunflower seeds when the beeper sounds or during the last 5 minutes of the final knead cycle.

MAXIM, SMALL OSTER, SANYO, SUNBEAM, SMALL PILLSBURY, SMALL TOASTMASTER, AND SMALL ZOJIRUSHI

2 teaspoons blackstrap molasses
1 tablespoon honey
1 tablespoon vegetable oil
½ cup plus 2 tablespoons water
¼ cup unprocessed bran flakes
¾ teaspoon salt
1 cup unbleached white flour

¼ cup whole wheat flour
1 tablespoon wheat germ
1½ tablespoons gluten OR 2 teaspoons
   Lora Brody's Bread Dough Enhancer™
   (optional for a higher loaf)
2 teaspoons yeast
¼ cup sunflower seeds

Place all the ingredients in the machine, program for Whole Wheat, Whole Grain, Standard, or Bread, and press Start.

SMALL WELBILT

2 teaspoons yeast
¼ cup unprocessed bran flakes
¾ teaspoon salt
1 cup unbleached white flour
¼ cup whole wheat flour
1 tablespoon wheat germ

1½ tablespoons gluten OR 2 teaspoons
   Lora Brody's Bread Dough Enhancer™
   (optional for a higher loaf)
2 teaspoons blackstrap molasses
1 tablespoon honey
1 tablespoon vegetable oil
½ cup plus 2 tablespoons water
¼ cup sunflower seeds

Have all the ingredients at room temperature. Place all the ingredients in the machine, program for Medium, and press Start.

SMALL PANASONIC/NATIONAL

¼ cup unprocessed bran flakes
¾ teaspoon salt
1 cup unbleached white flour
¼ cup whole wheat flour
1 tablespoon wheat germ
1½ tablespoons gluten OR 2 teaspoons
   Lora Brody's Bread Dough Enhancer™
   (optional for a higher loaf)

2 teaspoons blackstrap molasses
1 tablespoon honey
1 tablespoon vegetable oil
½ cup plus 2 tablespoons water
¼ cup sunflower seeds
2 teaspoons yeast

Place all the ingredients except the yeast and the sunflower seeds in the machine. Place the yeast in the dispenser. Program for Basic Bread and press Start. At the end of the second kneading, add the sunflower seeds.

SMOKED TEA GINGER BREAD

You've never tasted whole wheat bread like this before. Because this recipe has no white flour, the dough must go through two complete kneading cycles. (Or if your machine has a Whole Wheat Bread setting, use it instead of repeating the process.) To do this, simply stop or cancel your machine at the end of the first kneading cycle, then reset it at the beginning again for one more complete kneading cycle.

DAK/Welbilt

1 tablespoon yeast

3 cups whole wheat flour

2 tablespoons gluten OR 1 tablespoon Lora Brody's Bread Dough Enhancer™

1 teaspoon salt

1 teaspoon ground ginger

2 tablespoons honey

1 tablespoon vegetable oil

1 extra-large egg

1¼ cups very strong tea made with a smoky-flavored tea, such as Lapsang souchong

⅓ cup candied ginger, chopped

Have all the ingredients at room temperature. Place all the ingredients except the candied ginger in the machine, program for Manual, and press Start. At the end of the second kneading, cancel the machine, program for White Bread, and press Start again. Add the candied ginger when the beeper sounds at the end of the second kneading.

Black & Decker, Betty Crocker, Breadman/Trillium, Hitachi, Large Oster, Large Toastmaster, and Williams-Sonoma

2 tablespoons honey

1 tablespoon vegetable oil

1 extra-large egg

1¼ cups very strong tea made with a smoky-flavored tea, such as Lapsang souchong

3 cups whole wheat flour

2 tablespoons gluten OR 1 tablespoon Lora Brody's Bread Dough Enhancer™

1 teaspoon salt

1 teaspoon ground ginger

2 teaspoons yeast

⅓ cup candied ginger, chopped

Continued

Place all the ingredients except the candied ginger in the machine, program for Dough or Knead and First Rise, and press Start. At the end of the second kneading, cancel the machine, program for Mix Bread, Raisin Bread, Whole Wheat, Basic Wheat, Whole Wheat/Multigrain, White/Whole Grain, or Wheat, and press Start again. Add the candied ginger when the beeper sounds or during the last 5 minutes of the final knead cycle.

PANASONIC/NATIONAL

3 cups whole wheat flour

2 tablespoons gluten OR 1 tablespoon Lora Brody's Bread Dough Enhancer™

1 teaspoon salt

1 teaspoon ground ginger

2 tablespoons honey

1 tablespoon vegetable oil

1 extra-large egg

1¼ cups very strong tea made with a smoky-flavored tea, such as Lapsang souchong

2½ teaspoons yeast

⅓ cup candied ginger, chopped

Place all the ingredients except the yeast and candied ginger in the machine. Place the yeast in the dispenser. Program for Basic Bread and press Start. At the end of the second kneading, cancel the machine and press Off. Program for Basic Bread and press Start. Add the candied ginger 20 minutes into the prekneading cycle.

REGAL

2 tablespoons honey

1 tablespoon vegetable oil

1 extra-large egg

1¼ cups very strong tea made with a smoky-flavored tea, such as Lapsang souchong

3 cups whole wheat flour

2 tablespoons gluten OR 1 tablespoon Lora Brody's Bread Dough Enhancer™

1 teaspoon salt

1 teaspoon ground ginger

1 tablespoon yeast

⅓ cup candied ginger, chopped

Place all the ingredients except the candied ginger in the machine, program for Manual, and press Start. At the end of the second kneading, cancel the machine, program for Raisin Bread, and press Start again. Add the candied ginger when the beeper sounds at the end of the second kneading.

Large Pillsbury, Large Zojirushi, and West Bend

2 tablespoons honey

1 tablespoon vegetable oil

1 extra-large egg

1¼ cups very strong tea made with a smoky-flavored tea, such as Lapsang souchong

3 cups whole wheat flour

2 tablespoons gluten OR 1 tablespoon Lora Brody's Bread Dough Enhancer™

1 teaspoon salt

1 teaspoon ground ginger

1 tablespoon yeast

⅓ cup candied ginger, chopped

Place all the ingredients except the candied ginger in the machine, program for Manual, and press Start or On. At the end of the second kneading, cancel the machine, program for Raisin Bread, Whole Wheat, Basic Wheat, Whole Wheat/Multigrain, White/Whole Grain, or Wheat, and press Start again. Add the candied ginger when the beeper sounds or during the last 5 minutes of the final knead cycle.

Maxim, Small Oster, Small Pillsbury, Sanyo, Sunbeam, Small Toastmaster, and Small Zojirushi

2 teaspoons vegetable oil

1 medium egg

⅔ cup very strong tea made with a smoky-flavored tea, such as Lapsang souchong

1½ tablespoons honey

¼ cup candied ginger, chopped

1⅓ cups whole wheat flour

1½ tablespoons gluten OR 2 teaspoons Lora Brody's Bread Dough Enhancer™

½ teaspoon salt

¾ teaspoon ground ginger

2 teaspoons yeast

Place all the ingredients except the candied ginger in the machine, program for Dough or Manual, and press Start. At the end of the second kneading, cancel the machine, program for Standard, Bread, Whole Wheat, or Whole Grain, and press

Start again. Add the candied ginger when the beeper sounds or during the last 5 minutes of the final knead cycle.

SMALL WELBILT

2 teaspoons yeast

2 cups whole wheat flour

1½ tablespoons gluten OR 2 teaspoons Lora Brody's Bread Dough Enhancer™

½ teaspoon salt

¾ teaspoon ground ginger

1½ tablespoons honey

2 teaspoons vegetable oil

1 medium egg

⅔ cup very strong tea made with a smoky-flavored tea, such as Lapsang souchong

¼ cup candied ginger, chopped

Have all the ingredients at room temperature. Place all the ingredients except the candied ginger in the machine, program for Manual, and press Start. At the end of the second kneading, cancel the machine, program for Medium, and press Start again. Add the candied ginger when the beeper sounds at the end of the second kneading.

SMALL PANASONIC/NATIONAL

2 cups whole wheat flour

1½ tablespoons gluten OR 2 teaspoons Lora Brody's Bread Dough Enhancer™

½ teaspoon salt

¾ teaspoon ground ginger

2 teaspoons vegetable oil

1 medium egg

⅔ cup very strong tea made with a smoky-flavored tea, such as Lapsang souchong

1½ tablespoons honey

¼ cup candied ginger, chopped

2 teaspoons yeast

Place all the ingredients except the yeast and candied ginger in the machine. Place the yeast in the dispenser. Program for Basic Bread and press Start. At the end of the second kneading, cancel the machine, program for Basic Bread, and press Start again. Add the candied ginger at the end of the second kneading.

SWEET POTATO RYE BREAD

This recipe took many tries to perfect, but the results were worth the repeated efforts. This is a tall loaf with a light texture, a beautiful orangy color, and a tender, golden crust. The combination of spices makes for a splendid rainbow of flavors and the sweet potato adds just the right amount of moisture and sweetness.

This is a typically wet dough. Depending on the humidity the day you make it, you will need additional flour. If the dough at the bottom of the bowl looks "soupy" and hasn't incorporated into the rest of the mass after the first 10 minutes of kneading, add more flour (up to ¼ cup). Remember that the dough will look tacky even after adding more flour.

DAK/Welbilt

1 tablespoon yeast

4 tablespoons powdered buttermilk

¼ cup sugar

1 teaspoon salt

½ teaspoon ground nutmeg

½ teaspoon ground ginger

½ teaspoon ground mace

½ teaspoon freshly ground black pepper

½ cup baked, boiled, or canned sweet potatoes, mashed

Grated zest of 1 lemon

½ cup rye flour

2¾ cups unbleached white flour (plus up to an additional ¼ cup)

⅓ cup orange juice

⅔ cup water

1 tablespoon butter, at room temperature

Have all the ingredients at room temperature. Place all the ingredients in the machine, program for White Bread, and press Start.

BLACK & DECKER, BETTY CROCKER, BREADMAN/TRILLIUM, HITACHI, LARGE TOASTMASTER, AND WILLIAMS-SONOMA

1/3 cup orange juice

1/2 cup water

1 tablespoon butter, at room temperature

3 tablespoons powdered buttermilk

3 tablespoons sugar

1 teaspoon salt

1/2 teaspoon ground nutmeg

1/2 teaspoon ground ginger

1/2 teaspoon ground mace

1/2 teaspoon freshly ground black pepper

1/2 cup baked, boiled, or canned sweet potatoes, mashed

Grated zest of 1 lemon

1/4 cup rye flour

2 1/2 cups unbleached white flour (plus up to an additional 1/4 cup)

2 teaspoons yeast

Place all the ingredients in the machine, program for Bread, Basic, Basic Bread, Basic Wheat, or White/Whole Grain, and press Start.

....

PANASONIC/NATIONAL

1/3 cup orange juice

2/3 cup water

4 tablespoons powdered buttermilk

1/4 cup sugar

1 tablespoon butter, at room temperature

1 teaspoon salt

1/2 teaspoon ground nutmeg

1/2 teaspoon ground ginger

1/2 teaspoon ground mace

1/2 teaspoon freshly ground black pepper

1/2 cup baked, boiled, or canned sweet potatoes, mashed

Grated zest of 1 lemon

1/2 cup rye flour

2 3/4 cups unbleached white flour (plus up to an additional 1/4 cup)

1 tablespoon yeast

Place all the ingredients except the yeast in the machine. Place the yeast in the dispenser. Program for Basic Bread and press Start.

....

Large Pillsbury, Large Zojirushi, West Bend, Large Oster, and Regal

⅓ cup orange juice

⅔ cup water

4 tablespoons powdered buttermilk

¼ cup sugar

1 tablespoon butter, at room temperature

1 teaspoon salt

½ teaspoon ground nutmeg

½ teaspoon ground ginger

½ teaspoon ground mace

½ teaspoon freshly ground black pepper

½ cup baked, boiled, or canned sweet potatoes, mashed

Grated zest of 1 lemon

½ cup rye flour

2¾ cups unbleached white flour (plus up to an additional ¼ cup)

1 tablespoon yeast

Place all the ingredients in the machine, program for Bread, Basic White Bread, Basic, Basic Bread, Basic Wheat, White, or White/Whole Grain, and press Start or On.

Sweet Potato Rye Bread

Maxim, Small Oster, Small Pillsbury, Sanyo, Sunbeam, Small Toastmaster, and Small Zojirushi

¼ cup orange juice

¼ cup water

2 teaspoons butter, at room temperature

2 tablespoons powdered buttermilk

2 tablespoons sugar

½ teaspoon salt

¼ teaspoon ground nutmeg

¼ teaspoon ground ginger

¼ teaspoon ground mace

¼ teaspoon freshly ground black pepper

¼ cup baked, boiled, or canned sweet potatoes, mashed

Grated zest of 1 lemon

¼ cup rye flour

1¼ cups unbleached white flour (plus up to an additional ¼ cup)

1½ teaspoons yeast

Place all the ingredients in the machine, program for Basic, White, Basic Bread, Standard, or Bread, and press Start.

SMALL WELBILT

1½ teaspoons yeast

2 tablespoons powdered buttermilk

2 tablespoons sugar

½ teaspoon salt

¼ teaspoon ground nutmeg

¼ teaspoon ground ginger

¼ teaspoon ground mace

¼ teaspoon freshly ground black pepper

¼ cup baked, boiled, or canned sweet
    potatoes, mashed

Grated zest of 1 lemon

¼ cup rye flour

1¼ cups unbleached white flour (plus
    up to an additional ¼ cup)

¼ cup orange juice

¼ cup water

2 teaspoons butter, at room temperature

Have all the ingredients at room temperature. Place all the ingredients in the
machine, program for Medium, and press Start.

SMALL PANASONIC/NATIONAL

¼ cup rye flour

1¼ cups unbleached white flour (plus
    up to an additional ¼ cup)

2 tablespoons powdered buttermilk

2 tablespoons sugar

½ teaspoon salt

¼ teaspoon ground nutmeg

¼ teaspoon ground ginger

¼ teaspoon ground mace

¼ teaspoon freshly ground black pepper

¼ cup baked, boiled, or canned sweet
    potatoes, mashed

Grated zest of 1 lemon

¼ cup orange juice

¼ cup water

2 teaspoons butter, at room temperature

1½ teaspoons yeast

Place all the ingredients except the yeast in the machine. Place the yeast in the
dispenser. Program for Basic Bread and press Start.

SOURDOUGH BREADS

SOURDOUGH STARTER

STARTER (LARGE MACHINES)

STARTER (LARGE MACHINES)

1½ teaspoons yeast

¾ cup milk, heated to a simmer and then cooled to about 100°F

1 cup rye, whole wheat, or white whole wheat flour (see *The King Arthur Flour Baker's Catalogue*, page 339)

Yield: 1⅓ cups starter

Sprinkle the yeast on top of the warm milk, then stir until it dissolves completely. Stir in the rye flour. Store this, uncovered, at room temperature (at least 70° F) for 3 days, stirring once a day. Use this entire starter for the bread.

You can double the amount of starter and use half for the Sourdough Chèvre Bread (page 149) and half for the Sourdough Rye Bread (page 165). Or you can refrigerate the rest so the next time you want to make it you won't have to wait 3 days. Remember to stir the starter every few days. It will keep for months. You can refeed the starter by adding equal amounts of warm milk and flour equal to the amount of the remaining starter.

STARTER (SMALL MACHINES)

¾ teaspoon yeast

⅔ cup milk, heated to a simmer and then cooled to about 100°F

⅔ cup rye, whole wheat, or white whole wheat flour (see *The King Arthur Flour Baker's Catalogue*, page 339)

Yield: 1 cup starter

Sprinkle the yeast on top of the warm milk, then stir until it dissolves completely. Stir in the flour. Store this, uncovered, at room temperature (at least 70° F) for 3 days, stirring once a day. Use this entire starter for the bread.

You can double the amount of starter and use half for the Sourdough Chèvre Bread (page 149) and half for the Sourdough Rye Bread (page 165). Or you can refrigerate the rest so the next time you want to make it you won't have to wait 3 days. Remember to stir the starter every few days. It will keep for months. You can refeed the starter by adding equal amounts of warm milk and rye flour equal to the amount of the remaining starter.

You can buy packages of dry starters either in gourmet or health food stores, or by mail order (page 341), or you can buy fresh sourdough starter from *The King Arthur Flour Baker's Catalogue* (available seasonally, page 339). These will need to be reconstituted at least a day before using. Once you get into the habit of baking bread, which you will now that you own one of these wonderful machines, you'll start talking bread. Soon you'll discover friends, neighbors, and pals at work who have a jar of starter in their refrigerators. If you're really lucky, they will offer to give you some. Before you use this starter, you must add 1½ cups of flour and the same amount of warm (110°F) water to it. Stir well and let the mixture sit in a warm, draft-free spot for 24 hours. This is called feeding the starter. Stir it before using.

Several important things to remember: Once you have a starter you don't have to ever go through the acquisition process again. Reserve at least ½ cupful of the starter when making the bread. Refeed it—as explained above, let it sit out for another 24 hours, mix it well, then pour it into a sterilized crock or glass jar with a tight-fitting lid and refrigerate. Stir it every week or so. The starter will keep forever. If you have neglected your starter for several months, then give it a boost before using it by pouring it into a bowl, stirring well, adding 1 teaspoon of yeast, 1 cup of flour, and 1 cup of warm water. Then let it sit out overnight in a warm place.

If you share your starter with someone else, remember to add equal amounts of flour and water back into the starter, leave it out for 24 hours, and then refrigerate. Again, we strongly recommend using your starter at room temperature if possible. Try to take it out of the refrigerator at least 2 hours or up to 24 hours before you plan to make bread.

Even though the liquid that accumulates at the top of the starter looks and smells like something died in there—don't ever throw it away. It's supposed to look and smell like that.

SOURDOUGH BEER BREAD

This crusty, chewy bread rises over the top of the pan, making for a majestic-looking loaf, which has a pronounced tang. The results are better when the starter is at room temperature.

DAK/WELBILT

1½ teaspoons yeast

3 cups unbleached white flour

1½ teaspoons salt

1 tablespoon sugar

2 tablespoons vegetable oil

½ cup flat beer (see Note)

1⅓ cups Sourdough Starter (page 139)

¼ cup water

Have all the ingredients at room temperature. Place all the ingredients in the machine and program for White Bread. Set the temperature control halfway between Medium and Dark and press Start.

BLACK & DECKER, BETTY CROCKER, BREADMAN/TRILLIUM, HITACHI, LARGE OSTER, REGAL, LARGE TOASTMASTER, AND WILLIAMS-SONOMA

1⅓ cups Sourdough Starter (page 139), at room temperature

¼ cup water

½ cup flat beer (see Note)

2 tablespoons vegetable oil

3 cups unbleached white flour

1½ teaspoons salt

1 tablespoon sugar

1½ teaspoons yeast

Place all the ingredients in the machine, program for Bread, Whole Wheat, Basic Wheat, Whole Wheat/Multigrain, White/Whole Grain, or Wheat, and press Start.

PANASONIC/NATIONAL

3 cups unbleached white flour

1½ teaspoons salt

1 tablespoon sugar

1⅓ cups Sourdough Starter (page 139), at room temperature

¼ cup water

½ cup flat beer (see Note)

2 tablespoons vegetable oil

1½ teaspoons yeast

Place all the ingredients except the yeast in the machine. Place the yeast in the dispenser. Program for Basic Bread and press Start.

LARGE PILLSBURY, LARGE OSTER, LARGE ZOJIRUSHI, AND WEST BEND

1⅓ cups Sourdough Starter (page 139), at room temperature

¼ cup water

½ cup flat beer (see Note)

2 tablespoons vegetable oil

3 cups unbleached white flour

1½ teaspoons salt

1 tablespoon sugar

1½ teaspoons yeast

Place all the ingredients in the machine and program for Basic White Bread, Whole Wheat, Basic Wheat, Whole Wheat/Multigrain, White/Whole Grain, or Wheat, and press Start or On.

Sourdough Beer Bread

MAXIM, SMALL OSTER, SMALL PILLSBURY, SANYO, SUNBEAM, SMALL TOASTMASTER, AND SMALL ZOJIRUSHI

1 tablespoon vegetable oil

¼ cup flat beer (see Note)

¾ cup Sourdough Starter (page 139)

2 tablespoons water

2 cups unbleached white flour

1 teaspoon salt

2 teaspoons sugar

1 teaspoon yeast

Have all the ingredients at room temperature. Place all the ingredients in the machine, program for Whole Wheat, Whole Grain, Standard, or Bread, and press Start.

Small Welbilt

1 teaspoon yeast
2 cups unbleached white flour
1 teaspoon salt
2 teaspoons sugar

1 tablespoon vegetable oil
¼ cup flat beer (see Note)
¾ cup Sourdough Starter (page 139)
2 tablespoons water

Have all the ingredients at room temperature. Place all the ingredients in the machine, and press Start.

Small Panasonic/National

2 cups unbleached white flour
1 teaspoon salt
2 teaspoons sugar
1 tablespoon vegetable oil
¼ cup flat beer (see Note)

¾ cup Sourdough Starter (page 139),
    at room temperature
2 tablespoons water
1 teaspoon yeast

Place all the ingredients except the yeast in the machine. Place the yeast in the dispenser. Program for Basic Bread and press Start.

Note: If you don't want to wait around for the beer to become flat on its own, pour it into a small saucepan and heat it to a simmer. By the time the beer cools down, it will be flat.

Variation: Add 1 tablespoon of caraway seeds with the ingredients.

SOURDOUGH BUCKWHEAT BREAD

If you like a gutsy, chewy loaf that is packed with personality and flavor, then this one's for you. It's dense and compact with a crust that invites a hunk of Cheddar cheese or a hearty application of sweet butter. You get much better bread when the starter is at room temperature.

DAK/WELBILT

2 teaspoons yeast

4 tablespoons powdered buttermilk

2 cups unbleached white flour

⅔ cup buckwheat flour

⅓ cup cornmeal

1½ teaspoons salt

1 extra-large egg

½ cup Sourdough Starter (page 139)

½ cup plus 2 tablespoons flat beer
 (see Note)

1 tablespoon molasses

2 tablespoons honey

1½ tablespoons butter

1 tablespoon caraway seeds

Have all the ingredients at room temperature. Place all the ingredients except the caraway seeds in the machine and program for White Bread. Set the temperature control one third of the way past Medium toward Dark and press Start. When the beeper sounds at the end of the second kneading, add the caraway seeds.

BLACK & DECKER, BETTY CROCKER, BREADMAN/TRILLIUM, HITACHI, LARGE OSTER, LARGE TOASTMASTER, AND WILLIAMS-SONOMA

1 extra-large egg

½ cup Sourdough Starter (page 139)

½ cup plus 2 tablespoons flat beer (see Note)

1 tablespoon molasses

2 tablespoons honey

1½ tablespoons butter

4 tablespoons powdered buttermilk

2 cups plus 3 tablespoons unbleached white flour

½ cup buckwheat flour

⅓ cup cornmeal

1½ teaspoons salt

2 teaspoons yeast

1 tablespoon caraway seeds

Have all the ingredients at room temperature (even though the machine does not require this step, for this recipe it is necessary). Place all the ingredients except the caraway seeds in the machine, program for Mix Bread, Whole Wheat, Basic Wheat, Whole Wheat/Multigrain, White/Whole Grain, or Wheat, and press Start. Add the caraway seeds when the beeper sounds or during the last 5 minutes of the final knead cycle.

PANASONIC/NATIONAL

4 tablespoons powdered buttermilk

2 cups unbleached white flour

⅔ cup buckwheat flour

⅓ cup cornmeal

1½ teaspoons salt

1 extra-large egg

½ cup Sourdough Starter (page 139)

½ cup plus 2 tablespoons flat beer (see Note)

1 tablespoon molasses

2 tablespoons honey

1½ tablespoons butter

1 tablespoon caraway seeds

2 teaspoons yeast

Place all the ingredients except the yeast and caraway seeds in the machine. Place the yeast in the dispenser. Program for Basic Bread and press Start. Five minutes before the end of the second kneading cycle, add the caraway seeds.

REGAL

1 extra-large egg

½ cup Sourdough Starter (page 139)

½ cup plus 2 tablespoons flat beer (see Note)

1 tablespoon molasses

2 tablespoons honey

1½ tablespoons butter

4 tablespoons powdered buttermilk

2 cups plus 3 tablespoons unbleached white flour

⅔ cup buckwheat flour

⅓ cup cornmeal

1½ teaspoons salt

2 teaspoons yeast

1 tablespoon caraway seeds

Continued

145

Have all the ingredients at room temperature (even though the machine does not require this step, for this recipe it is necessary). Place all the ingredients except the caraway seeds in the machine, program for Bread, and press Start. When the beeper sounds at the end of the second kneading, add the caraway seeds.

....

LARGE PILLSBURY, LARGE ZOJIRUSHI, AND WEST BEND

1 extra-large egg

½ cup Sourdough Starter (page 139)

½ cup plus 2 tablespoons flat beer (see Note)

1 tablespoon molasses

2 tablespoons honey

1½ tablespoons butter

4 tablespoons powdered buttermilk

2 cups plus 3 tablespoons unbleached white flour

½ cup buckwheat flour

⅓ cup cornmeal

1½ teaspoons salt

2 teaspoons yeast

1 tablespoon caraway seeds

Have all the ingredients at room temperature (even though the machine does not require this step, for this recipe it is necessary). Place all the ingredients except the caraway seeds in the machine. Program for Basic White Bread, Whole Wheat, Basic Wheat, Whole Wheat/Multigrain, White/Whole Grain, or Wheat, and press Start or On. Add the caraway seeds when the beeper sounds or during the last 5 minutes of the final knead cycle.

....

MAXIM, SMALL PILLSBURY, AND SMALL ZOJIRUSHI

1 medium egg

⅓ cup Sourdough Starter (page 139)

½ cup flat beer (see Note)

1 tablespoon molasses

1 tablespoon honey

3 tablespoons powdered buttermilk

1½ cups plus 1 tablespoon unbleached white flour

½ cup buckwheat flour

¼ cup cornmeal

1 teaspoon salt

1½ teaspoons yeast

2 teaspoons caraway seeds

Have all the ingredients at room temperature (even though the machine does not require this step, for this recipe it is necessary). Place all the ingredients in the machine, program for Whole Wheat, Whole Grain, Standard, or Bread, and press Start.

Small Oster, Sanyo, Sunbeam, and Small Toastmaster

1 medium egg
⅓ cup Sourdough Starter (page 139)
½ cup flat beer (see Note)
1 tablespoon molasses
1 tablespoon honey
3 tablespoons powdered buttermilk

1¼ cups plus 1 tablespoon unbleached white flour
½ cup buckwheat flour
¼ cup cornmeal
1 teaspoon salt
1½ teaspoons yeast
2 teaspoons caraway seeds

Have all the ingredients at room temperature (even though the machine does not require this step, for this recipe it is necessary). Place all the ingredients except the caraway seeds in the machine, program for Bread, Whole Wheat, or Whole Grain, and press Start. When the beeper sounds, add the caraway seeds.

Small Welbilt

1½ teaspoons yeast
3 tablespoons powdered buttermilk
1¼ cups unbleached white flour
½ cup buckwheat flour
¼ cup cornmeal
1 teaspoon salt

1 medium egg
⅓ cup Sourdough Starter (page 139)
½ cup flat beer (see Note)
1 tablespoon molasses
1 tablespoon honey
2 teaspoons caraway seeds

Have all the ingredients at room temperature (even though the machine does not require this step, for this recipe it is necessary). Place all the ingredients except the caraway seeds in the machine and press Start. When the beeper sounds at the end of the second kneading, add the caraway seeds.

SMALL PANASONIC/NATIONAL

3 tablespoons powdered buttermilk

1½ cups plus 1 tablespoon unbleached white flour

½ cup buckwheat flour

¼ cup cornmeal

1 teaspoon salt

1 medium egg

⅓ cup Sourdough Starter (page 139)

½ cup flat beer (see Note)

1 tablespoon molasses

1 tablespoon honey

1½ teaspoons yeast

2 teaspoons caraway seeds

Place all the ingredients except the yeast and caraway seeds in the machine. Place the yeast in the dispenser. Program for Basic Bread and press Start. At the end of the prekneading cycle add the caraway seeds.

NOTE: If you don't want to wait around for the beer to become flat on its own, pour it into a small saucepan and heat it to a simmer. By the time the beer cools down, it will be flat.

SOURDOUGH CHÈVRE BREAD

Chèvre means "goat" in French. Goat cheese plus goat's milk give this bread a marvelously tangy flavor and an authentically chewy texture. When you make the sourdough starter on page 139 use rye flour for a particularly rustic result. I make the starter three or four days ahead of time and leave it at room temperature because I like my bread really sour. If you like it less so, then make the starter one to two days ahead. You will have better results if you allow the starter to come to room temperature before you make the bread.

Powdered goat's milk is available in most health food stores. Keep it in the refrigerator in a tightly sealed jar after opening.

DAK/WELBILT

2 teaspoons yeast

2¼ cups unbleached white flour

¾ cup rye flour

4 tablespoons powdered goat's milk

1½ teaspoons salt

1 extra-large egg

3 tablespoons honey

½ cup water

1⅓ cups Sourdough Starter
  (page 139)

5 ounces goat cheese, with or without
  herbs, crumbled

Have all the ingredients at room temperature. Place all the ingredients in the machine, program for White Bread, and press Start.

BLACK & DECKER, BETTY CROCKER, BREADMAN/TRILLIUM, HITACHI, LARGE OSTER, REGAL, LARGE TOASTMASTER, AND WILLIAMS-SONOMA

1 extra-large egg

3 tablespoons honey

½ cup water

1⅓ cups Sourdough Starter (page 139)

5 ounces goat cheese, with or without herbs, crumbled

2¼ cups unbleached white flour

¾ cup rye flour

4 tablespoons powdered goat's milk

1½ teaspoons salt

2 teaspoons yeast

Place all the ingredients in the machine, program for Bread, Whole Wheat, Basic Wheat, Whole Wheat/Multigrain, White/Whole Grain, or Wheat, and press Start.

PANASONIC/NATIONAL

2¼ cups unbleached white flour

¾ cup rye flour

4 tablespoons powdered goat's milk

1½ teaspoons salt

1 extra-large egg

3 tablespoons honey

½ cup water

1⅓ cups Sourdough Starter (page 139)

5 ounces goat cheese, with or without herbs, crumbled

2 teaspoons yeast

Place all the ingredients except the yeast in the machine. Place the yeast in the dispenser. Program for Basic Bread and press Start.

LARGE PILLSBURY, REGAL, LARGE ZOJIRUSHI, AND WEST BEND

1 extra-large egg

3 tablespoons honey

½ cup water

1⅓ cups Sourdough Starter (page 139)

5 ounces goat cheese, with or without herbs, crumbled

2¼ cups unbleached white flour

¾ cup rye flour

4 tablespoons powdered goat's milk

1½ teaspoons salt

2 teaspoons yeast

Place all the ingredients in the machine, program for Basic White Bread, Whole Wheat, Basic Wheat, Whole Wheat/Multigrain, White/Whole Grain, or Wheat, and press Start or On.

Maxim, Small Oster, Small Pillsbury, Sanyo, Sunbeam, Small Toastmaster, and Small Zojirushi

1 medium egg

2 tablespoons honey

⅓ cup water

1 cup Sourdough Starter
   (page 139)

3 ounces goat cheese, with or without
   herbs, crumbled

1½ cups unbleached white flour

½ cup rye flour

3 tablespoons powdered goat's milk

1 teaspoon salt

1½ teaspoons yeast

Place all the ingredients in the machine, program for Whole Wheat, Whole Grain, Standard, or Bread, and press Start.

Small Welbilt

1½ teaspoons yeast

1½ cups unbleached white flour

½ cup rye flour

3 tablespoons powdered goat's milk

1 teaspoon salt

1 medium egg

2 tablespoons honey

⅓ cup water

1 cup Sourdough Starter
   (page 139)

3 ounces goat cheese, with or without
   herbs, crumbled

Have all the ingredients at room temperature. Place all the ingredients in the machine, program for Dark, and press Start.

Small Panasonic/National

1½ cups unbleached white flour

½ cup rye flour

3 tablespoons powdered goat's milk

1 teaspoon salt

1 medium egg

2 tablespoons honey

⅓ cup water

1 cup Sourdough Starter
  (page 139)

3 ounces goat cheese, with or without
  herbs, crumbled

1½ teaspoons yeast

Place all the ingredients except the yeast in the machine. Place the yeast in the dispenser. Program for Basic Bread and press Start.

LYNNE BAIL'S SOURDOUGH CINNAMON ROLLS

Just when we were beginning to feel more than slightly overwhelmed testing twelve bread-baking machines, God sent Lynne Bail, who with great good cheer and never-flagging enthusiasm picked up the slack and guided us in almost on deadline.

This is her recipe for the most wonderful sweet sourdough buns you'll ever taste. You'll be licking your fingers! Lynne recommends using the strongest sourdough starter you can find. Leaving your starter out, uncovered, in a warm (but not hot) place for several days, and stirring it at least once a day, should do the trick. And you'll get much better bread when the starter is at room temperature.

DAK/WELBILT

1½ teaspoons yeast

3 cups unbleached white flour

1 teaspoon salt

¼ cup sugar

½ cup warm water

1 cup Sourdough Starter (page 139)

¼ cup butter OR margarine

Have all the ingredients at room temperature. Place all the ingredients in the machine, program for Dough or Manual, and press Start. Follow the Assembly Instructions on page 155.

BLACK & DECKER, BETTY CROCKER, BREADMAN/TRILLIUM, HITACHI, LARGE TOASTMASTER, AND WILLIAMS-SONOMA

½ cup warm water

1 cup Sourdough Starter (page 139)

¼ cup butter OR margarine, at room
  temperature

¼ cup sugar

3 cups unbleached white flour

1 teaspoon salt

1 teaspoon yeast

Place all the ingredients in the machine, program for Dough or Knead and First Rise, and press Start. Follow the Assembly Instructions on page 155.

Panasonic/National

3 cups unbleached white flour

1 teaspoon salt

¼ cup sugar

½ cup warm water

1 cup Sourdough Starter (page 139)

¼ cup butter OR margarine, at room temperature

1½ teaspoons yeast

Place all the ingredients except the yeast in the machine. Place the yeast in the dispenser. Program for Dough or Manual and press Start. Follow the Assembly Instructions on page 155.

Large Pillsbury, Regal, Large Oster, Large Zojirushi, and West Bend

½ cup warm water

1 cup Sourdough Starter (page 139)

¼ cup butter OR margarine, at room temperature

¼ cup sugar

3 cups unbleached white flour

1 teaspoon salt

1 teaspoon yeast

Place all the ingredients in the machine, program for Dough, and press Start or On. Follow the Assembly Instructions on page 155.

Maxim, Small Oster, Small Pillsbury, Sanyo, Sunbeam, Small Toastmaster, and Small Zojirushi

Sourdough Cinnamon Rolls

¼ cup warm water

½ cup Sourdough Starter (page 139)

2 tablespoons butter OR margarine, at room temperature

2 tablespoons sugar

2 cups unbleached white flour

½ teaspoon salt

1 teaspoon yeast

Place all the ingredients in the machine, program for Dough or Manual, and press Start. Follow the Assembly Instructions on page 156.

Small Welbilt

1 teaspoon yeast

2 cups unbleached white flour

½ teaspoon salt

2 tablespoons sugar

¼ cup warm water

½ cup Sourdough Starter (page 139)

2 tablespoons butter OR margarine

Have all the ingredients at room temperature. Place all the ingredients in the machine, program for Manual, and press Start. Follow the Assembly Instructions on page 156.

Small Panasonic/National

2 cups unbleached white flour

2 tablespoons sugar

½ teaspoon salt

¼ cup warm water

½ cup Sourdough Starter (page 139)

2 tablespoons butter OR margarine, at
   room temperature

1 teaspoon yeast

Place all the ingredients except the yeast in the machine. Place the yeast in the dispenser. Program for Dough or Manual and press Start. Follow the Assembly Instructions on page 156.

Assembly Instructions (large machines)

Filling

½ cup brown sugar

½ cup butter OR margarine, softened

½ teaspoon ground cinnamon

¼ teaspoon ground nutmeg

Assembly

2 tablespoons butter OR margarine,
   softened

Continued

Mix all of the ingredients for the filling together in a small bowl and set aside.

At the end of the cycle, remove the dough from the machine. Lightly grease a heavy baking sheet. On a lightly floured board, roll the dough to a 9 × 15-inch rectangle. Spread with the butter or margarine. Spread the filling up to the edges. Roll tightly starting from one of the 9-inch edges to form a 15-inch roll. Cut the roll into 9 equal slices and place each slice, cut side down, on the prepared sheet.

Cover with plastic wrap and let rise in a warm, draft-free place until doubled in size, about 1 hour.

Preheat the oven to 375°F with the rack in the center position. Bake the rolls for 20 to 25 minutes, or until golden brown.

Remove the rolls from the oven and prepare the following glaze:

1 cup confectioners' sugar, sifted	2 tablespoons Kahlúa
1 tablespoon hot coffee OR 1 teaspoon instant coffee dissolved in 1 tablespoon boiling water	

Add the coffee and Kahlúa to the sugar to form a thin glaze and drizzle it over the tops of the rolls while they are still warm. Use a metal spatula to remove the rolls to a wire rack to cool.

Assembly Instructions (small machines)

Filling

⅓ cup brown sugar	⅛ teaspoon (or a pinch) ground nutmeg
⅓ cup butter OR margarine, softened	
¼ teaspoon ground cinnamon	

Assembly

1½ tablespoons butter OR margarine, softened

Mix all of the ingredients for the filling together in a small bowl and set aside.

At the end of the cycle, remove the dough from the machine. Lightly grease a heavy baking sheet. On a lightly floured board, roll the dough to a 9 × 9-inch rectangle. Spread with the butter or margarine. Spread the filling up to the edges. Roll tightly starting from one of the 9-inch edges to form a 9-inch roll. Cut the roll into 6 equal slices and place each slice, cut side down, on the prepared sheet.

Cover with plastic wrap and let rise in a warm, draft-free place until doubled in size, about 1 hour.

Preheat the oven to 375°F with the rack in the center position. Bake the rolls for 20 to 25 minutes, or until golden brown.

Remove the rolls from the oven and prepare the following glaze:

¾ cup confectioners' sugar, sifted

3 teaspoons hot coffee OR ¾ teaspoon
   instant coffee dissolved in 1 to 3
   teaspoons boiling water

2 teaspoons Kahlúa

Add the coffee and Kahlúa to the sugar to form a thin glaze and drizzle it over the tops of the rolls while they are still warm. Use a spatula to remove the rolls to a wire rack to cool.

SOURDOUGH CORNMEAL BREAD

You must give this bread a long second rise out of the machine and bake it out of the machine as well. You cannot do this on a timer overnight, so it means you must start the machine as soon as you place in the ingredients. It doesn't matter in which order. And you get much better bread when the starter is at room temperature.

DAK/WELBILT

2 teaspoons yeast

2 tablespoons powdered skim milk

2 tablespoons wheat germ

2 tablespoons wheat bran

1 cup unbleached white flour

1 cup whole wheat flour

1 cup cornmeal

1½ teaspoons salt

1 cup Sourdough Starter (page 139)

2 tablespoons honey

1 cup water

Have all the ingredients at room temperature. Place all the ingredients in the machine, program for Dough or Manual, and press Start. Follow the Baking Instructions on page 160.

BLACK & DECKER, BETTY CROCKER, BREADMAN/TRILLIUM, HITACHI, LARGE OSTER, REGAL, LARGE TOASTMASTER, WILLIAMS-SONOMA, WEST BEND, LARGE PILLSBURY, AND LARGE ZOJIRUSHI

1 cup Sourdough Starter (page 139), at
   room temperature

1 cup water

2 tablespoons honey

2 tablespoons powdered skim milk

2 tablespoons wheat germ

2 tablespoons wheat bran

1 cup unbleached white flour

1 cup whole wheat flour

1 cup cornmeal

1½ teaspoons salt

2 teaspoons yeast

Place all the ingredients in the machine, program for Dough or Manual, and press Start or On. Follow the Baking Instructions on page 160.

PANASONIC/NATIONAL

1 cup unbleached white flour
1 cup whole wheat flour
1 cup cornmeal
1½ teaspoons salt
2 tablespoons wheat germ
2 tablespoons honey
2 tablespoons wheat bran
2 tablespoons powdered skim milk
1 cup Sourdough Starter (page 139), at room temperature
1 cup water
2 teaspoons yeast

Place all the ingredients except the yeast in the machine. Place the yeast in the dispenser. Program for Dough or Manual and press Start. Follow the Baking Instructions on page 160.

MAXIM, SMALL OSTER, SMALL PILLSBURY, SANYO, SUNBEAM, SMALL TOASTMASTER, SMALL ZOJIRUSHI, AND SMALL WELBILT

⅔ cup Sourdough Starter (page 139)
⅔ cup water
1 tablespoon plus 1 teaspoon honey
1 tablespoon plus 1 teaspoon powdered skim milk
1 tablespoon plus 1 teaspoon wheat germ
1 tablespoon plus 1 teaspoon wheat bran
1 cup unbleached white flour
⅓ cup whole wheat flour
⅓ cup plus 1 tablespoon cornmeal
1 teaspoon salt
1½ teaspoons yeast

Have all the ingredients at room temperature. Place all the ingredients in the machine, program for Dough or Manual, and press Start. Follow the Baking Instructions on page 160.

Small Panasonic/National

1 tablespoon plus 1 teaspoon powdered
  skim milk
1 tablespoon plus 1 teaspoon wheat
  germ
1 tablespoon plus 1 teaspoon wheat
  bran
1 cup unbleached white flour
⅓ cup whole wheat flour

⅓ cup plus 1 tablespoon cornmeal
1 teaspoon salt
1 tablespoon plus 1 teaspoon honey
⅔ cup Sourdough Starter (page 139),
  at room temperature
⅔ cup water
1½ teaspoons yeast

Place all the ingredients except the yeast in the machine. Place the yeast in the dispenser. Program for Dough or Manual and press Start. Follow the Baking Instructions below.

Baking Instructions

At the end of the cycle, grease well either 2 small or 1 regular-size loaf pan(s). Punch the dough down (it may be on the loose side), divide the dough, and place it in the pan(s). Let it rise, uncovered, in a warm, draft-free place for 1 hour. Preheat the oven to 350°F and bake for 30 to 40 minutes until well browned.

SOURDOUGH POTATO DILL BREAD

This makes a light brown, compact, moist, dense loaf with lots of character, a classic sourdough flavor, and a crunchy, chewy crust. And you get much better bread when the starter is at room temperature.

DAK/Welbilt

2 teaspoons yeast

1 cup unbleached white flour (plus an additional 1 or 2 tablespoons if the dough looks very wet after the first 10 minutes of kneading)

1 cup whole wheat flour

1 cup rye flour

⅓ cup cornmeal

1½ teaspoons salt

1 teaspoon freshly ground black pepper

4 tablespoons powdered buttermilk

1 tablespoon dillseed

¾ cup Sourdough Starter (page 139)

1 cup mashed potato (see Note)

¼ cup potato cooking liquid

2 tablespoons vegetable oil

2 tablespoons honey

1 tablespoon molasses

Have all the ingredients at room temperature. Place all the ingredients in the machine, program for White Bread, and press Start.

Black & Decker, Betty Crocker, Breadman/Trillium, Hitachi, Large Oster, Regal, Large Toastmaster, Williams-Sonoma, Large Pillsbury, Large Zojirushi, and West Bend

¾ cup Sourdough Starter (page 139)

1 cup mashed potato (see Note)

¼ cup potato cooking liquid

2 tablespoons vegetable oil

2 tablespoons honey

1 tablespoon molasses

1½ teaspoons salt

1 teaspoon freshly ground black pepper

4 tablespoons powdered buttermilk

1 tablespoon dillseed

1 cup whole wheat flour

1 cup rye flour

⅓ cup cornmeal

1 cup unbleached white flour (plus an additional 1 or 2 tablespoons if the dough looks very wet after the first 10 minutes of kneading)

2 teaspoons yeast

Place all the ingredients in the machine, program for Bread, Basic White Bread, Whole Wheat, Basic Wheat, Whole Wheat/Multigrain, White/Whole Grain, or Wheat, and press Start or On.

Panasonic/National

¾ cup Sourdough Starter (page 139)

1 cup mashed potato (see Note)

¼ cup potato cooking liquid

2 tablespoons vegetable oil

2 tablespoons honey

1 tablespoon molasses

1½ teaspoons salt

1 teaspoon freshly ground black pepper

4 tablespoons powdered buttermilk

1 tablespoon dillseed

1 cup whole wheat flour

1 cup rye flour

⅓ cup cornmeal

1 cup unbleached white flour (plus an additional 1 or 2 tablespoons if the dough looks very wet after the first 10 minutes of kneading)

2 teaspoons yeast

Place all the ingredients except the yeast in the machine. Place the yeast in the dispenser. Program for Basic Bread and press Start.

162

½ cup Sourdough Starter (page 139)

½ cup mashed potato (see Note)

2 tablespoons potato cooking liquid

1 tablespoon vegetable oil

1 tablespoon honey

2 teaspoons molasses

¾ teaspoon salt

½ teaspoon freshly ground black pepper

2 tablespoons powdered buttermilk

2 teaspoons dillseed

½ cup unbleached white flour (plus an additional 1 or 2 tablespoons if the dough looks very wet after the first 10 minutes of kneading)

½ cup whole wheat flour

½ cup rye flour

¼ cup cornmeal

1 teaspoon yeast

Place all the ingredients in the machine, program for Whole Wheat, Whole Grain, Standard, or Bread, and press Start.

SMALL WELBILT

1 teaspoon yeast

½ cup unbleached white flour (plus an additional 1 or 2 tablespoons if the dough looks very wet after the first 10 minutes of kneading)

½ cup whole wheat flour

½ cup rye flour

¼ cup cornmeal

¾ teaspoon salt

½ teaspoon freshly ground black pepper

2 tablespoons powdered buttermilk

2 teaspoons dillseed

½ cup Sourdough Starter (page 139)

½ cup mashed potato (see Note)

2 tablespoons potato cooking liquid

1 tablespoon vegetable oil

1 tablespoon honey

2 teaspoons molasses

Have all the ingredients at room temperature. Place all the ingredients in the machine, program for Dark, and press Start.

Small Panasonic/National

½ cup unbleached white flour (plus an additional 1 or 2 tablespoons if the dough looks very wet after the first 10 minutes of kneading)

½ cup whole wheat flour

½ cup rye flour

¼ cup cornmeal

¾ teaspoon salt

½ teaspoon freshly ground black pepper

2 tablespoons powdered buttermilk

2 teaspoons dillseed

½ cup Sourdough Starter (page 139)

½ cup mashed potato (see Note)

2 tablespoons potato cooking liquid

1 tablespoon vegetable oil

1 tablespoon honey

2 teaspoons molasses

1 teaspoon yeast

Place all the ingredients except the yeast in the machine. Place the yeast in the dispenser. Program for Basic Bread and press Start.

NOTE: When you boil the potato, save the water to use as an ingredient.

SOURDOUGH RYE BREAD

This bread requires a special sourdough starter that must be prepared at least three days before you make the bread and be at room temperature when you begin.

....

DAK/Welbilt

1½ teaspoons yeast

2¼ cups unbleached white flour

¾ cup rye flour

2 tablespoons caraway seeds

1½ teaspoons salt

2 tablespoons vegetable oil

1½ tablespoons molasses

1½ tablespoons honey

1 extra-large egg

½ cup water

1⅓ cups Sourdough Starter
   (page 139)

Have all the ingredients at room temperature. Place all the ingredients in the machine, program for White Bread, and press Start.

....

Black & Decker, Betty Crocker, Breadman/Trillium, Hitachi, Large Oster, Large Toastmaster, and Williams-Sonoma

2 tablespoons vegetable oil

1½ tablespoons molasses

1½ tablespoons honey

1 extra-large egg

½ cup water

1⅓ cups Sourdough Starter (page 139)

2¼ cups plus 1 tablespoon unbleached
   white flour

¾ cup rye flour

2 tablespoons caraway seeds

1½ teaspoons salt

1½ teaspoons yeast (1 teaspoon for the
   Black & Decker, Breadman/Trillium,
   and Toastmaster)

Place all the ingredients in the machine, program for Bread, Whole Wheat, Basic Wheat, Whole Wheat/Multigrain, White/Whole Grain, or Wheat, and press Start.

PANASONIC/NATIONAL

2¼ cups unbleached white flour

¾ cup rye flour

2 tablespoons caraway seeds

1½ teaspoons salt

2 tablespoons vegetable oil

1½ tablespoons molasses

1½ tablespoons honey

1 extra-large egg

½ cup water

1⅓ cups Sourdough Starter
 (page 139)

1½ teaspoons yeast

Place all the ingredients except the yeast in the machine. Place the yeast in the dispenser. Program for Basic Bread and press Start.

....

LARGE PILLSBURY, REGAL, LARGE ZOJIRUSHI, AND WEST BEND

2 tablespoons vegetable oil

1½ tablespoons molasses

1½ tablespoons honey

1 extra-large egg

½ cup water

1⅓ cups Sourdough Starter
 (page 139)

2¼ cups unbleached white flour

¾ cup rye flour

2 tablespoons caraway seeds

1½ teaspoons salt

1½ teaspoons yeast

Place all the ingredients in the machine, program for Basic White Bread, Whole Wheat, Basic Wheat, Whole Wheat/Multigrain, White/Whole Grain, or Wheat, and press Start or On.

....

Sourdough Rye

MAXIM, SMALL OSTER, SMALL PILLSBURY, SANYO, SUNBEAM, SMALL TOASTMASTER, AND SMALL ZOJIRUSHI

1 tablespoon plus 1 teaspoon vegetable oil

1 tablespoon molasses

1 tablespoon honey

1 medium egg

⅓ cup water

1 cup Sourdough Starter (page 139)

1½ cups unbleached white flour

½ cup rye flour

1 tablespoon caraway seeds

1 teaspoon salt

1 teaspoon yeast

Place all the ingredients in the machine, program for Whole Wheat, Whole Grain, Standard, or Bread, and press Start.

....

SMALL WELBILT

1 teaspoon yeast

1½ cups unbleached white flour

½ cup rye flour

1 tablespoon caraway seeds

1 teaspoon salt

1 tablespoon plus 1 teaspoon vegetable oil

1 tablespoon molasses

1 tablespoon honey

1 medium egg

⅓ cup water

1 cup Sourdough Starter (page 139)

Have all the ingredients at room temperature. Place all the ingredients in the machine, program for Medium, and press Start.

....

Small Panasonic/National

1½ cups unbleached white flour

½ cup rye flour

1 tablespoon caraway seeds

1 teaspoon salt

1 tablespoon plus 1 teaspoon vegetable
  oil

1 tablespoon molasses

1 tablespoon honey

1 medium egg

⅓ cup water

1 cup Sourdough Starter
  (page 139)

1 teaspoon yeast

Place all the ingredients except the yeast in the machine. Place the yeast in the dispenser. Program for Basic Bread and press Start.

VEGETABLE AND HERB BREADS

NO-FAT POTATO BREAD

This simple, wholesome loaf is filled with good-for-you ingredients. It has a delicious springy texture and a gutsy homespun flavor. You can use freshly made, leftover, or reconstituted granulated instant mashed potatoes.

DAK/WELBILT

2½ teaspoons yeast

2½ cups unbleached white flour

½ cup whole wheat flour

1 teaspoon salt

1 teaspoon caraway seeds

2 tablespoons sprouted wheat berries, soaked in water overnight and then drained, OR 2 tablespoons bran

½ cup mashed potato

1 cup water

Have all the ingredients at room temperature. Place all the ingredients in the machine, program for White Bread, and press Start.

BLACK & DECKER, BETTY CROCKER, BREADMAN/TRILLIUM, HITACHI, LARGE TOASTMASTER, AND WILLIAMS-SONOMA

2 tablespoons sprouted wheat berries, soaked in water overnight and then drained, OR 2 tablespoons bran

1 cup water

½ cup mashed potatoes

2½ cups unbleached white flour

½ cup whole wheat flour

1 teaspoon salt

1 teaspoon caraway seeds

2 teaspoons yeast

Place all the ingredients in the machine, program for Bread, Basic Bread, Basic Wheat, Basic White, or White/Whole Grain, and press Start.

Panasonic/National

2½ cups unbleached white flour
½ cup whole wheat flour
1 teaspoon salt
1 teaspoon caraway seeds
1 cup water

2 tablespoons sprouted wheat berries, soaked in water overnight and then drained, OR 2 tablespoons bran
½ cup mashed potatoes
2½ teaspoons yeast

Place all the ingredients except the yeast in the machine. Place the yeast in the dispenser. Program for Basic Bread and press Start.

Large Pillsbury, Regal, Large Oster, Large Zojirushi, and West Bend

2 tablespoons sprouted wheat berries, soaked in water overnight and then drained, OR 2 tablespoons bran
1 cup water
½ cup mashed potatoes

2½ cups unbleached white flour
½ cup whole wheat flour
1 teaspoon salt
1 teaspoon caraway seeds
2½ teaspoons yeast

Place all the ingredients in the machine, program for Basic White Bread, Basic Bread, Basic Wheat, Basic White, or White/Whole Grain, and press Start or On.

Maxim, Small Oster, Small Pillsbury, Sanyo, Sunbeam, Small Toastmaster, and Small Zojirushi

1½ tablespoons sprouted wheat berries, soaked in water overnight and then drained, OR 1½ tablespoons bran
¾ cup water
1½ cups plus 1 tablespoon unbleached white flour

¼ cup whole wheat flour
¼ cup mashed potatoes
½ teaspoon salt
½ teaspoon caraway seeds
1½ teaspoons yeast

Continued

Have all the ingredients at room temperature. Place all the ingredients in the machine, program for Standard, Bread, Basic, White, or Basic Bread, and press Start.

SMALL WELBILT

1½ teaspoons yeast

1½ cups unbleached white flour

¼ cup whole wheat flour

¼ cup mashed potatoes

½ teaspoon salt

½ teaspoon caraway seeds

1½ tablespoons sprouted wheat berries, soaked in water overnight and then drained, OR 1½ tablespoons bran

¾ cup water

Have all the ingredients at room temperature. Place all the ingredients in the machine, program for Medium, and press Start.

SMALL PANASONIC/NATIONAL

¾ cup water

1½ cups plus 1 tablespoon unbleached white flour

¼ cup whole wheat flour

¼ cup mashed potatoes

½ teaspoon salt

½ teaspoon caraway seeds

1½ tablespoons sprouted wheat berries, soaked overnight in water and then drained, OR 1½ tablespoons bran

1½ teaspoons yeast

Place all the ingredients except the yeast in the machine. Place the yeast in the dispenser. Program for Basic Bread and press Start.

Variation: Program the machine for Manual or Dough and remove the dough at the end of the cycle. Sprinkle a baking sheet with cornmeal and form the dough into a dome. Let it rise, uncovered, in a warm, draft-free place until doubled in bulk, about 1 to 1½ hours. Bake in a preheated 350°F oven for 40 to 50 minutes, or until the bottom sounds hollow when tapped.

LEMON PEPPER BREAD

Lemon pepper is a spice blend that is available in specialty food shops, especially those that sell Middle Eastern foods. High-gluten flour can be found in health food stores. Or you can mail-order both of these (page 337).

....

DAK/WELBILT

2½ teaspoons yeast

1 teaspoon salt

1¼ teaspoons lemon pepper

¼ teaspoon baking soda

3 cups unbleached white flour

3 tablespoons gluten OR 1 tablespoon Lora
  Brody's Bread Dough Enhancer™

1 tablespoon vegetable oil

1 extra-large egg

½ cup cottage cheese (creamy style)

½ cup sour cream

Grated zest of 2 lemons

3 tablespoons water

1 tablespoon powdered buttermilk

Have all the ingredients at room temperature. Place all the ingredients in the machine, program for White Bread, and press Start.

....

BLACK & DECKER, BETTY CROCKER, BREADMAN/TRILLIUM, HITACHI, LARGE TOASTMASTER, AND WILLIAMS-SONOMA

1 tablespoon vegetable oil

3 tablespoons water

1 tablespoon powdered buttermilk

1 large egg

½ cup cottage cheese (creamy style)

½ cup sour cream

Grated zest of 2 lemons

1 teaspoon salt

1¼ teaspoons lemon pepper

¼ teaspoon baking soda

3 cups plus 2 tablespoons unbleached
  white flour

3 tablespoons gluten OR 1 tablespoon Lora
  Brody's Bread Dough Enhancer™

2 teaspoons yeast

Continued

Place all the ingredients in the machine, program for Bread, Basic Bread, Basic Wheat, White, Basic White, or White/Whole Grain, and press Start.

PANASONIC/NATIONAL

1 teaspoon salt

1¼ teaspoons lemon pepper

¼ teaspoon baking soda

3 cups unbleached white flour

3 tablespoons gluten OR 1 tablespoon Lora Brody's Bread Dough Enhancer™

1 tablespoon powdered buttermilk

1 large egg

1 tablespoon vegetable oil

½ cup cottage cheese (creamy style)

½ cup sour cream

3 tablespoons water

Grated zest of 2 lemons

2½ teaspoons yeast

Place all the ingredients except the yeast in the machine. Place the yeast in the dispenser. Program for Basic Bread and press Start.

REGAL

1 tablespoon vegetable oil

3 tablespoons water

1 tablespoon powdered buttermilk

1 large egg

½ cup cottage cheese (creamy style)

½ cup sour cream

Grated zest of 2 lemons

1 teaspoon salt

1¼ teaspoons lemon pepper

¼ teaspoon baking soda

3 cups plus 2 tablespoons unbleached white flour

3 tablespoons gluten OR 1 tablespoon Lora Brody's Bread Dough Enhancer™

2 teaspoons yeast

Place all the ingredients in the machine, program for Standard, and press Start.

Large Oster, West Bend, Large Pillsbury, and Large Zojirushi

1 tablespoon vegetable oil
1 extra-large egg
½ cup cottage cheese (creamy style)
½ cup sour cream
Grated zest of 2 lemons
1 teaspoon salt
1¼ teaspoons lemon pepper

¼ teaspoon baking soda
3 cups unbleached white flour
3 tablespoons gluten OR 1 tablespoon Lora
   Brody's Bread Dough Enhancer™
2½ teaspoons yeast
3 tablespoons water
1 tablespoon powdered buttermilk

Place all the ingredients in the machine, program for Basic White Bread, Basic Bread, Basic Wheat, Basic, White, Basic White, or White/Whole Grain, and press Start or On.

Maxim, Small Oster, Small Pillsbury, Sanyo, Sunbeam, Small Toastmaster, and Small Zojirushi

2 teaspoons vegetable oil
1 large egg
⅓ cup cottage cheese (creamy style)
⅓ cup sour cream
Grated zest of 2 lemons
¾ teaspoon salt
1 teaspoon lemon pepper

¼ teaspoon baking soda
2 cups unbleached white flour
2 tablespoons gluten OR 2 teaspoons Lora
   Brody's Bread Dough Enhancer™
1½ teaspoons yeast
2 tablespoons water
2 teaspoons powdered buttermilk

Place all the ingredients in the machine, program for Standard, Basic, White, Basic Bread, or Bread, and press Start.

Small Welbilt

2 teaspoons yeast

¼ teaspoon baking soda

2 cups unbleached white flour

2 tablespoons gluten OR 2 teaspoons Lora
  Brody's Bread Dough Enhancer™

¾ teaspoon salt

1 teaspoon lemon pepper

2 teaspoons vegetable oil

1 large egg

⅓ cup cottage cheese (creamy style)

⅓ cup sour cream

Grated zest of 2 lemons

2 tablespoons water

2 teaspoons powdered buttermilk

Have all the ingredients at room temperature. Place all the ingredients in the machine, program for Medium, and press Start.

Small Panasonic/National

¾ teaspoon salt

1 teaspoon lemon pepper

¼ teaspoon baking soda

2 cups unbleached white flour

2 tablespoons gluten OR 2 teaspoons Lora
  Brody's Bread Dough Enhancer™

2 teaspoons powdered buttermilk

2 teaspoons vegetable oil

2 tablespoons water

1 large egg

⅓ cup cottage cheese (creamy style)

⅓ cup sour cream

Grated zest of 2 lemons

1½ teaspoons yeast

Place all the ingredients except the yeast in the machine. Place the yeast in the dispenser. Program for Basic Bread and press Start.

KAREN'S HERB OATMEAL-POTATO BREAD

Our dear friend Karen Slater rose to the challenge of testing all of these recipes on three bread machines. We don't know how she ever found time to create this one, but we're glad she did. Wait until you taste its delightful savory flavor and see its homespun texture. Hot from the oven (we mean, machine), it is heavenly. You can use homemade, leftover, or instant mashed potatoes.

DAK/Welbilt

1 tablespoon yeast

2½ cups unbleached white flour

½ cup quick-cooking oats

1 teaspoon salt

1 tablespoon sugar

½ cup mashed potato

1 extra-large egg

4 tablespoons butter OR vegetable oil

¾ cup water

¾ teaspoon dried thyme, rosemary, oregano, or basil OR a combination

2 tablespoons sunflower seeds

Have all the ingredients at room temperature. Place all the ingredients except the sunflower seeds in the machine, program for White Bread, and press Start. When the beeper sounds, add the sunflower seeds.

BLACK & DECKER, BETTY CROCKER, BREADMAN/TRILLIUM, HITACHI, LARGE TOASTMASTER, WILLIAMS-SONOMA, REGAL, LARGE OSTER, WEST BEND, LARGE PILLSBURY, AND LARGE ZOJIRUSHI

½ cup mashed potato

1 extra-large egg

4 tablespoons butter, at room temperature, OR vegetable oil

¾ cup water

¾ teaspoon dried thyme, rosemary, oregano, or basil OR a combination

2½ cups unbleached white flour

½ cup quick-cooking oats

1 teaspoon salt

1 tablespoon sugar

1 tablespoon yeast (2 teaspoons for the Black & Decker, Breadman/Trillium, and Toastmaster)

2 tablespoons sunflower seeds

Continued

177

Place all the ingredients except the sunflower seeds in the machine, program for Raisin Bread, Mix Bread, Basic Bread, Basic Wheat, Basic, White, Basic White, or White/Whole Grain, and press Start or On. Add the sunflower seeds when the beeper sounds during the last 5 minutes of the final knead cycle.

PANASONIC/NATIONAL

½ cup mashed potato

1 extra-large egg

4 tablespoons butter, at room temperature, OR vegetable oil

¾ cup water

¾ teaspoon dried thyme, rosemary, oregano, or basil OR a combination

2½ cups unbleached white flour

½ cup quick-cooking oats

1 teaspoon salt

1 tablespoon sugar

1 tablespoon yeast

2 tablespoons sunflower seeds

Place all the ingredients except the yeast and the sunflower seeds in the machine. Place the yeast in the dispenser. Program for Basic Bread and press Start. Add the sunflower seeds 20 minutes into the first kneading cycle.

MAXIM, SMALL OSTER, SMALL PILLSBURY, SANYO, SUNBEAM, SMALL TOASTMASTER, AND SMALL ZOJIRUSHI

⅓ cup mashed potato

1 medium egg

2 tablespoons butter, at room temperature, OR vegetable oil

½ cup water

½ teaspoon dried thyme, rosemary, oregano, or basil OR a combination

1⅔ cups unbleached white flour

½ cup quick-cooking oats

½ teaspoon salt

3 teaspoons sugar

2 teaspoons yeast

2 tablespoons sunflower seeds

Place all the ingredients except the sunflower seeds in the machine, program for Standard, Basic, White, Basic Bread, or Bread, and press Start. Add the sunflower seeds when the beeper sounds or during the last 5 minutes of the final knead cycle.

Small Welbilt

1²⁄₃ cups unbleached white flour

½ cup quick-cooking oats

½ teaspoon salt

3 teaspoons sugar

2 teaspoons yeast

⅓ cup mashed potato

1 medium egg

2 tablespoons butter OR vegetable oil

½ cup water

½ teaspoon dried thyme, rosemary, oregano, or basil OR a combination

2 tablespoons sunflower seeds

Have all the ingredients at room temperature. Place all the ingredients except the sunflower seeds in the machine, program for Medium, and press Start. When the beeper sounds, add the sunflower seeds.

Small Panasonic/National

½ teaspoon dried thyme, rosemary, oregano, or basil OR a combination

1²⁄₃ cups unbleached white flour

½ cup quick-cooking oats

½ teaspoon salt

3 teaspoons sugar

⅓ cup mashed potato

1 medium egg

2 tablespoons butter, at room temperature, OR vegetable oil

½ cup water

2 teaspoons yeast

2 tablespoons sunflower seeds

Place all the ingredients except the yeast and the sunflower seeds in the machine. Place the yeast in the dispenser. Program for Basic Bread and press Start. Add the sunflower seeds 20 minutes into the kneading.

GREEN PEPPERCORN SAGE BREAD

A high riser with real zing! This bread goes well with Brie or Camembert.

....

DAK/Welbilt

2½ teaspoons yeast

1 teaspoon salt

¼ cup cornmeal

3 cups unbleached white flour

2 tablespoons fresh sage, chopped, OR 2
  teaspoons dried sage (do not use
  ground sage)

1 tablespoon green peppercorns, rinsed
  in a small strainer and shaken dry

5 tablespoons powdered buttermilk

1¼ cups water

2 tablespoons butter

2 tablespoons honey

Have all the ingredients at room temperature. Place all the ingredients in the
machine, program for White Bread, and press Start.

....

Black & Decker, Betty Crocker, Breadman/Trillium, Hitachi, Large Toastmaster, and Williams-Sonoma

1 tablespoon green peppercorns, rinsed
  in a small strainer and shaken dry

5 tablespoons powdered buttermilk

1¼ cups water

2 tablespoons butter, at room
  temperature

2 tablespoons honey

1 teaspoon salt

¼ cup cornmeal

3 cups unbleached white flour

2 tablespoons fresh sage, chopped, OR 2
  teaspoons dried sage (do not use
  ground sage)

2½ teaspoons yeast (2 teaspoons for
  the Black & Decker, Toastmaster,
  and Breadman/Trillium)

Place all the ingredients in the machine, program for Bread, Basic Bread, Basic
Wheat, Basic, White, Basic White, or White/Whole Grain, and press Start.

Panasonic/National

1 teaspoon salt
¼ cup cornmeal
3 cups unbleached white flour
2 tablespoons fresh sage, chopped, OR 2 teaspoons dried sage (do not use ground sage)
1 tablespoon green peppercorns, rinsed in a small strainer and shaken dry

5 tablespoons powdered buttermilk
1¼ cups water
2 tablespoons butter, at room temperature
2 tablespoons honey
2½ teaspoons yeast

Place all the ingredients except the yeast in the machine. Place the yeast in the dispenser. Program for Basic Bread and press Start.

....

Regal

1 tablespoon green peppercorns, rinsed in a small strainer and shaken dry
4 tablespoons powdered buttermilk
1 cup water
2 tablespoons butter, at room temperature
1 tablespoon honey

1 teaspoon salt
2 tablespoons cornmeal
3 cups unbleached white flour
1½ tablespoons fresh sage, chopped OR 2 teaspoons dried sage (do not use ground sage)
2½ teaspoons yeast

Place all the ingredients in the machine, program for Bread, and press Start.

....

Large Oster, West Bend, Large Pillsbury, and Large Zojirushi

5 tablespoons powdered buttermilk

1¼ cups water

2 tablespoons butter, at room temperature

2 tablespoons honey

1 teaspoon salt

¼ cup cornmeal

3 cups unbleached white flour

2 tablespoons fresh sage, chopped OR 2 teaspoons dried sage (do not use ground sage)

1 tablespoon green peppercorns, rinsed in a small strainer and shaken dry

2½ teaspoons yeast

Place all the ingredients in the machine, program for Basic White Bread, Basic Bread, Basic Wheat, Basic, White, Basic White, or White/Whole Grain, and press Start or On.

Maxim, Small Oster, Small Pillsbury, Sanyo, Sunbeam, Small Toastmaster, and Small Zojirushi

2 teaspoons green peppercorns, rinsed in a small strainer and shaken dry

3 tablespoons powdered buttermilk

¾ cup water

1½ tablespoons butter, at room temperature

1½ tablespoons honey

½ teaspoon salt

3 tablespoons cornmeal

2 cups unbleached white flour

1½ tablespoons fresh sage, chopped OR 1½ teaspoons dried sage (do not use ground sage)

2 teaspoons yeast

Place all the ingredients in the machine, program for Standard, Basic, White, Basic Bread, or Bread, and press Start.

Small Welbilt

2 teaspoons yeast

½ teaspoon salt

3 tablespoons cornmeal

2 cups unbleached white flour

1½ tablespoons fresh sage, chopped OR
   1½ teaspoons dried sage (do not use
   ground sage)

2 teaspoons green peppercorns, rinsed
   in a small strainer and shaken dry

3 tablespoons powdered buttermilk

¾ cup water

1½ tablespoons butter

1½ tablespoons honey

Have all the ingredients at room temperature. Place all the ingredients in the machine, program for Medium, and press Start.

Small Panasonic/National

½ teaspoon salt

3 tablespoons cornmeal

2 cups unbleached white flour

1½ tablespoons fresh sage, chopped, OR
   1½ teaspoons dried sage (do not use
   ground sage)

2 teaspoons green peppercorns, rinsed
   in a small strainer and shaken dry

3 tablespoons powdered buttermilk

¾ cup water

1½ tablespoons butter, at room
   temperature

1½ tablespoons honey

2 teaspoons yeast

Place all the ingredients except the yeast in the machine. Place the yeast in the dispenser. Program for Basic Bread and press Start.

Green Peppercorn Sage Dinner Rolls: To make the dinner rolls, program for Dough or Manual. When the beeper sounds, remove the dough and divide it into 10 pieces and form small balls. Let them rise 1½ inches apart on a greased baking sheet set in a warm, draft-free place, uncovered, until doubled in bulk, about 1 hour.

Continued

Brush with a mixture of 1 egg white combined with 1 tablespoon water. Sprinkle with sesame seeds, if desired.

Preheat the oven to 350°F with the rack in the center position. Bake for 15 to 20 minutes, or until the tops are brown and the rolls sound hollow when tapped on the bottom.

FOCACCIA BREAD WITH SUN-DRIED TOMATOES

Whether flat or loaf-shaped, this unforgettably delicious bread is a beautiful speckled rose color and long on tomato flavor.

DAK/WELBILT

1 tablespoon yeast

⅓ cup cornmeal

3 cups unbleached white flour

1¼ cups water

3 tablespoons olive oil

2 teaspoons chopped garlic OR 3 tablespoons garlic oil

1 teaspoon salt

½ cup sun-dried tomatoes, coarsely chopped

⅓ cup grated Parmesan cheese

Have all the ingredients at room temperature. Place all the ingredients except the tomatoes and Parmesan cheese in the machine, program for White Bread, and press Start. When the beeper sounds, add the tomatoes and cheese.

BLACK & DECKER, BETTY CROCKER, BREADMAN/TRILLIUM, HITACHI, LARGE TOASTMASTER, AND WILLIAMS-SONOMA

1¼ cups water

3 tablespoons olive oil

2 teaspoons chopped garlic OR 3 tablespoons garlic oil

⅓ cup cornmeal

3 cups unbleached white flour

1 teaspoon salt

2 teaspoons yeast

½ cup sun-dried tomatoes, coarsely chopped

⅓ cup grated Parmesan cheese

Place all the ingredients except the tomatoes and Parmesan cheese in the machine, program for Mix Bread, Raisin Bread, Fruit and Nut, Basic Bread, Basic Wheat, Basic, White, Basic White, or White/Whole Grain, and press Start. When the beeper sounds or during the last 5 minutes of the final knead cycle, add the tomatoes and cheese.

PANASONIC/NATIONAL

⅓ cup cornmeal

3 cups unbleached white flour

1¼ cups water

3 tablespoons olive oil

2 teaspoons chopped garlic OR 3
tablespoons garlic oil

1 teaspoon salt

2½ teaspoons yeast

½ cup sun-dried tomatoes, coarsely
chopped

⅓ cup grated Parmesan cheese

Place all the ingredients except the yeast, tomatoes, and Parmesan cheese in the machine. Add the yeast to the dispenser. Program for Basic Bread and press Start. Add the tomatoes and cheese after the first 20 minutes of processing.

REGAL

1¼ cups water

3 tablespoons olive oil

2 teaspoons chopped garlic OR 3
tablespoons garlic oil

⅓ cup cornmeal

3 cups unbleached white flour

1 teaspoon salt

2¾ teaspoons yeast

½ cup sun-dried tomatoes, coarsely
chopped

⅓ cup grated Parmesan cheese

Place all the ingredients except the tomatoes and Parmesan cheese in the machine, program for Raisin Bread, and press Start. When the beeper sounds, add the tomatoes and cheese.

LARGE OSTER, WEST BEND, LARGE PILLSBURY, AND LARGE ZOJIRUSHI

1¼ cups water

3 tablespoons olive oil

2 teaspoons chopped garlic OR 3
tablespoons garlic oil

⅓ cup cornmeal

3 cups unbleached white flour

1 teaspoon salt

1 tablespoon yeast

½ cup sun-dried tomatoes, coarsely
chopped

⅓ cup grated Parmesan cheese

Place all the ingredients except the tomatoes and Parmesan cheese in the machine, program for Raisin Bread, Basic Bread, Basic Wheat, Basic, White, Basic White, or White/Whole Grain, and press Start or On. Add the tomatoes and cheese when the beeper sounds or during the last 5 minutes of the final knead cycle.

Foccasia Bread ō Sundried Tomatoes.

Maxim, Small Oster, Small Pillsbury, Sanyo, Sunbeam, Small Toastmaster, and Small Zojirushi

¾ cup water

2 tablespoons olive oil

1½ teaspoons chopped garlic OR 2½ tablespoons garlic oil

¼ cup cornmeal

2 cups unbleached white flour

½ teaspoon salt

2 teaspoons yeast

⅓ cup sun-dried tomatoes, coarsely chopped

¼ cup grated Parmesan cheese

Have all the ingredients at room temperature. Place all the ingredients except the tomatoes and Parmesan cheese in the machine, program for Standard, Bread, Basic, White, or Basic Bread, and press Start. Add the tomatoes and cheese when the beeper sounds or during the last 5 minutes of the final knead cycle.

Small Welbilt

2 teaspoons yeast

¼ cup cornmeal

2 cups unbleached white flour

¾ cup water

2 tablespoons olive oil

1½ teaspoons chopped garlic OR 2½ tablespoons garlic oil

½ teaspoon salt

⅓ cup sun-dried tomatoes, coarsely chopped

¼ cup grated Parmesan cheese

Have all the ingredients at room temperature. Place all the ingredients except the tomatoes and Parmesan cheese in the machine, program for Medium, and press Start. When the beeper sounds, add the tomatoes and cheese.

Small Panasonic/National

¼ cup cornmeal

2 cups unbleached white flour

½ teaspoon salt

¾ cup water

2 tablespoons olive oil

1½ teaspoons chopped garlic OR 2½ tablespoons garlic oil

2 teaspoons yeast

⅓ cup sun-dried tomatoes, coarsely chopped

¼ cup grated Parmesan cheese

Place all the ingredients except the yeast, tomatoes, and Parmesan cheese in the machine. Place the yeast in the dispenser. Program for Basic Bread and press Start. Add the tomatoes and cheese after the first 20 minutes of processing.

Variation: Real Italian focaccia is shaped like a thick-crust pizza. To make it, remove the dough from the machine after the tomatoes and cheese are incorporated. Sprinkle a wooden pizza paddle or flat cookie sheet with cornmeal. If you have a pizza stone or baker's tiles, place them in the oven. Preheat the oven to 425°F with the rack in the center position. When the oven is hot, brush the top of the bread with 1 tablespoon olive oil and sprinkle with 2 teaspoons coarse salt. Either slide the bread off the paddle onto the tiles or simply slide the cookie sheet into the oven. Bake for 15 to 20 minutes, until the top is golden brown and the underside is browned as well. Use the point of a long knife to test the dough in the center for doneness before removing the focaccia from the oven. Slice and serve hot or at room temperature.

PESTO BREAD

Pesto is a pungent Italian sauce made from ground-up basil, pine nuts, and Parmesan cheese. It used to be available only in the summer when fresh basil is plentiful. Now you can buy it in most groceries bottled, in the refrigerator case, or even in a tube! While we think homemade is the best, for this recipe store-bought is just fine.

....

DAK/WELBILT

2½ teaspoons yeast
3 cups unbleached white flour
1 tablespoon sugar
1 teaspoon salt
1 extra-large egg
¼ cup dry vermouth OR any dry white wine

1 clove garlic, finely chopped, plus 3 tablespoons olive oil OR 3 tablespoons garlic oil
½ cup pesto
⅓ cup plus 2 tablespoons water
½ cup toasted pine nuts (see Note)

Have all the ingredients at room temperature. Place all the ingredients except the pine nuts in the machine, program for White Bread, and press Start. When the beeper sounds, add the pine nuts.

....

BLACK & DECKER, BETTY CROCKER, BREADMAN/TRILLIUM, HITACHI, LARGE TOASTMASTER, AND WILLIAMS-SONOMA

1 extra-large egg
¼ cup vermouth OR any dry white wine
1 clove garlic, finely chopped, plus 3 tablespoons olive oil OR 3 tablespoons garlic oil
3 cups unbleached white flour

½ cup pesto
⅓ cup plus 2 tablespoons water
1 tablespoon sugar
1 teaspoon salt
2 teaspoons yeast
½ cup toasted pine nuts (see Note)

Continued

Place all the ingredients except the pine nuts in the machine, program for Mix Bread, Raisin Bread, Fruit and Nut, Basic Bread, Basic Wheat, Basic, White, Basic White, or White/Whole Grain, and press Start. When the beeper sounds during the last kneading, add the pine nuts.

PANASONIC/NATIONAL

3 cups unbleached white flour

1 tablespoon sugar

1 teaspoon salt

1 extra-large egg

¼ cup dry vermouth OR any dry white wine

1 clove garlic, finely chopped, plus 3 tablespoons olive oil OR 3 tablespoons garlic oil

½ cup pesto

⅓ cup plus 2 tablespoons water

2½ teaspoons yeast

½ cup toasted pine nuts (see Note)

Place all the ingredients except the yeast and pine nuts in the machine. Place the yeast in the dispenser. Program for Basic Bread and press Start. Add the pine nuts after 20 minutes of kneading.

REGAL, LARGE OSTER, WEST BEND, LARGE PILLSBURY, AND LARGE ZOJIRUSHI

1 extra-large egg

¼ cup dry vermouth OR any dry white wine

1 clove garlic, finely chopped, plus 3 tablespoons olive oil OR 3 tablespoons garlic oil

½ cup pesto

⅓ cup plus 2 tablespoons water

3 cups unbleached white flour

1 tablespoon sugar

1 teaspoon salt

2½ teaspoons yeast

½ cup toasted pine nuts (see Note)

Place all the ingredients except the pine nuts in the machine, program for Raisin Bread, Basic Bread, Basic Wheat, Basic, White, Basic White, or White/Whole Grain, and press Start or On. Add the pine nuts when the beeper sounds or during the last 5 minutes of the final knead cycle.

MAXIM, SMALL OSTER, SMALL PILLSBURY, SANYO, SUNBEAM, SMALL TOASTMASTER, AND SMALL ZOJIRUSHI

1 medium egg

3 tablespoons dry vermouth OR any dry white wine

1 clove garlic, finely chopped, plus 2 tablespoons olive oil OR 2 tablespoons garlic oil

2 cups unbleached white flour

⅓ cup pesto

¼ cup plus 2 tablespoons water

2 teaspoons sugar

¾ teaspoon salt

2 teaspoons yeast

⅓ cup toasted pine nuts (see Note)

Place all the ingredients except the pine nuts in the machine, program for Standard, Bread, Basic, White, or Basic Bread, and press Start. Add the pine nuts 5 minutes before the end of the last kneading cycle.

SMALL WELBILT

2 teaspoons yeast

2 cups unbleached white flour

2 teaspoons sugar

¾ teaspoon salt

1 medium egg

3 tablespoons dry vermouth OR any dry white wine

1 clove garlic, finely chopped, plus 2 tablespoons olive oil OR 2 tablespoons garlic oil

⅓ cup pesto

¼ cup plus 2 tablespoons water

⅓ cup toasted pine nuts (see Note)

Have all the ingredients at room temperature. Place all the ingredients except the pine nuts in the machine, program for Medium, and press Start. Add the pine nuts when the beeper sounds during the final kneading cycle.

Small Panasonic/National

2 cups unbleached white flour

2 teaspoons sugar

¾ teaspoon salt

1 medium egg

3 tablespoons dry vermouth OR any dry white wine

1 clove garlic, finely chopped, plus 2 tablespoons olive oil OR 2 tablespoons garlic oil

⅓ cup pesto

¼ cup plus 2 tablespoons water

2 teaspoons yeast

⅓ cup toasted pine nuts (see Note)

Place all the ingredients except the yeast and pine nuts in the machine. Place the yeast in the dispenser. Program for Basic Bread and press Start. Add the pine nuts 20 minutes into the kneading process.

NOTE: To toast pine nuts, place a small strainer in a metal bowl. In a small frying pan, heat 2 tablespoons vegetable oil. Add the pine nuts and shake the pan back and forth continuously over the burner (to roll the nuts around) until they are golden brown. Immediately empty the entire contents of the pan into the strainer. Shake to eliminate the excess oil.

OLIVE ONION BREAD

This makes a marbleized loaf, dark tan and deep brown, from the olives. It's a Mediterranean delight, gutsy thick bread with a hearty flavor and the salty zest of the olives.

It is essential to use high-quality oil and cured Greek or Italian black olives, which are available in many ethnic markets and some delis. These are the only types sturdy enough to withstand the action of the kneading blade without turning into mush, though you must pit them yourself. Use a small knife, slit the olives in two pieces, then slip out the pits.

DAK/WELBILT

1 tablespoon yeast

3 cups unbleached white flour

1 teaspoon sugar

1 teaspoon salt

1 teaspoon dried thyme

1¼ cups water

3 tablespoons olive oil OR garlic oil

½ cup pitted oil-cured black olives, each cut into 2 pieces

½ cup finely chopped red (Bermuda) onions

Have all the ingredients at room temperature. Place all the ingredients except the olives and onions in the machine, program for White Bread, and press Start. Add the olives and onions when the beeper sounds.

BLACK & DECKER, BETTY CROCKER, BREADMAN/TRILLIUM, HITACHI, LARGE TOASTMASTER, AND WILLIAMS-SONOMA

1¼ cups water

3 tablespoons olive oil OR garlic oil

3 cups unbleached white flour

1 teaspoon sugar

1 teaspoon salt

1 teaspoon dried thyme

2 teaspoons yeast

½ cup pitted oil-cured black olives, each cut into 2 pieces

½ cup finely chopped red (Bermuda) onions

Continued

Place all the ingredients except the olives and onions in the machine, program for Mix Bread, Raisin Bread, Fruit and Nut, Basic Bread, Basic Wheat, Basic, White, Basic White, or White/Whole Grain, and press Start. Add the olives and onions when the beeper sounds or during the last 5 minutes of the final knead cycle.

PANASONIC/NATIONAL

3 cups unbleached white flour

1 teaspoon sugar

1 teaspoon salt

1 teaspoon dried thyme

1¼ cups water

3 tablespoons olive oil OR garlic oil

1 tablespoon yeast

½ cup pitted oil-cured black olives, each cut into 2 pieces

½ cup finely chopped red (Bermuda) onions

Place all the ingredients except the yeast, olives, and onions in the machine. Place the yeast in the dispenser. Program for Basic Bread and press Start. Add the olives and onions just before the end of the first kneading (20 minutes into the cycle).

REGAL, LARGE OSTER, WEST BEND, LARGE PILLSBURY, AND LARGE ZOJIRUSHI

1¼ cups water

3 tablespoons olive oil OR garlic oil

1 teaspoon sugar

1½ teaspoons salt

1 teaspoon dried thyme

3 cups unbleached white flour

1 tablespoon yeast

½ cup pitted oil-cured black olives, each cut into 2 pieces

½ cup finely chopped red (Bermuda) onions

Place all the ingredients except the olives and onions in the machine, program for Raisin Bread, Basic Bread, Basic Wheat, Basic, White, Basic White, or White/Whole Grain, and press Start or On. Add the olives and onions when the beeper sounds or during the last 5 minutes of the final knead cycle.

Maxim, Small Oster, Small Pillsbury, Sanyo, Sunbeam, Small Toastmaster, and Small Zojirushi

½ cup plus 2 tablespoons water

1½ tablespoons olive oil OR garlic oil

½ teaspoon sugar

½ teaspoon salt

1 teaspoon dried thyme

1½ cups unbleached white flour

1½ teaspoons yeast

¼ cup pitted oil-cured black olives, each cut into 2 pieces

¼ cup finely chopped red (Bermuda) onions

Place all the ingredients except the olives and onions in the machine, program for Standard, Bread, Basic, White, or Basic Bread, and press Start. Add the olives and onions when the beeper sounds or during the last 5 minutes of the final knead cycle.

....

Small Welbilt

1½ teaspoons yeast

1½ cups unbleached white flour

½ teaspoon sugar

½ teaspoon salt

1 teaspoon dried thyme

½ cup plus 2 tablespoons water

1½ tablespoons olive oil OR garlic oil

¼ cup pitted oil-cured black olives, each cut into 2 pieces

¼ cup finely chopped red (Bermuda) onions

Have all the ingredients at room temperature. Place all the ingredients except the olives and onions in the machine, program for Medium, and press Start. Add the olives and onions when the beeper sounds.

....

Small Panasonic/National

½ teaspoon sugar

½ teaspoon salt

1 teaspoon dried thyme

1½ cups unbleached white flour

½ cup plus 2 tablespoons water

1½ tablespoons olive oil OR garlic oil

1½ teaspoons yeast

¼ cup pitted oil-cured black olives, each cut into 2 pieces

¼ cup finely chopped red (Bermuda) onions

Place all the ingredients except the yeast, olives, and onions in the machine. Place the yeast in the dispenser. Program for Basic Bread and press Start. Add the olives and onions just before the end of the second kneading (20 minutes into the cycle).

RANCH ONION BREAD

Boy, was this a tasty surprise! The beer and salad dressing mix give this bread terrific flavor and the onions give it moistness and additional flavor as well. The combination of the whole-grain flour and cornmeal makes for a hearty, wholesome loaf that's loaded with personality. We loved it to make grilled cheese sandwiches with thick slices of Vermont Cheddar cheese and a slice of Bermuda onion.

We made this bread up when there was a blizzard and we couldn't get to the store. We ransacked the refrigerator and cabinets and came up with what we thought might be compatible ingredients—and were delighted with the results. You can easily substitute any envelope of powdered dressing mix.

DAK/WELBILT

1 tablespoon yeast

2 cups unbleached white flour

3/4 cup plus 2 tablespoons whole wheat flour

1/2 cup cornmeal

1/2 teaspoon salt

1 1-ounce envelope Hidden Valley Ranch dressing mix

4 tablespoons powdered buttermilk

1/2 cup ricotta cheese

1 extra-large egg

1/2 cup flat beer (see Note)

2 tablespoons honey

2 tablespoons vegetable oil OR garlic oil

2/3 cup chopped fresh scallions, both white and green parts

Have all the ingredients at room temperature. Place all the ingredients in the machine, program for White Bread, and press Start.

BLACK & DECKER, BETTY CROCKER, BREADMAN/TRILLIUM, HITACHI, LARGE TOASTMASTER, AND WILLIAMS-SONOMA

½ cup ricotta cheese

1 extra-large egg

½ cup flat beer (see Note)

2 tablespoons honey

⅓ cup chopped fresh scallions, both white and green parts

2 tablespoons vegetable oil OR garlic oil

½ teaspoon salt

1 1-ounce envelope Hidden Valley Ranch dressing mix

4 tablespoons powdered buttermilk

2 cups unbleached white flour

¾ cup plus 2 tablespoons whole wheat flour

½ cup cornmeal

2½ teaspoons yeast (2 teaspoons for the Black & Decker, Breadman/Trillium, and Toastmaster)

Place all the ingredients in the machine, program for Bread, Basic Bread, Basic Wheat, Basic, White, Basic White, or White/Whole Grain, and press Start.

....

PANASONIC/NATIONAL

2 cups unbleached white flour

¾ cup plus 2 tablespoons whole wheat flour

½ cup cornmeal

½ teaspoon salt

1 1-ounce envelope Hidden Valley Ranch dressing mix

4 tablespoons powdered buttermilk

½ cup ricotta cheese

1 extra-large egg

½ cup flat beer (see Note)

2 tablespoons honey

2 tablespoons vegetable oil OR garlic oil

⅔ cup chopped fresh scallions, both white and green parts

1 tablespoon yeast

Place all the ingredients except the yeast in the machine. Place the yeast in the dispenser. Program for Basic Bread and press Start.

....

198

REGAL, LARGE OSTER, WEST BEND, LARGE PILLSBURY, AND LARGE ZOJIRUSHI

½ cup ricotta cheese

1 extra-large egg

½ cup flat beer (see Note)

2 tablespoons honey

2 tablespoons vegetable oil OR garlic oil

½ teaspoon salt

1 1-ounce envelope Hidden Valley
   Ranch dressing mix

4 tablespoons powdered buttermilk

2 cups unbleached white flour

¾ cup plus 2 tablespoons whole wheat
   flour

½ cup cornmeal

⅔ cup chopped fresh scallions, both
   white and green parts

1 tablespoon yeast

Place all the ingredients in the machine, program for Basic White Bread, Basic Bread, Basic Wheat, Basic, White, Basic White, or White/Whole Grain, and press Start or On.

MAXIM, SMALL OSTER, SMALL PILLSBURY, SANYO, SUNBEAM, SMALL TOASTMASTER, AND SMALL ZOJIRUSHI

¼ cup ricotta cheese

1 medium egg

¼ cup flat beer (see Note)

1 tablespoon honey

1 tablespoon vegetable oil OR garlic oil

⅓ cup chopped fresh scallions, both
   white and green parts

1 cup plus 2 tablespoons unbleached
   white flour

⅓ cup whole wheat flour

¼ cup cornmeal

¼ teaspoon salt

½ 1-ounce envelope Hidden Valley
   Ranch dressing mix

2 tablespoons powdered buttermilk

2 teaspoons yeast

Place all the ingredients in the machine, program for Standard, Basic, White, Basic Bread, or Bread, and press Start.

SMALL WELBILT

2 teaspoons yeast
1 cup unbleached white flour
⅓ cup whole wheat flour
¼ cup cornmeal
¼ teaspoon salt
½ 1-ounce envelope Hidden Valley
   Ranch dressing mix
2 tablespoons powdered buttermilk

¼ cup ricotta cheese
1 medium egg
¼ cup flat beer (see Note)
1 tablespoon honey
1 tablespoon vegetable oil OR garlic oil
⅓ cup chopped fresh scallions, both
   white and green parts

Have all the ingredients at room temperature. Place all the ingredients in the machine, program for Medium, and press Start.

SMALL PANASONIC/NATIONAL

1 cup plus 2 tablespoons unbleached
   white flour
⅓ cup whole wheat flour
¼ cup cornmeal
¼ teaspoon salt
½ 1-ounce envelope Hidden Valley
   Ranch dressing mix
2 tablespoons powdered buttermilk

¼ cup ricotta cheese
1 medium egg
¼ cup flat beer (see Note)
1 tablespoon honey
1 tablespoon vegetable oil OR garlic oil
⅓ cup chopped fresh scallions, both
   white and green parts
2 teaspoons yeast

Place all the ingredients except the yeast in the machine. Place the yeast in the dispenser. Program for Basic Bread and press Start.

NOTE: If you don't want to wait around for the beer to become flat on its own, pour it into a small saucepan and heat it to a simmer. By the time the beer cools down, it will be flat.

ROSEMARY PEPPER BREAD

While baking, this bread made the whole house smell like the South of France in the summertime. The texture is incredibly light, studded with bits of herbs and pepper that will warm your mouth with a lingering flavor. Try a slice toasted and spread with goat cheese.

This recipe calls for fresh rosemary. While it is possible to substitute dried rosemary (not ground rosemary, however), it's worth the search to find fresh. More and more fresh herbs are available in supermarkets and health food stores.

....

DAK/WELBILT

1 tablespoon yeast
½ cup quick-cooking oats
¼ cup cornmeal
3 cups unbleached white flour
1 teaspoon salt
1½ teaspoons coarsely ground black
    pepper

2 generous tablespoons fresh rosemary
    (use only the leaves, discard the
    stems) OR 1 tablespoon dried
    rosemary
2 tablespoons honey
2 tablespoons vegetable oil
4 tablespoons nonfat dry milk
1 cup plus 1 tablespoon water

Have all the ingredients at room temperature. Place all the ingredients in the machine, program for White Bread, and press Start.

....

Black & Decker, Betty Crocker, Breadman/Trillium, Hitachi, Large Toastmaster, Regal, and Williams-Sonoma

1½ generous tablespoons fresh
rosemary (use only the leaves,
discard the stems) OR 1 tablespoon
dried rosemary
1½ tablespoons honey
1½ tablespoons vegetable oil
¾ cup plus 1 tablespoon water
⅓ cup quick-cooking oats
3 tablespoons cornmeal

2½ cups unbleached white flour
1 teaspoon salt
3 tablespoons nonfat dry milk
1 teaspoon coarsely ground black
pepper
2 teaspoons yeast (1½ teaspoons for
the Black & Decker, the
Toastmaster, and Breadman/Trillium)

Place all the ingredients in the machine, program for Bread, Basic Bread, Basic Wheat, Basic, White, Basic White, or White/Whole Grain, and press Start.

Panasonic/National

½ cup quick-cooking oats
¼ cup cornmeal
3 cups unbleached white flour
1 teaspoon salt
4 tablespoons nonfat dry milk
1½ teaspoons coarsely ground black
pepper

2 generous tablespoons fresh rosemary
(use only the leaves, discard the
stems) OR 1 tablespoon dried
rosemary
2 tablespoons honey
2 tablespoons vegetable oil
1 cup plus 1 tablespoon water
1 tablespoon yeast

Place all the ingredients except the yeast in the machine. Place the yeast in the dispenser. Program for Basic Bread and press Start.

REGAL, LARGE OSTER, WEST BEND, LARGE PILLSBURY, AND LARGE ZOJIRUSHI

2 generous tablespoons fresh rosemary (use only the leaves, discard the stems) OR 1 tablespoon dried rosemary

2 tablespoons honey

2 tablespoons vegetable oil

4 tablespoons nonfat dry milk

1 cup plus 1 tablespoon water

½ cup quick-cooking oats

¼ cup cornmeal

3 cups unbleached white flour

1 teaspoon salt

1½ teaspoons coarsely ground black pepper

1 tablespoon yeast

Place all the ingredients in the machine, program for Basic White Bread, Basic Bread, Basic Wheat, Basic, White, Basic White, or White/Whole Grain, and press Start or On.

....

MAXIM, SMALL OSTER, SMALL PILLSBURY, SANYO, SUNBEAM, SMALL TOASTMASTER, AND SMALL ZOJIRUSHI

1 tablespoon honey

1 tablespoon vegetable oil

½ cup plus 1 tablespoon water

¼ cup quick-cooking oats

2 tablespoons nonfat dry milk

2 tablespoons cornmeal

1½ cups unbleached white flour

½ teaspoon salt

1 generous tablespoon fresh rosemary (use only the leaves, discard the stems) OR ½ tablespoon dried rosemary

¾ teaspoon coarsely ground black pepper

1½ teaspoons yeast

Place all the ingredients in the machine, program for Standard, Basic, White, Basic Bread, or Bread, and press Start.

....

SMALL WELBILT

1½ teaspoons yeast

¼ cup quick-cooking oats

2 tablespoons cornmeal

1½ cups unbleached white flour

½ teaspoon salt

¾ teaspoon coarsely ground black
   pepper

1 generous tablespoon fresh rosemary
   (use only the leaves, discard the
   stems) OR ½ tablespoon dried
   rosemary

1 tablespoon honey

1 tablespoon vegetable oil

2 tablespoons nonfat dry milk

½ cup plus 1 tablespoon water

Have all the ingredients at room temperature. Place all the ingredients in the machine, program for Medium, and press Start.

SMALL PANASONIC/NATIONAL

¼ cup quick-cooking oats

2 tablespoons nonfat dry milk

2 tablespoons cornmeal

1½ cups unbleached white flour

½ teaspoon salt

¾ teaspoon coarsely ground black
   pepper

1 generous tablespoon fresh rosemary
   (use only the leaves, discard the
   stems) OR ½ tablespoon dried
   rosemary

1 tablespoon honey

1 tablespoon vegetable oil

½ cup plus 1 tablespoon water

1½ teaspoons yeast

Place all the ingredients except the yeast in the machine. Place the yeast in the dispenser. Program for Basic Bread and press Start.

RITA FRIED'S GARLIC HERB BREAD

Several years ago a dear friend Rita Fried raved about her brand-new toy, an automatic bread machine. We didn't pay much attention until she brought a sample from it to try. We were hooked. It's in large part because of Rita that this book of recipes came about. This special recipe comes from her creative hand. Do not use garlic salt in place of the garlic powder in this recipe—the former would stall the yeast and you'll end up with a loaf that didn't rise.

DAK/Welbilt

2½ teaspoons yeast
2⅔ cups unbleached white flour
⅓ cup nonfat dry milk
1 teaspoon salt
¼ cup plus 1 tablespoon grated
   Parmesan cheese

1 teaspoon dried oregano
¼ teaspoon dried basil
1 teaspoon garlic powder (not garlic
   salt)
1 cup plus 1 tablespoon water
¼ cup olive oil

Have all the ingredients at room temperature. Place all the ingredients in the machine, program for White Bread, and press Start.

Black & Decker, Betty Crocker, Breadman/Trillium, Hitachi, Large Toastmaster, and Williams-Sonoma

¼ cup plus 1 tablespoon grated
   Parmesan cheese
1 teaspoon oregano
¼ teaspoon dried basil
1 teaspoon garlic powder (not garlic
   salt)
1 cup water

¼ cup olive oil
2⅔ cups unbleached white flour
⅓ cup nonfat dry milk
1 teaspoon salt
2 teaspoons yeast (1½ teaspoons for the
   Black & Decker, the Breadman/
   Trillium, and Toastmaster)

Place all the ingredients in the machine, program for Bread, Basic Bread, Basic Wheat, Basic, White, Basic White, or White/Whole Grain, and press Start.

PANASONIC/NATIONAL

2⅔ cups unbleached white flour
⅓ cup nonfat dry milk
1 teaspoon salt
¼ cup plus 1 tablespoon grated
   Parmesan cheese
1 teaspoon oregano

¼ teaspoon dried basil
1 teaspoon garlic powder (not garlic
   salt)
1 cup plus 1 tablespoon water
¼ cup olive oil
2½ teaspoons yeast

Place all the ingredients except the yeast in the machine. Place the yeast in the dispenser. Program for Basic Bread and press Start.

REGAL, LARGE OSTER, WEST BEND, LARGE PILLSBURY, AND LARGE ZOJIRUSHI

¼ cup plus 1 tablespoon grated
   Parmesan cheese
1 teaspoon oregano
¼ teaspoon dried basil
1 teaspoon garlic powder (not garlic
   salt)

1 cup plus 1 tablespoon water
¼ cup olive oil
2⅔ cups unbleached white flour
⅓ cup nonfat dry milk
1 teaspoon salt
2½ teaspoons yeast

Place all the ingredients in the machine, program for Bread, Basic, White, Basic White, or White/Whole Grain, and press Start or On.

MAXIM, SMALL OSTER, SMALL PILLSBURY, SANYO, SUNBEAM, SMALL TOASTMASTER, AND SMALL ZOJIRUSHI

¼ cup olive oil
½ cup plus 2 tablespoons water
¼ cup grated Parmesan cheese
½ teaspoon oregano
¼ teaspoon dried basil

½ teaspoon garlic powder (not garlic salt)
2 cups unbleached white flour
3 tablespoons nonfat dry milk
½ teaspoon salt
2 teaspoons yeast

Place all the ingredients in the machine, program for Standard, Basic, White, Basic Bread, or Bread, and press Start.

SMALL WELBILT

2 teaspoons yeast
2 cups unbleached white flour
3 tablespoons nonfat dry milk
½ teaspoon salt
¼ cup grated Parmesan cheese
½ teaspoon oregano

¼ teaspoon dried basil
½ teaspoon garlic powder (not garlic salt)
½ cup plus 2 tablespoons water
¼ cup olive oil

Have all the ingredients at room temperature. Place all the ingredients in the machine, program for Medium, and press Start.

SMALL PANASONIC/NATIONAL

2 cups unbleached white flour
3 tablespoons nonfat dry milk
½ teaspoon salt
¼ cup grated Parmesan cheese
½ teaspoon oregano
¼ teaspoon dried basil

½ teaspoon garlic powder (not garlic salt)
½ cup plus 2 tablespoons water
¼ cup olive oil
2 teaspoons yeast

Place all the ingredients except the yeast in the machine. Place the yeast in the dispenser. Program for Basic Bread and press Start.

Variation: To make hot garlic bread, cut the loaf into ¾-inch slices, brushing each side with olive oil or soft butter. Place the slices back together, wrap them securely in foil, and then place them in a preheated 400°F oven for 15 minutes. Serve hot.

CARAMELIZED ONION BRAID

There is nothing more delicious than the combination of onions, slowly sautéed in butter until they are golden brown and caramelized from their natural sugar, and a soft, rich egg braid.

This showpiece bread looks like something you'd find in a pastry shop designed by *Vogue* and executed by Rolls-Royce. The braid is high and generously elegant with a shiny, deep golden brown top. The taste and texture are sublime with the sweetness of caramelized onions and the subtle crunch of poppy seeds.

DAK/Welbilt

For the Onion

1 large onion, peeled and thinly sliced	4 tablespoons butter

For the Bread

2 teaspoons yeast	1 extra-large egg
3 cups unbleached white flour	3 tablespoons butter and onion cooking
1½ teaspoons salt	liquid (see below)
1 tablespoon honey	1 cup caramelized onions (see below)
¾ cup water	¼ cup poppy seeds

In a skillet, sauté the onions in the butter over low heat, stirring occasionally, until they are golden brown, about 20 minutes. Don't try to rush them or they will burn. Pour the contents of the skillet into a strainer set over a bowl. Use the back of a spoon to gently push out the butter and some juice from the onions. Measure out 3 tablespoons of liquid and reserve.

Have all the ingredients at room temperature. Place all the ingredients except the onions and poppy seeds in the machine, program for Manual, and press Start.

At the beginning of the second kneading, add the onions and poppy seeds. At the end of the second rise, remove the dough (it will be sticky) and place it in a well-oiled bowl. Cover the bowl tightly and place it in the refrigerator for at least 2 hours or as long as overnight. Follow the Baking Instructions on page 214.

BLACK & DECKER, BETTY CROCKER, BREADMAN/TRILLIUM, HITACHI, LARGE TOASTMASTER, AND WILLIAMS-SONOMA

FOR THE ONION

1 large onion, peeled and thinly sliced   4 tablespoons butter

FOR THE BREAD

1 tablespoon honey

¾ cup water

1 extra-large egg

3 tablespoons butter and onion cooking
    liquid (see below)

3 cups unbleached white flour

1½ teaspoons salt

2 teaspoons yeast (1½ teaspoons for
    the Black & Decker, the Breadman/
    Trillium, and Toastmaster)

1 cup caramelized onions (see below)

¼ cup poppy seeds

In a skillet, sauté the onions in the butter over low heat, stirring occasionally, until they are golden brown, about 20 minutes. Don't try to rush them or they will burn. Pour the contents of the skillet into a strainer set over a bowl. Use the back of a spoon to gently push out the butter and some juice from the onions. Measure out 3 tablespoons of liquid and reserve.

Place all the ingredients except the onions and poppy seeds in the machine, program for Dough or Knead and First Rise, and press Start.

When the beeper sounds or during the last 5 minutes of the final knead cycle, add the onions and poppy seeds. When the machine is through, remove the dough (it will be sticky) and place it in a well-oiled bowl. Cover the bowl tightly and place it in the refrigerator for at least 2 hours or as long as overnight. Follow Baking Instructions on page 214.

PANASONIC/NATIONAL
FOR THE ONION

1 large onion, peeled and thinly sliced   4 tablespoons butter

FOR THE BREAD

3 cups unbleached white flour
1½ teaspoons salt
1 tablespoon honey
¾ cup water
1 extra-large egg

3 tablespoons butter and onion cooking
   liquid (see below)
2 teaspoons yeast
1 cup caramelized onions (see below)
¼ cup poppy seeds

In a skillet, sauté the onions in the butter over low heat, stirring occasionally, until they are golden brown, about 20 minutes. Don't try to rush them or they will burn. Pour the contents of the skillet into a strainer set over a bowl. Use the back of a spoon to gently push out the butter and some juice from the onions. Measure out 3 tablespoons of liquid and reserve.

     Place all the ingredients except the yeast, onions, and poppy seeds in the machine. Place the yeast in the dispenser. Program for Dough or Manual and press Start.

     Toward the end of the kneading cycle, add the onions and poppy seeds. A beeper will sound when the dough is ready to be removed from the machine. Remove the dough (it will be sticky) and place it in a well-oiled bowl. Cover the bowl tightly and place it in the refrigerator for at least 2 hours or as long as overnight. Follow the Baking Instructions on page 214.

....

REGAL, LARGE OSTER, WEST BEND, LARGE PILLSBURY, AND LARGE ZOJIRUSHI
FOR THE ONION

1 large onion, peeled and thinly sliced   4 tablespoons butter

For the Bread

For the Bread

1 tablespoon honey	3 cups unbleached white flour
¾ cup water	1½ teaspoons salt
1 extra-large egg	2 teaspoons yeast
3 tablespoons butter and onion cooking liquid (see below)	1 cup caramelized onions (see below)
	¼ cup poppy seeds

In a skillet, sauté the onions in the butter over low heat, stirring occasionally, until they are golden brown, about 20 minutes. Don't try to rush them or they will burn. Pour the contents of the skillet into a strainer set over a bowl. Use the back of a spoon to gently push out the butter and some juice from the onions. Measure out 3 tablespoons of liquid and reserve.

Place all the ingredients except the onions and poppy seeds in the machine, program for Dough or Manual, and press Start.

When the beeper sounds or during the last 5 minutes of the final knead cycle, add the onions and poppy seeds. At the end of the second rise, remove the dough (it will be sticky) and place it in a well-oiled bowl. Cover the bowl tightly and place it in the refrigerator for at least 2 hours or as long as overnight. Follow the Baking Instructions on page 214.

Maxim, Small Oster, Small Pillsbury, Sanyo, Sunbeam, Small Toastmaster, and Small Zojirushi

For the Onion

1 medium onion, peeled and thinly sliced, to equal 1 generous cup	2½ tablespoons butter

For the Bread

2 teaspoons honey	2 cups unbleached white flour
¼ cup plus 2 tablespoons water	1 teaspoon salt
1 medium egg	1½ teaspoons yeast
3 tablespoons butter and onion cooking liquid (see page 212)	⅔ cup caramelized onions (see page 212)
	2½ tablespoons poppy seeds

Continued

In a skillet, sauté the onions in the butter over low heat, stirring occasionally, until they are golden brown, about 20 minutes. Don't try to rush them or they will burn. Pour the contents of the skillet into a strainer set over a bowl. Use the back of a spoon to gently push out the butter and some juice from the onions. Measure out 3 tablespoons of liquid and reserve.

Place all the ingredients except the onions and poppy seeds in the machine, program for Dough or Manual, and press Start.

When the beeper sounds or during the last 5 minutes of the final knead cycle, add the onions and poppy seeds. At the end of the second rise, remove the dough (it will be sticky) and place it in a well-oiled bowl. Cover the bowl tightly and place it in the refrigerator for at least 2 hours or as long as overnight. Follow the Baking Instructions on page 214.

....

SMALL WELBILT

FOR THE ONION

1 medium onion, peeled and thinly sliced, to equal 1 generous cup

2½ tablespoons butter

FOR THE BREAD

1½ teaspoons yeast
2 cups unbleached white flour
1 teaspoon salt
2 teaspoons honey
¼ cup plus 2 tablespoons water

1 medium egg
2 tablespoons butter and onion cooking liquid (see below)
⅔ cup caramelized onions (see below)
2½ tablespoons poppy seeds

In a skillet, sauté the onions in the butter over low heat, stirring occasionally, until they are golden brown, about 20 minutes. Don't try to rush them or they will burn. Pour the contents of the skillet into a strainer set over a bowl. Use the back of a spoon to gently push out the butter and some juice from the onions. Measure out 2 tablespoons of liquid and reserve.

Have all the ingredients at room temperature. Place all the ingredients except the onions and poppy seeds in the machine, program for Manual, and press Start.

At the beginning of the second kneading, add the onions and poppy seeds. At the end of the second rise, remove the dough (it will be sticky) and place it in a well-oiled bowl. Cover the bowl tightly and place it in the refrigerator for at least 2 hours or as long as overnight. Follow the Baking Instructions on page 214.

....

SMALL PANASONIC/NATIONAL
FOR THE ONION

1 medium onion, peeled and thinly sliced, to equal 1 generous cup

2½ tablespoons butter

FOR THE BREAD

2 cups unbleached white flour

1 teaspoon salt

2 teaspoons honey

¼ cup plus 2 tablespoons water

1 medium egg

2 tablespoons butter and onion cooking liquid (see below)

1½ teaspoons yeast

⅔ cup caramelized onions (see below)

2½ tablespoons poppy seeds

In a skillet, sauté the onions in the butter over low heat, stirring occasionally, until they are golden brown, about 20 minutes. Don't try to rush them or they will burn. Pour the contents of the skillet into a strainer set over a bowl. Use the back of a spoon to gently push out the butter and some juice from the onions. Measure out 2 tablespoons of liquid and reserve.

Place all the ingredients except the yeast, onions, and poppy seeds in the machine. Place the yeast in the dispenser. Program for Dough or Manual and press Start.

Toward the end of the kneading cycle, add the onions and poppy seeds. When the beeper sounds, remove the dough (it will be sticky) and place it in a well-oiled bowl. Cover the bowl tightly and place it in the refrigerator for at least 2 hours or as long as overnight. Follow the Baking Instructions on page 214.

BAKING INSTRUCTIONS (LARGE MACHINES)

1 egg beaten with 1 tablespoon water

Lightly butter or grease a heavy-duty cookie sheet. On a lightly floured board, pat the cold dough into a fat log and then cut the log into 3 equal pieces. With the palms of your hands, form each piece into a 16- to 17-inch length. Pinch 3 of the ends together, then make a fairly tight braid, pinching the other ends together. Place on the prepared cookie sheet.

Generously brush the top of the braid with the egg glaze and reserve the egg glaze. Let the braid rise, uncovered, in a warm, draft-free place for about 1 hour, or until almost doubled in size.

Preheat the oven to 350°F with the rack in the lower third, but not the bottom, position. Repaint the braid with the reserved egg glaze. Bake for 50 to 60 minutes, or until deep golden brown and the inside is done (check by inserting a small sharp knife between the braids to make sure the bread is cooked throughout).

BAKING INSTRUCTIONS (SMALL MACHINES)

1 egg beaten with 1 tablespoon water

Lightly butter or grease a heavy-duty cookie sheet. On a lightly floured board, pat the cold dough into a fat log and then cut the log into 3 equal pieces. With the palms of your hands, form each piece into a 8- to 10-inch length. Pinch 3 of the ends together, then make a fairly tight braid, pinching the other ends together. Place on the prepared cookie sheet.

Generously brush the top of the braid with the egg glaze and reserve the egg glaze. Let the braid rise, uncovered, in a warm, draft-free place for about 1 hour, or until almost doubled in size.

Preheat the oven to 350°F with the rack in the lower third, but not the bottom, position. Repaint the braid with the reserved egg glaze. Bake for 50 to 60 minutes, or until deep golden brown and the inside is done (check by inserting a small sharp knife between the braids to make sure the bread is cooked throughout).

CURRIED PISTACHIO BREAD

A loaf that is tall and golden with a hint of green, studded with pistachios, and slightly exotic. A true masterpiece.

DAK/WELBILT

1 tablespoon yeast

4 tablespoons nonfat dry milk

1½ teaspoons salt

2 teaspoons curry powder

2½ cups unbleached white flour

½ cup bran flakes

½ cup oatmeal

1 extra-large egg

¾ cup water

2 tablespoons honey

2 tablespoons butter

½ cup unsalted pistachios, shelled

Have all the ingredients at room temperature. Place all the ingredients except the pistachios in the machine, program for White Bread, and press Start. When the beeper sounds during the second kneading, add the pistachios.

BLACK & DECKER, BETTY CROCKER, BREADMAN/TRILLIUM, HITACHI, LARGE TOASTMASTER, AND WILLIAMS-SONOMA

1 extra-large egg

¾ cup water

2 tablespoons honey

2 tablespoons butter, at room temperature

2¼ cups unbleached white flour

3 tablespoons nonfat dry milk

1 teaspoon salt

1½ teaspoons curry powder

½ cup bran flakes

½ cup oatmeal

2 teaspoons yeast

½ cup unsalted pistachios, shelled

Place all the ingredients except the pistachios in the machine, program for Mix Bread, Raisin Bread, Fruit and Nut, Basic, Basic Bread, White, or Basic Wheat, and press Start. Add the pistachios when the beeper sounds or during the last 5 minutes of the final knead cycle.

PANASONIC/NATIONAL

2¼ cups unbleached white flour

3 tablespoons nonfat dry milk

1 teaspoon salt

1½ teaspoons curry powder

½ cup bran flakes

½ cup oatmeal

1 extra-large egg

¾ cup water

2 tablespoons honey

2 tablespoons butter, at room temperature

1 tablespoon yeast

½ cup unsalted pistachios, shelled

Place all the ingredients except the yeast and pistachios in the machine. Place the yeast in the dispenser. Program for Basic Bread and press Start. Add the pistachios when the prekneading is completed, 20 minutes into processing.

REGAL

1 extra-large egg

¾ cup water

2 tablespoons honey

2 tablespoons butter, at room temperature

2¼ cups unbleached white flour

3 tablespoons nonfat dry milk

1 teaspoon salt

1½ teaspoons curry powder

½ cup bran flakes

½ cup oatmeal

2½ teaspoons yeast

½ cup unsalted pistachios, shelled

Place all the ingredients except the pistachios in the machine, program for Raisin Bread, and press Start. Add the pistachios when the beeper sounds.

Large Oster, West Bend, Large Pillsbury, and Large Zojirushi

1 extra-large egg

¾ cup water

2 tablespoons honey

2 tablespoons butter, at room
temperature

4 tablespoons nonfat dry milk

1½ teaspoons salt

2 teaspoons curry powder

2½ cups unbleached white flour

½ cup bran flakes

½ cup oatmeal

1 tablespoon yeast

½ cup unsalted pistachios, shelled

Place all the ingredients except the pistachios in the machine, program for Raisin Bread, Basic, White, or White/Whole Grain, and press Start or On. Add the pistachios when the beeper sounds or during the last 5 minutes of the final knead cycle.

Maxim, Small Oster, Small Pillsbury, Sanyo, Sunbeam, Small Toastmaster, and Small Zojirushi

1 medium egg

½ cup water

1½ tablespoons honey

1½ tablespoons butter, at room
temperature

3 tablespoons nonfat dry milk

1 teaspoon salt

1½ teaspoons curry powder

1½ cups plus 2 tablespoons unbleached
white flour

¼ cup bran flakes

¼ cup oatmeal

2 teaspoons yeast

⅓ cup unsalted pistachios, shelled

Place all the ingredients except the pistachios in the machine, program for Standard, Basic, White, Basic Bread, or Bread, and press Start. Add the pistachios when the beeper sounds or during the last 5 minutes of the final knead cycle.

Small Welbilt

2 teaspoons yeast

3 tablespoons nonfat dry milk

1 teaspoon salt

1½ teaspoons curry powder

1½ cups unbleached white flour

¼ cup bran flakes

¼ cup oatmeal

1 medium egg

½ cup water

1½ tablespoons honey

1½ tablespoons butter

⅓ cup unsalted pistachios, shelled

Have all the ingredients at room temperature. Place all the ingredients except the pistachios in the machine, program for Medium, and press Start. When the beeper sounds during the second kneading, add the pistachios.

Small Panasonic/National

3 tablespoons nonfat dry milk

1 teaspoon salt

1½ teaspoons curry powder

1½ cups plus 2 tablespoons unbleached white flour

¼ cup bran flakes

¼ cup oatmeal

1 medium egg

½ cup water

1½ tablespoons honey

1½ tablespoons butter, at room temperature

2 teaspoons yeast

⅓ cup unsalted pistachios, shelled

Place all the ingredients except the yeast and pistachios in the machine. Place the yeast in the dispenser. Program for Basic Bread and press Start. Add the pistachios when the prekneading is completed.

FENNEL PEPPERONI BREAD

While this bread baked, the house was filled with a tantalizing aroma. The family gathered as it was removed from the machine, each person clamoring for a taste. This sturdy loaf is high and studded with tiny bits of pepperoni and fennel seed. Perfect for sandwiches or canapés and wonderful toasted and served with omelets.

DAK/Welbilt

1 tablespoon yeast

3 cups unbleached white flour

¼ cup rye flour

1 tablespoon fennel seeds

1 cup flat beer (see Note)

1 tablespoon Dijon mustard

2 tablespoons olive oil OR garlic oil

1 teaspoon garlic salt OR 1 teaspoon salt
and 1 teaspoon chopped garlic

¾ cup hard pepperoni, sliced into very
thin rounds and then cut in half

Have all the ingredients at room temperature. Place all the ingredients in the machine, program for White Bread, and press Start.

Black & Decker, Betty Crocker, Breadman/Trillium, Hitachi, Large Toastmaster, and Williams-Sonoma

¾ cup flat beer (see Note)

1 tablespoon Dijon mustard

2 tablespoons olive oil OR garlic oil

1 teaspoon garlic salt OR 1 teaspoon salt
and 1 teaspoon chopped garlic

½ cup hard pepperoni, sliced into very
thin rounds and then cut in half

2¼ cups unbleached white flour

¼ cup rye flour

1 tablespoon fennel seeds

2½ teaspoons yeast (2 teaspoons for
the Black & Decker, the Breadman/
Trillium, and Toastmaster)

Place all the ingredients in the machine, program for Bread, Basic Bread, Basic Wheat, Basic, or White/Whole Grain, and press Start.

219

PANASONIC/NATIONAL

2¾ cups unbleached white flour

¼ cup rye flour

1 tablespoon fennel seeds

1 cup flat beer (see Note)

1 tablespoon Dijon mustard

2 tablespoons olive oil OR garlic oil

1 teaspoon garlic salt OR 1 teaspoon salt
  and 1 teaspoon chopped garlic

¾ cup hard pepperoni, sliced into very
  thin rounds and then cut in half

2½ teaspoons yeast

Place all the ingredients except the yeast in the machine. Place the yeast in the dispenser. Program for Basic Bread and press Start.

REGAL

¾ cup flat beer (see Note)

1 tablespoon Dijon mustard

2 tablespoons olive oil OR garlic oil

1 teaspoon garlic salt OR 1 teaspoon salt
  and 1 teaspoon chopped garlic

½ cup hard pepperoni, sliced into very
  thin rounds and then cut in half

2¼ cups unbleached white flour

¼ cup rye flour

1 tablespoon fennel seeds

2½ teaspoons yeast

Place all the ingredients in the machine, program for Bread, and press Start.

LARGE OSTER, WEST BEND, LARGE PILLSBURY, AND LARGE ZOJIRUSHI

1 cup flat beer (see Note)

1 tablespoon Dijon mustard

2 tablespoons olive oil OR garlic oil

1 teaspoon garlic salt OR 1 teaspoon salt
  and 1 teaspoon chopped garlic

3 cups unbleached white flour

¼ cup rye flour

1 tablespoon fennel seeds

¾ cup hard pepperoni, sliced into very
  thin rounds and then cut in half

1 tablespoon yeast

Place all the ingredients in the machine, program for Basic White Bread, Basic, White, or White/Whole Grain, and press Start or On.

....

MAXIM, SMALL OSTER, SMALL PILLSBURY, SANYO, SUNBEAM, SMALL TOASTMASTER, AND SMALL ZOJIRUSHI

⅔ cup flat beer (see Note)

2 teaspoons Dijon mustard

1 tablespoon olive oil OR garlic oil

½ teaspoon garlic salt OR ½ teaspoon salt and ½ teaspoon chopped garlic

½ cup hard pepperoni, sliced into very thin rounds and then cut in half

1½ cups unbleached white flour

2 tablespoons rye flour

2 teaspoons fennel seeds

1½ teaspoons yeast

Place all the ingredients in the machine, program for Standard, Basic, White, Basic Bread, or Bread, and press Start.

....

SMALL WELBILT

1½ teaspoons yeast

1½ cups unbleached white flour

2 tablespoons rye flour

2 teaspoons fennel seeds

⅔ cup flat beer (see Note)

2 teaspoons Dijon mustard

1 tablespoon olive oil OR garlic oil

½ teaspoon garlic salt OR ½ teaspoon salt and ½ teaspoon chopped garlic

½ cup hard pepperoni, sliced into very thin rounds and then cut in half

Have the ingredients at room temperature. Place all the ingredients in the machine, program for Medium, and press Start.

....

221

Small Panasonic/National

1½ cups unbleached white flour

2 tablespoons rye flour

2 teaspoons fennel seeds

½ teaspoon garlic salt OR ½ teaspoon
salt and ½ teaspoon chopped garlic

⅔ cup flat beer (see Note)

2 teaspoons Dijon mustard

1 tablespoon olive oil OR garlic oil

½ cup hard pepperoni, sliced into very
thin rounds and then cut in half

1½ teaspoons yeast

Place all the ingredients except the yeast in the machine. Place the yeast in the dispenser. Program for Basic Bread and press Start.

NOTE: If you are in a hurry and only have fizzy beer, heat it in a small pan and then let it cool in the freezer until it is just warm.

CHEESE
BREADS

STILTON PARMESAN BREAD

This magnificently aromatic loaf rises about two thirds high in the machine. It has a heavy, moist, rich texture, it's golden yellow in color, and has a powerfully assertive cheese aroma and taste.

DAK/Welbilt

1 tablespoon yeast

2½ cups unbleached white flour

⅓ cup water

⅓ cup chopped red (Bermuda) onions

2 extra-large eggs

5 tablespoons butter

5 ounces Stilton cheese, crumbled

1 cup freshly grated Parmesan cheese

Have all the ingredients at room temperature. Place all the ingredients in the machine, program for White Bread, and press Start.

Black & Decker, Betty Crocker, Breadman/Trillium, Hitachi, Regal, Large Toastmaster, and Williams-Sonoma

⅓ cup water

2 extra-large eggs

⅓ cup chopped red (Bermuda) onions

5 tablespoons butter, softened

2½ cups unbleached white flour

5 ounces Stilton cheese, crumbled

1 cup freshly grated Parmesan cheese

2½ teaspoons yeast

Place all the ingredients in the machine, program for Bread, Basic Bread, Basic Wheat, or Basic, and press Start.

PANASONIC/NATIONAL

2½ cups unbleached white flour

5 tablespoons butter, softened

2 extra-large eggs

1 cup freshly grated Parmesan cheese

5 ounces Stilton cheese, crumbled

⅓ cup water

⅓ cup chopped red (Bermuda) onions

1 tablespoon yeast

Place all the ingredients except the yeast in the machine. Place the yeast in the dispenser. Program for Basic Bread and press Start.

LARGE OSTER, WEST BEND, LARGE PILLSBURY, AND LARGE ZOJIRUSHI

⅓ cup water

2 extra-large eggs

⅓ cup chopped red (Bermuda) onions

5 tablespoons butter, softened

5 ounces Stilton cheese, crumbled

1 cup freshly grated Parmesan cheese

2½ cups unbleached white flour

1 tablespoon yeast

Place all the ingredients in the machine, program for Basic White Bread, Basic, White, or White/Whole Grain, and press Start or On.

MAXIM, SMALL OSTER, SMALL PILLSBURY, SANYO, SUNBEAM, SMALL TOASTMASTER, AND SMALL ZOJIRUSHI

¼ cup water

2 medium eggs OR 1 extra-large egg

¼ cup chopped red (Bermuda) onions

3 tablespoons butter

⅓ cup Stilton cheese, crumbled

½ cup freshly grated Parmesan cheese

1¼ cups unbleached white flour

2 teaspoons yeast

Have all the ingredients at room temperature. Place all the ingredients in the machine, program for Standard, Basic, White, Basic Bread, or Bread, and press Start.

SMALL WELBILT

2 teaspoons yeast
1¼ cups unbleached white flour
¼ cup water
2 medium eggs OR 1 extra-large egg

3 tablespoons butter
¼ cup chopped red (Bermuda) onions
⅓ cup Stilton cheese, crumbled
½ cup freshly grated Parmesan cheese

Have all the ingredients at room temperature. Place all the ingredients in the machine, program for Medium, and press Start.

SMALL PANASONIC/NATIONAL

1¼ cups unbleached white flour
¼ cup water
2 medium eggs OR 1 extra-large egg
3 tablespoons butter, softened

¼ cup chopped red (Bermuda) onions
⅓ cup Stilton cheese, crumbled
½ cup freshly grated Parmesan cheese
2 teaspoons yeast

Place all the ingredients except the yeast in the machine. Place the yeast in the dispenser. Program for Basic Bread and press Start.

Variation: Substitute Roquefort cheese for Stilton.

CHEESE CHILE CORN BREAD

Although this loaf will sink a bit in the center, that won't affect its sweet and spicy taste, or the texture, which is moist, yet crunchy. Serve this with a bowl of chili or as the base for Sloppy Joes.

DAK/Welbilt

2½ teaspoons yeast

2½ cups unbleached white flour

¾ cup cornmeal

1 teaspoon salt

½ cup corn (canned, fresh, or defrosted frozen), drained

½ cup freshly grated Cheddar cheese

1 tablespoon chopped canned chiles (mild, medium, or hot, depending on your taste)

2 tablespoons chili oil

1 extra-large egg

¾ cup flat beer (see Note)

Have all the ingredients at room temperature. Place all the ingredients in the machine, program for White Bread, and press Start.

Black & Decker, Betty Crocker, Breadman/Trillium, Hitachi, Large Toastmaster, and Williams-Sonoma

½ cup corn (canned, fresh, or defrosted frozen), drained

½ cup freshly grated Cheddar cheese

1 tablespoon chopped canned chiles (mild, medium, or hot, depending on your taste)

2 tablespoons chili oil

1 extra-large egg

¾ cup flat beer (see Note)

2½ cups unbleached white flour

¾ cup cornmeal

1 teaspoon salt

2½ teaspoons yeast (2 teaspoons for the Black & Decker, Large Toastmaster and Breadman/Trillium)

Place all the ingredients in the machine, program for Bread, Basic Bread, Basic Wheat, Basic, White, or White/Whole Grain, and press Start.

....

PANASONIC/NATIONAL

2½ cups unbleached white flour

¾ cup cornmeal

1 teaspoon salt

½ cup corn (canned, fresh, or defrosted frozen), drained

½ cup freshly grated Cheddar cheese

1 tablespoon chopped canned chiles (mild, medium, or hot, depending on your taste)

2 tablespoons chili oil

1 extra-large egg

¾ cup flat beer (see Note)

2½ teaspoons yeast

Place all the ingredients except the yeast in the machine. Place the yeast in the dispenser. Program for Basic Bread and press Start.

....

REGAL, LARGE OSTER, WEST BEND, LARGE PILLSBURY, AND LARGE ZOJIRUSHI

½ cup corn (canned, fresh, or defrosted frozen), drained

⅓ cup freshly grated Cheddar cheese

1 tablespoon chopped canned chiles (mild, medium, or hot, depending on your taste)

2 tablespoons chili oil

1 extra-large egg

¾ cup flat beer (see Note)

3 cups unbleached white flour

½ cup cornmeal

1½ teaspoons salt

2½ teaspoons yeast

Place all the ingredients in the machine, program for Bread, Basic Bread, Basic Wheat, Basic, White, White/Whole Grain, or Basic White Bread, and press Start or On.

....

MAXIM, SMALL OSTER, SMALL PILLSBURY, SANYO, SUNBEAM, SMALL TOASTMASTER, AND SMALL ZOJIRUSHI

⅓ cup corn (canned, fresh, or defrosted frozen), drained

¼ cup freshly grated Cheddar cheese

2 teaspoons chopped canned chiles (mild, medium, or hot, depending on your taste)

1 tablespoon chili oil

1 medium egg

½ cup flat beer (see Note)

2 cups unbleached white flour

⅓ cup cornmeal

1 teaspoon salt

1¾ teaspoons yeast

Place all the ingredients in the machine, program for Standard, Bread, Basic Bread, or White, and press Start.

SMALL WELBILT

1¾ teaspoons yeast

2 cups unbleached white flour

⅓ cup cornmeal

1 teaspoon salt

⅓ cup corn (canned, fresh, or defrosted frozen), drained

¼ cup freshly grated Cheddar cheese

2 teaspoons chopped canned chiles (mild, medium, or hot, depending on your taste)

1 tablespoon chili oil

1 medium egg

½ cup flat beer (see Note)

Have all the ingredients at room temperature. Place all the ingredients in the machine, program for Medium, and press Start.

Small Panasonic/National

2 cups unbleached white flour

⅓ cup cornmeal

1 teaspoon salt

⅓ cup corn (canned, fresh, or defrosted frozen), drained

¼ cup freshly grated Cheddar cheese

2 teaspoons chopped canned chiles (mild, medium, or hot, depending on your taste)

1 tablespoon chili oil

1 medium egg

½ cup flat beer (see Note)

1¾ teaspoons yeast

Place all the ingredients except the yeast in the machine. Place the yeast in the dispenser. Program for Basic Bread and press Start.

NOTE: If you don't want to wait around for the beer to become flat on its own, pour it into a small saucepan and heat it to a simmer. By the time the beer cools down, it will be flat.

Cheese and Chile Corn Bread Rolls: Place all the ingredients in the machine, program for Dough, and press Start. Remove the dough at the end of the cycle and place it on a floured board. Cover with a cloth and allow to rest for 20 minutes. Butter or grease a baking sheet or 12-cup muffin tin. Divide the dough into 12 pieces (large machines) or 8 pieces (small machines) and shape into balls. Place the balls in the muffin tin or 3 inches apart on the cookie sheet. In a small bowl, lightly beat 1 egg white and 1 tablespoon water. Brush the rolls with the egg glaze and sprinkle with grated Parmesan cheese or sesame seeds, if desired. Allow the dough to rise, uncovered, in a warm, draft-free place for about 40 minutes, or until doubled in bulk.

Preheat the oven to 375°F with the rack in the center position. Bake for 15 to 20 minutes, or until the tops are brown.

PIZZAGENA–BOSTON EASTER BREAD

This glorious bread served with salad can be a meal in itself. The compact loaf won't rise very much and tends to sink in a bit at the top because of the cheese. However, the taste is sublime. This bread is a tapestry of Italian flavors and should be enjoyed either right out of the machine or as soon as possible after baking.

....

DAK/Welbilt

1 tablespoon yeast

2 tablespoons sugar

2½ cups unbleached white flour

½ cup cornmeal

¾ cup plus 2 tablespoons water

1 extra-large egg

2 tablespoons vegetable oil OR garlic oil

½ cup diced hard smoked cheese (such as smoked Gouda)

½ cup prosciutto, cut into ½-inch slices and then cubed

Have all the ingredients at room temperature. Place all the ingredients except the prosciutto in the machine, program for White Bread, and press Start. When the beeper sounds at the end of the second kneading, add the prosciutto.

....

Black & Decker, Betty Crocker, Breadman/Trillium, Hitachi, Large Toastmaster, and Williams-Sonoma

¾ cup plus 2 tablespoons water

1 extra-large egg

2 tablespoons vegetable oil OR garlic oil

2 tablespoons sugar

2½ cups plus 1 tablespoon unbleached white flour

½ cup cornmeal

½ cup diced hard smoked cheese (such as smoked Gouda)

2½ teaspoons yeast (1½ teaspoons for the Black & Decker and Large Toastmaster, 1 teaspoon for the Breadman/Trillium)

½ cup prosciutto, cut into ½-inch slices and then cubed

Place all the ingredients except the prosciutto in the machine, program for Mix Bread, Raisin Bread, Fruit and Nut, Basic Bread, Basic Wheat, or Basic, and press Start. Add the prosciutto when the beeper sounds or during the last 5 minutes of the final knead cycle.

....

PANASONIC/NATIONAL

2½ cups minus 2 tablespoons
   unbleached white flour

½ cup cornmeal

1 extra-large egg

¾ cup plus 2 tablespoons water

2 tablespoons vegetable oil OR garlic oil

2 tablespoons sugar

½ cup diced hard smoked cheese (such
   as smoked Gouda)

2¾ teaspoons yeast

½ cup prosciutto, cut into ½-inch
   slices and then cubed

Place all the ingredients except the yeast and prosciutto in the machine. Place the yeast in the dispenser. Program for Basic Bread and press Start. Add the prosciutto at the end of the prekneading cycle.

....

REGAL, LARGE OSTER, WEST BEND, LARGE PILLSBURY, AND LARGE ZOJIRUSHI

¾ cup plus 2 tablespoons water

1 extra-large egg

2 tablespoons vegetable oil OR garlic oil

2 tablespoons sugar

2½ cups minus 2 tablespoons
   unbleached white flour

½ cup cornmeal

½ cup diced hard smoked cheese (such
   as smoked Gouda)

1 tablespoon yeast

½ cup prosciutto, cut into ½-inch
   slices and then cubed

Place all the ingredients except the prosciutto in the machine, program for Raisin Bread, Basic, White, or White/Whole Grain, and press Start or On. Add the prosciutto when the beeper sounds or during the last 5 minutes of the final knead cycle.

....

Maxim, Small Oster, Small Pillsbury, Sanyo, Sunbeam, Small Toastmaster, and Small Zojirushi

⅓ cup water

1 medium egg

1 tablespoon plus 1 teaspoon vegetable oil OR garlic oil

⅓ cup diced hard smoked cheese (such as smoked Gouda)

⅓ cup prosciutto, cut into ½-inch slices and then cubed

1 tablespoon plus 1 teaspoon sugar

1⅔ cups unbleached white flour

⅓ cup cornmeal

2½ teaspoons yeast

Place all the ingredients except the prosciutto in the machine, program for Standard, Basic, White, Basic Bread, or Bread, and press Start. Add the prosciutto when the beeper sounds or during the last 5 minutes of the final knead cycle.

Small Welbilt

2 teaspoons yeast

1 tablespoon plus 1 teaspoon sugar

1⅔ cups unbleached white flour

⅓ cup cornmeal

⅓ cup water

1 medium egg

1 tablespoon plus 1 teaspoon vegetable oil OR garlic oil

⅓ cup diced hard smoked cheese (such as smoked Gouda)

⅓ cup prosciutto, cut into ½-inch slices and then cubed

Have all the ingredients at room temperature. Place all the ingredients except the prosciutto in the machine, program for Medium, and press Start. When the beeper sounds at the end of the second kneading, add the prosciutto.

Small Panasonic/National

1 tablespoon plus 1 teaspoon sugar
1⅔ cups unbleached white flour
⅓ cup cornmeal
⅓ cup water
1 medium egg
1 tablespoon plus 1 teaspoon vegetable
   oil OR garlic oil

⅓ cup diced hard smoked cheese (such
   as smoked Gouda)
⅓ cup prosciutto, cut into ½-inch
   slices and then cubed
2½ teaspoons yeast

Place all the ingredients except the yeast and prosciutto in the machine. Place the yeast in the dispenser. Program for Basic Bread and press Start. Add the prosciutto at the end of the prekneading cycle.

AVERY ISLAND HOT BREAD

This jump-in-your-mouth loaf stars one of our all-time favorite condiments—Tabasco Sauce, which is made in only one place in this country, Avery Island, Louisiana. Accept no substitutes if you want the authentic version of this bread. The other special ingredients are chili honey, which is available by mail order (page 337), and pepper-flavored vodka, which is readily available in liquor stores. You may substitute regular vodka if you wish.

....

DAK/Welbilt

1 tablespoon yeast

2 teaspoons salt

½ teaspoon ground coriander

1 cup cornmeal

2 cups unbleached white flour

1 cup coarsely chopped red peppers, sautéed in 3 tablespoons olive oil, OR chili oil

1 tablespoon chopped garlic

1 tablespoon chopped canned chiles (mild, medium, or hot is up to you)

½ cup sour cream

⅓ cup freshly grated Cheddar cheese

1 extra-large egg

10 drops Tabasco Sauce

1 tablespoon regular honey OR chili honey

¼ cup pepper-flavored (or regular) vodka

Have all the ingredients at room temperature. Place all the ingredients in the machine, program for White Bread, and press Start.

....

BLACK & DECKER, BETTY CROCKER, BREADMAN/TRILLIUM, HITACHI, LARGE TOASTMASTER, AND WILLIAMS-SONOMA

1 cup coarsely chopped red peppers, sautéed in 3 tablespoons olive oil, OR chili oil

1 tablespoon chopped garlic

1 tablespoon chopped canned chiles (mild, medium, or hot is up to you)

½ cup sour cream

⅓ cup freshly grated Cheddar cheese

1 extra-large egg

10 drops Tabasco Sauce

1 tablespoon regular honey OR chili honey

¼ cup pepper-flavored (or regular) vodka

2 teaspoons salt

½ teaspoon ground coriander

1 cup cornmeal

2 cups unbleached white flour

2½ teaspoons yeast (2 teaspoons for the Black & Decker, Large Toastmaster, and Breadman/Trillium)

Have all the ingredients at room temperature (even though the machine doesn't specify this, for this recipe it is necessary). Place all the ingredients in the machine, program for Bread, Basic Bread, Basic Wheat, or Basic, and press Start.

PANASONIC/NATIONAL

1 cup coarsely chopped red peppers, sautéed in 3 tablespoons olive oil, OR chili oil

1 tablespoon chopped garlic

1 tablespoon chopped canned chiles (mild, medium, or hot is up to you)

½ cup sour cream

⅓ cup freshly grated Cheddar cheese

1 extra-large egg

10 drops Tabasco Sauce

1 tablespoon regular honey OR chili honey

¼ cup pepper-flavored (or regular) vodka

2 teaspoons salt

½ teaspoon ground coriander

1 cup cornmeal

2 cups unbleached white flour

2½ teaspoons yeast

Have all the ingredients at room temperature. Place all the ingredients except the yeast in the machine. Place the yeast in the dispenser. Program for Basic Bread and press Start.

Regal

½ cup sour cream

⅓ cup freshly grated Cheddar cheese

1 extra-large egg

10 drops Tabasco Sauce

1 tablespoon regular honey OR chili
   honey

¼ cup pepper-flavored (or regular)
   vodka

2 teaspoons salt

½ teaspoon ground coriander

1 cup cornmeal

2 cups unbleached white flour

1 cup coarsely chopped red peppers,
   sautéed in 3 tablespoons olive oil, OR
   chili oil

1 tablespoon chopped garlic

1 tablespoon chopped canned chiles
   (mild, medium, or hot is up to you)

2½ teaspoons yeast

Have all the ingredients at room temperature. Place all the ingredients in the machine, program for Bread, and press Start.

....

Large Oster, West Bend, Large Pillsbury, and Large Zojirushi

1 cup coarsely chopped red peppers,
   sautéed in 3 tablespoons olive oil, OR
   chili oil

1 tablespoon chopped garlic

1 tablespoon chopped canned chiles
   (mild, medium, or hot is up to you)

½ cup sour cream

⅓ cup freshly grated Cheddar cheese

1 extra-large egg

1 tablespoon regular honey OR chili
   honey

¼ cup pepper-flavored (or regular)
   vodka

2 teaspoons salt

10 drops Tabasco Sauce

½ teaspoon ground coriander

1 cup cornmeal

2 cups unbleached white flour

1 tablespoon yeast

Have all the ingredients at room temperature (even though the machine doesn't specify this, for this recipe it is necessary). Place all the ingredients in the machine, program for White Bread, Basic, White, or White/Whole Grain, and press Start or On.

Maxim, Small Oster, Small Pillsbury, Sanyo, Sunbeam, Small Toastmaster, and Small Zojirushi

⅔ cup coarsely chopped red peppers, sautéed in 2 tablespoons olive oil, OR chili oil

2 teaspoons chopped garlic

2 teaspoons chopped canned chiles (mild, medium, or hot is up to you)

⅓ cup sour cream

¼ cup freshly grated Cheddar cheese

1 medium egg

7 to 8 drops Tabasco Sauce

2 teaspoons regular honey OR chili honey

3 tablespoons pepper-flavored (or regular) vodka

1 teaspoon salt

¼ teaspoon ground coriander

⅔ cup cornmeal

1⅓ cups plus 2 tablespoons unbleached white flour

2 teaspoons yeast

Have all the ingredients at room temperature. Place all the ingredients in the machine, program for Standard, Basic, White, Basic Bread, or Bread, and press Start.

....

Small Welbilt

2 teaspoons yeast

1 teaspoon salt

¼ teaspoon ground coriander

⅔ cup cornmeal

1⅓ cups unbleached white flour

⅔ cup coarsely chopped red peppers, sautéed in 2 tablespoons olive oil, OR chili oil

2 teaspoons chopped garlic

2 teaspoons chopped canned chiles (mild, medium, or hot is up to you)

⅓ cup sour cream

¼ cup freshly grated Cheddar cheese

1 medium egg

7 to 8 drops Tabasco Sauce

2 teaspoons regular honey OR chili honey

3 tablespoons pepper-flavored (or regular) vodka

Have all the ingredients at room temperature. Place all the ingredients in the machine, program for Medium, and press Start.

SMALL PANASONIC/NATIONAL

3 tablespoons pepper-flavored (or regular) vodka

1 teaspoon salt

¼ teaspoon ground coriander

⅔ cup cornmeal

1⅓ cups plus 2 tablespoons unbleached white flour

⅔ cup coarsely chopped red peppers, sautéed in 2 tablespoons olive oil, OR chili oil

2 teaspoons chopped garlic

2 teaspoons chopped canned chiles (mild, medium, or hot is up to you)

⅓ cup sour cream

¼ cup freshly grated Cheddar cheese

1 medium egg

7 to 8 drops Tabasco Sauce

2 teaspoons regular honey OR chili honey

2 teaspoons yeast

Have all the ingredients at room temperature. Place all the ingredients except the yeast in the machine. Place the yeast in the dispenser. Program for Basic Bread and press Start.

FRUIT
AND SPICE
BREADS

MARY ANN MCKENNA'S OATMEAL APPLESAUCE BREAD

Lora talked her beloved mailman, Bob McKenna, into getting a bread machine for his family for Christmas last year. Among the triumphs from their kitchen is the following recipe created by Mary Ann McKenna, Bob and Ann's eldest daughter, who is a student at Brandeis University. This is a moist and fragrant bread that tastes great with a slice of Cheddar cheese melted on top.

DAK/Welbilt

1 tablespoon yeast

3 cups unbleached white flour

⅓ cup quick-cooking oatmeal

1½ tablespoons sugar

2 tablespoons nonfat dry milk

1 teaspoon salt

2 teaspoons apple pie spice

1 cup minus 2 tablespoons apple cider
  OR apple juice

2 tablespoons butter

1 cup peeled and chopped apple

Have all the ingredients at room temperature. Place all the ingredients in the machine, program for White Bread, and press Start.

Large Oster, West Bend, Large Pillsbury, Large Zojirushi, Betty Crocker, Hitachi, and Williams-Sonoma

¾ cup plus 2 tablespoons apple cider OR
  apple juice

1 cup peeled and chopped apple

1½ tablespoons butter

3 cups unbleached white flour

⅓ cup quick-cooking oatmeal

1½ tablespoons sugar

2 tablespoons nonfat dry milk

1 teaspoon salt

2 teaspoons apple pie spice

2½ teaspoons yeast

Place all the ingredients in the machine, program for Bread, Basic Bread, Basic Wheat, Basic, White, White/Whole Grain, or Basic White Bread, and press Start or On.

PANASONIC/NATIONAL

3 cups unbleached white flour

⅓ cup quick-cooking oatmeal

1½ tablespoons sugar

2 tablespoons nonfat dry milk

1 teaspoon salt

2 teaspoons apple pie spice

¾ cup minus 2 tablespoons apple cider
  OR apple juice

1 cup peeled and chopped apple

1½ tablespoons butter

2½ teaspoons yeast

Place all the ingredients except the yeast in the machine. Place the yeast in the dispenser. Program for Basic Bread and press Start.

REGAL, BLACK & DECKER, BREADMAN/TRILLIUM, AND LARGE TOASTMASTER

¾ cup apple cider OR apple juice

1 tablespoon butter

1 medium apple, peeled and chopped

2 cups plus 2 tablespoons unbleached
  white flour

¼ cup quick-cooking oatmeal

1 tablespoon sugar

1 tablespoon nonfat dry milk

1 teaspoon salt

1 teaspoon apple pie spice

2 teaspoons yeast

Place all the ingredients in the machine, program for Standard, and press Start.

MAXIM, SMALL OSTER, SMALL PILLSBURY, SANYO, SUNBEAM, SMALL TOASTMASTER, AND SMALL ZOJIRUSHI

⅔ cup apple cider OR apple juice

1 tablespoon butter, at room
  temperature

1 medium apple, peeled and chopped

1 tablespoon nonfat dry milk

¼ cup quick-cooking oatmeal

1 tablespoon sugar

2¼ cups unbleached white flour

1 teaspoon salt

1 teaspoon apple pie spice

1½ teaspoons yeast

Place all the ingredients in the machine, program for Standard, Basic, White, Basic Bread, or Bread, and press Start.

Small Welbilt

1½ teaspoons yeast

2¼ cups unbleached white flour

¼ cup quick-cooking oatmeal

1 tablespoon sugar

1 tablespoon nonfat dry milk

1 teaspoon salt

1 teaspoon apple pie spice

⅔ cup apple cider OR apple juice

1 tablespoon butter

1 medium apple, peeled and chopped

Have all the ingredients at room temperature. Place all the ingredients in the machine, program for White Bread, and press Start.

Small Panasonic/National

2¼ cups unbleached white flour

¼ cup quick-cooking oatmeal

1 tablespoon sugar

1 tablespoon nonfat dry milk

1 teaspoon salt

1 teaspoon apple pie spice

⅔ cup apple cider OR apple juice

1 tablespoon butter, at room temperature

1 medium apple, peeled and chopped

1½ teaspoons yeast

Place all the ingredients except the yeast in the machine. Place the yeast in the dispenser. Program for Basic Bread and press Start.

BANANA OATMEAL BREAD

Karen Slater invented this recipe. It has all the wonderful qualities of a banana quick bread—flavor and moistness—plus the characteristics that we love in yeast bread—great texture and a heavenly crust. The riper the bananas, the more flavor you'll get. Steel-cut oats are the old-fashioned kind that are not precooked, quick-cooking, or instant. You can find them in health food stores or through many of the resources listed at the end of the book.

DAK/Welbilt

1 tablespoon yeast

1½ teaspoons salt

4 tablespoons powdered buttermilk

1 cup quick-cooking oats

2½ cups unbleached white flour

3 tablespoons brown sugar

¼ cup water

⅓ cup steel-cut oats, soaked in ⅓ cup boiling water until the mixture is at room temperature

1 extra-large egg

2 tablespoons vegetable oil

1 cup mashed very ripe bananas

Have all the ingredients at room temperature. Place all the ingredients in the machine, program for White Bread, and press Start.

Black & Decker, Betty Crocker, Breadman/Trillium, Hitachi, Large Toastmaster, and Williams-Sonoma

¼ cup water

1 extra-large egg

2 tablespoons vegetable oil

1 cup mashed very ripe bananas

3 tablespoons brown sugar

1½ teaspoons salt

4 tablespoons powdered buttermilk

1 cup quick-cooking oats

2½ cups unbleached white flour

⅓ cup steel-cut oats, soaked in ⅓ cup boiling water until the mixture is at room temperature

2 teaspoons yeast

246

Place all the ingredients in the machine, program for Bread, Basic Bread, Basic Wheat, Basic, White, or White/Whole Grain, and press Start.

PANASONIC/NATIONAL

1½ teaspoons salt

4 tablespoons powdered buttermilk

1 cup quick-cooking oats

2½ cups unbleached white flour

3 tablespoons brown sugar

⅓ cup steel-cut oats, soaked in ⅓ cup
    boiling water until the mixture is at
    room temperature

¼ cup water

1 extra-large egg

2 tablespoons vegetable oil

1 cup mashed very ripe bananas

1 tablespoon yeast

Place all the ingredients except the yeast in the machine. Place the yeast in the dispenser. Program for Basic Bread and press Start.

REGAL, LARGE OSTER, WEST BEND, LARGE PILLSBURY, AND LARGE ZOJIRUSHI

¼ cup water

1 extra-large egg

2 tablespoons vegetable oil

1 cup mashed very ripe bananas

3 tablespoons brown sugar

1½ teaspoons salt

4 tablespoons powdered buttermilk

1 cup quick-cooking oats

2½ cups unbleached white flour

⅓ cup steel-cut oats, soaked in ⅓ cup
    boiling water until the mixture is at
    room temperature

1 tablespoon yeast

Place all the ingredients in the machine, program for Bread, Basic Bread, Basic Wheat, Basic, White, White/Whole Grain, or White Bread, and press Start or On.

Maxim, Small Oster, Small Pillsbury, Sanyo, Sunbeam, Small Toastmaster, and Small Zojirushi

¼ cup steel-cut oats, soaked in ¼ cup
   boiling water until the mixture is at
   room temperature
3 tablespoons water
1 medium egg
1½ tablespoons vegetable oil
⅔ cup mashed very ripe bananas

1 teaspoon salt
3 tablespoons powdered buttermilk
¾ cup quick-cooking oats
1½ cups unbleached white flour
2 tablespoons brown sugar
2 teaspoons yeast

Place all the ingredients in the machine, program for Standard, Basic, White, Basic Bread, or Bread, and press Start.

Small Welbilt

2 teaspoons yeast
1 teaspoon salt
3 tablespoons powdered buttermilk
¾ cup quick-cooking oats
1½ cups unbleached white flour
2 tablespoons brown sugar

¼ cup steel-cut oats, soaked in ¼ cup
   boiling water until the mixture is at
   room temperature
3 tablespoons water
1 medium egg
1½ tablespoons vegetable oil
⅔ cup mashed very ripe bananas

Have all the ingredients at room temperature. Place all the ingredients in the machine, program for Medium, and press Start.

Small Panasonic/National

¼ cup steel-cut oats, soaked in ¼ cup
boiling water until the mixture is at
room temperature

1 teaspoon salt

3 tablespoons powdered buttermilk

¾ cup quick-cooking oats

1½ cups unbleached white flour

2 tablespoons brown sugar

3 tablespoons water

1 medium egg

1½ tablespoons vegetable oil

⅔ cup mashed very ripe bananas

2 teaspoons yeast

Place all the ingredients except the yeast in the machine. Place the yeast in the
dispenser. Program for Basic Bread and press Start.

Variation: Program for Raisin Bread (or White Bread in machines without Raisin
Bread settings). When the beeper sounds, add ½ cup raisins, currants, or other dried
fruit such as apricots, prunes, pears, or peaches, cut into small pieces; or add ½ cup
chopped nuts of your choice.

RAISIN BUTTERMILK BREAD

A raisin bread that makes eating breakfast something to look forward to. Tender and fragrant with raisins and the nuts of your choice.

....

DAK/Welbilt

2½ teaspoons yeast

2 cups unbleached white flour

1 cup whole wheat flour

1 teaspoon salt

1 cup plus 1 tablespoon buttermilk OR 1 cup plus 1 tablespoon water and 5 tablespoons powdered buttermilk

2 tablespoons vegetable oil (we used canola)

⅓ cup raisins

⅓ cup coarsely broken nuts of your choice, such as walnuts, pecans, hazelnuts, or pistachios

Have all the ingredients at room temperature. Place all the ingredients except the raisins and nuts in the machine, program for White Bread, and press Start. Add the raisins and nuts when the beeper sounds during the last part of the second kneading.

....

Black & Decker, Betty Crocker, Breadman/Trillium, Hitachi, Large Toastmaster, Williams-Sonoma, Regal, Large Oster, West Bend, Large Pillsbury, and Large Zojirushi

2 tablespoons vegetable oil (we used canola)

1 cup plus 1 tablespoon buttermilk OR 1 cup plus 1 tablespoon water and 5 tablespoons powdered buttermilk

2 cups unbleached white flour

1 cup whole wheat flour

1 teaspoon salt

2½ teaspoons yeast

⅓ cup raisins

⅓ cup coarsely broken nuts of your choice, such as walnuts, pecans, hazelnuts, or pistachios

Place all the ingredients except the raisins and nuts in the machine, program for Mix Bread, Fruit and Nut, Raisin Bread, Basic Bread, Basic Wheat, Basic, White, or

White/Whole Grain, and press Start or On. Add the raisins and nuts when the beeper sounds or during the last 5 minutes of the final knead cycle.

....

PANASONIC/NATIONAL

2 cups unbleached white flour

1 cup whole wheat flour

1 teaspoon salt

2 tablespoons vegetable oil (we used canola)

1 cup plus 1 tablespoon buttermilk OR 1 cup plus 1 tablespoon water and 5 tablespoons powdered buttermilk

2½ teaspoons yeast

⅓ cup raisins

⅓ cup coarsely broken nuts of your choice, such as walnuts, pecans, hazelnuts, or pistachios

Place all the ingredients except the yeast, raisins, and nuts in the machine. Place the yeast in the dispenser. Program for Basic Bread and press Start. Add the raisins and nuts at the end of the prekneading cycle.

....

MAXIM, SMALL OSTER, SMALL PILLSBURY, SANYO, SUNBEAM, SMALL TOASTMASTER, AND SMALL ZOJIRUSHI

2 tablespoons vegetable oil (we used canola)

¾ cup plus 2 tablespoons buttermilk OR ¾ cup plus 2 tablespoons water and 5 tablespoons powdered buttermilk

1 cup unbleached white flour

1 cup whole wheat flour

½ teaspoon salt

1½ teaspoons yeast

⅓ cup raisins

⅓ cup coarsely broken nuts of your choice, such as walnuts, pecans, hazelnuts, or pistachios

Place all the ingredients except the raisins and nuts in the machine, program for Standard, Basic, White, Basic Bread, or Bread, and press Start. Add the raisins and nuts when the beeper sounds or during the last 5 minutes of the final knead cycle.

SMALL WELBILT

1½ teaspoons yeast

1 cup unbleached white flour

1 cup whole wheat flour

½ teaspoon salt

2 tablespoons vegetable oil (we used canola)

¾ cup plus 2 tablespoons buttermilk OR
¾ cup plus 2 tablespoons water and
5 tablespoons powdered buttermilk

⅓ cup raisins

⅓ cup coarsely broken nuts of your choice, such as walnuts, pecans, hazelnuts, or pistachios

Have all the ingredients at room temperature. Place all the ingredients except the raisins and nuts in the machine, program for Medium, and press Start. Add the raisins and nuts when the beeper sounds or during the last 5 minutes of the final knead cycle.

SMALL PANASONIC/NATIONAL

1 cup unbleached white flour

1 cup whole wheat flour

½ teaspoon salt

2 tablespoons vegetable oil (we used canola)

¾ cup plus 2 tablespoons buttermilk OR
¾ cup plus 2 tablespoons water and
5 tablespoons powdered buttermilk

1½ teaspoons yeast

⅓ cup raisins

⅓ cup coarsely broken nuts of your choice, such as walnuts, pecans, hazelnuts, or pistachios

Place all the ingredients except the yeast, raisins, and nuts in the machine. Place the yeast in the dispenser. Program for Basic Bread and press Start. Add the raisins and nuts during the last part of the second kneading.

SHERRIED PRUNE PECAN BREAD

To make this exquisite loaf, you must remove the dough from the machine, let it rise, and bake in a conventional oven. Even though the package says "pitted" prunes, it's a good idea to check.

....

DAK/WELBILT

¾ cup pitted prunes   ½ cup medium or dry (not cream)
                                              sherry

Combine the prunes and sherry in a small pan or covered microwavable bowl. Either simmer over medium heat for 5 minutes or microwave on high for 2 minutes. Cool to room temperature and drain off the sherry into a 1-cup glass measure.

For the Dough

1 extra-large egg, reserved sherry, and   ½ teaspoon ground cinnamon
   enough orange juice to equal 1 cup   1 teaspoon salt
   liquid total   ½ cup oat flour
1 tablespoon molasses   ½ cup oatmeal
1 tablespoon honey   ⅓ cup miller's bran
2 tablespoons vegetable oil OR 1   2⅓ cups unbleached white flour
   tablespoon vegetable oil and 1   1 tablespoon yeast
   tablespoon walnut oil   ½ cup pecans (optional—but
½ teaspoon orange oil (optional)   wonderful)
4 tablespoons powdered buttermilk

Have all the ingredients at room temperature. Place all the ingredients except the pecans in the machine in this order: the yeast first, then all the dry ingredients, then the liquid ingredients. Program for Manual and press Start. Toward the end of the second kneading, when the beeper sounds, add the pecans.

Continued

Remove the dough after the second kneading, form it into a round loaf, and place it on a greased baking sheet. Cover it with a clean cloth and place in a warm, draft-free place for 2 to 2½ hours, or until the dough has doubled in bulk. Preheat the oven to 375°F with the rack in the center position. Bake for 45 to 55 minutes, or until the bottom of the loaf sounds hollow when tapped, or until the bread has an internal temperature of 190° to 200°F.

BLACK & DECKER, BETTY CROCKER, BREADMAN/TRILLIUM, HITACHI, LARGE TOASTMASTER, AND WILLIAMS-SONOMA

¾ cup pitted prunes

½ cup medium or dry (not cream) sherry

Combine the prunes and sherry in a small pan or covered microwavable bowl. Either simmer over medium heat for 5 minutes or microwave on high for 2 minutes. Cool to room temperature and drain off the sherry into a 1-cup glass measure.

FOR THE DOUGH

1 extra-large egg, reserved sherry, and enough orange juice to equal 1-cup liquid total

1 tablespoon molasses

1 tablespoon honey

2 tablespoons vegetable oil OR 1 tablespoon vegetable oil and 1 tablespoon walnut oil

1 teaspoon salt

½ teaspoon orange oil (optional)

4 tablespoons powdered buttermilk

½ teaspoon ground cinnamon

½ cup oat flour

½ cup oatmeal

⅓ cup miller's bran

2⅓ cups unbleached white flour

2½ teaspoons yeast

½ cup pecans (optional—but wonderful)

Place all the ingredients except the pecans in the machine, program for Dough or Knead and First Rise, and press Start. When the beeper sounds or during the last 5 minutes of the final knead cycle, add the pecans.

Remove the dough after the kneading cycle, form it into a round loaf, and place it on a greased baking sheet. Cover it with a clean cloth and place in a warm, draft-free place for 2 to 2½ hours, or until the dough has doubled in bulk. Preheat the oven to 375°F with the rack in the center position. Bake for 45 to 55 minutes, or until the bottom of the loaf sounds hollow when tapped, or until the bread has an internal temperature of 190° to 200°F.

Panasonic/National

¾ cup pitted prunes

½ cup medium or dry (not cream) sherry

Combine the prunes and sherry in a small pan or covered microwavable bowl. Either simmer over medium heat for 5 minutes or microwave on high for 2 minutes. Cool to room temperature and drain off the sherry into a 1-cup glass measure.

For the Dough

1 extra-large egg, reserved sherry, and enough orange juice to equal 1-cup liquid total

1 tablespoon molasses

1 tablespoon honey

2 tablespoons vegetable oil OR 1 tablespoon vegetable oil and 1 tablespoon walnut oil

1 teaspoon salt

½ teaspoon orange oil (optional)

4 tablespoons powdered buttermilk

½ teaspoon ground cinnamon

½ cup oat flour

½ cup oatmeal

⅓ cup miller's bran

2⅓ cups unbleached white flour

1 tablespoon yeast

½ cup pecans (optional—but wonderful)

Place all the ingredients except the yeast and pecans in the machine in this order: all the dry ingredients first, then all the liquid ingredients. Place the yeast in the dispenser. Program for Dough or Manual, and press Start. Add the pecans when the beeper sounds or during the last 5 minutes of the final knead cycle.

Continued

255

Remove the dough after the kneading cycle, form it into a round loaf, and place it on a greased baking sheet. Cover it with a clean cloth and place in a warm, draft-free place for 2 to 2½ hours, or until the dough has doubled in bulk. Preheat the oven to 375°F with the rack in the center position. Bake for 45 to 55 minutes, or until the bottom of the loaf sounds hollow when tapped, or until the bread has an internal temperature of 190° to 200°F.

Regal, Large Oster, West Bend, Large Pillsbury, and Large Zojirushi

¾ cup pitted prunes

½ cup medium or dry (not cream) sherry

Combine the prunes and sherry in a small pan or covered microwavable bowl. Either simmer over medium heat for 5 minutes or microwave on high for 2 minutes. Cool to room temperature and drain off the sherry into a 1-cup glass measure.

For the Dough

1 extra-large egg, reserved sherry, and enough orange juice to equal 1-cup liquid total

1 tablespoon molasses

1 tablespoon honey

2 tablespoons vegetable oil OR 1 tablespoon vegetable oil and 1 tablespoon walnut oil

1 teaspoon salt

½ teaspoon orange oil (optional)

4 tablespoons powdered buttermilk

½ teaspoon ground cinnamon

½ cup oat flour

½ cup oatmeal

⅓ cup miller's bran

2⅓ cups unbleached white flour

1 tablespoon yeast

½ cup pecans (optional—but wonderful)

Place all the ingredients except the pecans in the machine, program for Manual or Dough, and press Start or On. Add the pecans when the beeper sounds or during the last 5 minutes of the final knead cycle.

Remove the dough after the second kneading, form it into a round loaf, and

place it on a greased baking sheet. Cover it with a clean cloth and place in a warm, draft-free place for 2 to 2½ hours, or until the dough has doubled in bulk. Preheat the oven to 375°F with the rack in the center position. Bake for 45 to 55 minutes, or until the bottom of the loaf sounds hollow when tapped, or until the bread has an internal temperature of 190° to 200°F.

Maxim, Small Oster, Small Pillsbury, Sanyo, Sunbeam, Small Toastmaster, and Small Zojirushi

½ cup pitted prunes

⅓ cup medium or dry (not cream) sherry

Combine the prunes and sherry in a small pan or covered microwavable bowl. Either simmer over medium heat for 5 minutes or microwave on high for 2 minutes. Cool to room temperature and drain off the sherry into a 1-cup glass measure.

For the Dough

1 medium egg, reserved sherry, and enough orange juice to equal ⅔-cup liquid total

2 teaspoons molasses

2 teaspoons honey

1½ tablespoons vegetable oil OR 1 tablespoon vegetable oil and 2 teaspoons walnut oil

¼ teaspoon orange oil (optional)

3 tablespoons powdered buttermilk

¼ teaspoon ground cinnamon

½ teaspoon salt

¼ cup oat flour

¼ cup oatmeal

¼ cup miller's bran

1½ cups unbleached white flour

2 teaspoons yeast

½ cup pecans (optional—but wonderful)

Have all the ingredients at room temperature. Place all the ingredients except the pecans in the machine, program for Dough or Manual, and press Start. Add the pecans when the beeper sounds or during the last 5 minutes of the final knead cycle.

Remove the dough after the second kneading, form it into a round loaf, and

place it on a greased baking sheet. Cover it with a clean cloth and place in a warm, draft-free place for 2 to 2½ hours, or until the dough has doubled in bulk. Preheat the oven to 375°F with the rack in the center position. Bake for 45 to 55 minutes, or until the bottom of the loaf sounds hollow when tapped, or until the bread has an internal temperature of 190° to 200°F.

Small Welbilt

½ cup pitted prunes

⅓ cup medium or dry (not cream) sherry

Combine the prunes and sherry in a small pan or covered microwavable bowl. Either simmer over medium heat for 5 minutes or microwave on high for 2 minutes. Cool to room temperature and drain off the sherry into a 1-cup glass measure.

For the Dough

1 medium egg, reserved sherry, and enough orange juice to equal ⅔-cup liquid total

2 teaspoons molasses

2 teaspoons honey

1½ tablespoons vegetable oil or 1 tablespoon vegetable oil and 2 teaspoons walnut oil

¼ teaspoon orange oil (optional)

3 tablespoons powdered buttermilk

¼ teaspoon ground cinnamon

½ teaspoon salt

¼ cup oat flour

¼ cup oatmeal

¼ cup miller's bran

1½ cups unbleached white flour

2 teaspoons yeast

½ cup pecans (optional—but wonderful)

Have all the ingredients at room temperature. Place all the ingredients except the pecans in the machine in this order: the yeast first, then all the dry ingredients, then the liquid ingredients. Program for Manual and press Start. Add the pecans when the beeper sounds or during the last 5 minutes of the final knead cycle.

Remove the dough after the second kneading, form it into a round loaf, and

place it on a greased baking sheet. Cover it with a clean cloth and place in a warm, draft-free place for 2 to 2½ hours, or until the dough has doubled in bulk. Preheat the oven to 375°F with the rack in the center position. Bake for 45 to 55 minutes, or until the bottom of the loaf sounds hollow when tapped, or until the bread has an internal temperature of 190° to 200°F.

SMALL PANASONIC/NATIONAL

½ cup pitted prunes

⅓ cup medium or dry (not cream) sherry

Combine the prunes and sherry in a small pan or covered microwavable bowl. Either simmer over medium heat for 5 minutes or microwave on high for 2 minutes. Cool to room temperature and drain off the sherry into a 1-cup glass measure.

FOR THE DOUGH

1 medium egg, reserved sherry, and enough orange juice to equal ⅔-cup liquid total
2 teaspoons molasses
2 teaspoons honey
1½ tablespoons vegetable oil OR 1 tablespoon vegetable oil and 2 teaspoons walnut oil
¼ teaspoon orange oil (optional)
3 tablespoons powdered buttermilk

¼ teaspoon ground cinnamon
½ teaspoon salt
¼ cup oat flour
¼ cup oatmeal
¼ cup miller's bran
1½ cups unbleached white flour
2 teaspoons yeast
½ cup pecans (optional—but wonderful)

Place all the ingredients except the yeast and pecans in the machine in this order: all the dry ingredients first, then all the liquid ingredients. Place the yeast in the dispenser. Program for Dough or Manual and press Start. Add the pecans when the beeper sounds or during the last 5 minutes of the final knead cycle.

Continued

Remove the dough after the second kneading, form it into a round loaf, and place it on a greased baking sheet. Cover it with a clean cloth and place in a warm, draft-free place for 2 to 2½ hours, or until the dough has doubled in bulk. Preheat the oven to 375°F with the rack in the center position. Bake for 45 to 55 minutes, or until the bottom of the loaf sounds hollow when tapped, or until the bread has an internal temperature of 190° to 200°F.

SAFFRON CURRANT BREAD

Saffron adds a beautiful color and the brandy adds a subtle taste to this elegant bread. This bread makes wonderful French toast.

DAK/Welbilt
Ahead of Time

¾ cup water   1 generous pinch saffron

Heat the water to a simmer and stir in the saffron. Cool to lukewarm.

⅔ cup currants   3 tablespoons brandy

Place the currants and brandy in a small pan, heat to a low simmer, and let soak until ready to add. You can also do this in the microwave in a small glass dish covered with plastic wrap.

In the Bread Machine

1 tablespoon yeast   3 tablespoons honey
3 cups unbleached white flour   Water/saffron mixture (add the grains
1 teaspoon salt   of saffron)
4 tablespoons butter   3 tablespoons powdered skim milk
2 extra-large eggs

Have all the ingredients at room temperature. Place all the ingredients except the currants in the machine, program for White Bread, and press Start. When the beeper sounds, drain the currants and add them to the dough.

Black & Decker, Betty Crocker, Breadman/Trillium, Hitachi, Regal, Large Toastmaster, and Williams-Sonoma

Ahead of Time

¾ cup water   1 generous pinch saffron

Heat the water to a simmer and stir in the saffron. Cool to lukewarm.

⅔ cup currants   3 tablespoons brandy

Place the currants and brandy in a small pan, heat to a low simmer, and let soak until ready to add. You can also do this in the microwave in a small glass dish covered with plastic wrap.

In the Bread Machine

4 tablespoons butter, at room temperature   3 tablespoons powdered skim milk
2 extra-large eggs   3 cups plus 2 tablespoons unbleached
3 tablespoons honey   white flour
Water/saffron mixture (add the grains   1 teaspoon salt
   of saffron)   2 teaspoons yeast

Place all the ingredients except the currants in the machine, program for Mix Bread, Raisin Bread, Fruit and Nut, Basic, Basic Bread, White, Basic Wheat, White/Whole Grain, or Sweet, and press Start. When the beeper sounds or during the last 5 minutes of the final knead cycle, drain the currants and add them to the dough.

Panasonic/National

Ahead of Time

¾ cup water   1 generous pinch saffron

Heat the water to a simmer and stir in the saffron. Cool to lukewarm.

| ⅔ cup currants | 3 tablespoons brandy |

Place the currants and brandy in a small pan, heat to a low simmer, and let soak until ready to add. You can also do this in the microwave in a small glass dish covered with plastic wrap.

IN THE BREAD MACHINE

3 tablespoons powdered skim milk	2 extra-large eggs
3 cups unbleached white flour	3 tablespoons honey
1 teaspoon salt	Water/saffron mixture (add the grains
4 tablespoons butter, at room	of saffron)
temperature	1 tablespoon yeast

Place all the ingredients except the yeast and the currants in the machine. Place the yeast in the dispenser. Program for Basic Bread and press Start. Drain the currants and add them to the dough after the first 20 minutes of kneading.

LARGE OSTER, WEST BEND, LARGE PILLSBURY, AND LARGE ZOJIRUSHI
AHEAD OF TIME

| ¾ cup water | 1 generous pinch saffron |

Heat the water to a simmer and stir in the saffron. Cool to lukewarm.

| ⅔ cup currants | 3 tablespoons brandy |

Place the currants and brandy in a small pan, heat to a low simmer, and let soak until ready to add. You can also do this in the microwave in a small glass dish covered with plastic wrap.

Continued

IN THE BREAD MACHINE

4 tablespoons butter, at room temperature

2 extra-large eggs

3 tablespoons honey

Water/saffron mixture (add the grains of saffron)

3 tablespoons powdered skim milk

3 cups unbleached white flour

1 teaspoon salt

1 tablespoon yeast

Place all the ingredients except the currants in the machine, program for Basic, Basic Bread, White, Basic Wheat, White/Whole Grain, Sweet, or Raisin Bread, and press Start or On. When the beeper sounds or during the last 5 minutes of the final knead cycle, drain the currants and add them to the dough.

MAXIM, SMALL OSTER, SMALL PILLSBURY, SANYO, SUNBEAM, SMALL TOASTMASTER, AND SMALL ZOJIRUSHI

AHEAD OF TIME

½ cup water

1 generous pinch saffron

Heat the water to a simmer and stir in the saffron. Cool to lukewarm.

½ cup currants

2 tablespoons brandy

Place the currants and brandy in a small pan, heat to a low simmer, and let soak until ready to add. You can also do this in the microwave in a small glass dish covered with plastic wrap.

IN THE BREAD MACHINE

Water/saffron mixture (add the grains of saffron)

2 medium eggs

2 tablespoons honey

2 tablespoons powdered skim milk

2¼ cups unbleached white flour

1 teaspoon salt

2 tablespoons butter, at room temperature

1½ teaspoons yeast (1 teaspoon for the Small Zojirushi)

Place all the ingredients except the currants in the machine, program for Standard, Bread, Basic, Basic Bread, White, Basic Wheat, White/Whole Grain, or Sweet, and press Start. When the beeper sounds or during the last 5 minutes of the final knead cycle, drain the currants and add them to the dough.

....

Small Welbilt
Ahead of Time

½ cup water   1 generous pinch saffron

Heat the water to a simmer and stir in the saffron. Cool to lukewarm.

½ cup currants   2 tablespoons brandy

Place the currants and brandy in a small pan, heat to a low simmer, and let soak until ready to add. You can also do this in the microwave in a small glass dish covered with plastic wrap.

In the Bread Machine

2 teaspoons yeast   2 medium eggs
2 tablespoons powdered skim milk   2 tablespoons honey
2¼ cups unbleached white flour   Water/saffron mixture (add the grains
1 teaspoon salt   of saffron)
2 tablespoons butter

Have all the ingredients at room temperature. Place all the ingredients except the currants in the machine, program for Medium, and press Start. When the beeper sounds, drain the currants and add them to the dough.

....

Small Panasonic/National

Ahead of Time

½ cup water   1 generous pinch saffron

Heat the water to a simmer and stir in the saffron. Cool to lukewarm.

½ cup currants   2 tablespoons brandy

Place the currants and brandy in a small pan, heat to a low simmer, and let soak until ready to add. You can also do this in the microwave in a small glass dish covered with plastic wrap.

In the Bread Machine

2 tablespoons powdered skim milk   2 medium eggs
2¼ cups unbleached white flour   2 tablespoons honey
1 teaspoon salt   Water/saffron mixture (add the grains
2 tablespoons butter, at room   of saffron)
   temperature   1½ teaspoons yeast

Place all the ingredients except the yeast and currants in the machine. Place the yeast in the dispenser. Program for Basic Bread and press Start. Drain the currants and add them to the dough after the first 20 minutes of kneading.

PRUNE BREAD

If you like raisin bread, you'll love this moist, flavorful, crusty loaf. Great for breakfast or tea. Even though the package says "pitted" prunes, it's a good idea to check very carefully.

DAK/WELBILT

2½ teaspoons yeast

2½ cups unbleached white flour

½ cup whole wheat flour

2 tablespoons nonfat dry milk

3 tablespoons brown sugar

1 teaspoon ground cinnamon

1 teaspoon salt

1 tablespoon butter

1¼ cups warm water

1 cup pitted prunes, quartered

½ cup chopped walnuts (optional)

Have all the ingredients at room temperature. Place all the ingredients except the walnuts in the machine, program for White Bread, and press Start. If you wish to add walnuts, add them when the beeper sounds.

BLACK & DECKER, BETTY CROCKER, BREADMAN/TRILLIUM, HITACHI, LARGE TOASTMASTER, AND WILLIAMS-SONOMA

1¼ cups warm water (plus an
   additional 2 to 3 tablespoons if the
   dough appears very dry after the first
   10 minutes of kneading)

1 tablespoon butter, softened

1 cup pitted prunes, quartered

2 cups unbleached white flour

1 cup whole wheat flour

2 tablespoons nonfat dry milk

3 tablespoons brown sugar

1 teaspoon ground cinnamon

1 teaspoon salt

2 teaspoons yeast

½ cup chopped walnuts (optional)

Place all the ingredients except the walnuts in the machine, program for Mix Bread, Raisin Bread, Fruit and Nut, Basic, Basic Bread, White, Basic Wheat, White/ Whole

Grain, or Sweet, and press Start. If you wish to add walnuts, add them when the beeper sounds or during the last 5 minutes of the final knead cycle,.

PANASONIC/NATIONAL

2 cups unbleached white flour
1 cup whole wheat flour
2 tablespoons nonfat dry milk
3 tablespoons brown sugar
1 teaspoon ground cinnamon
1 teaspoon salt
1 tablespoon butter, softened

1 cup pitted prunes, quartered
1¼ cups warm water (plus an
    additional 2 to 3 tablespoons if the
    dough appears very dry after the first
    10 minutes of kneading)
2½ teaspoons yeast
½ cup chopped walnuts (optional)

Place all the ingredients except the yeast and walnuts in the machine. Place the yeast in the dispenser. Program for Basic Bread and press Start. Toward the end of the prekneading cycle, add the walnuts if desired.

REGAL, LARGE OSTER, WEST BEND, LARGE PILLSBURY, AND LARGE ZOJIRUSHI

1¼ cups warm water (plus an
    additional 2 to 3 tablespoons if the
    dough appears very dry after the first
    10 minutes of kneading)
1 tablespoon butter, softened
1 cup pitted prunes, quartered
2 cups unbleached white flour

1 cup whole wheat flour
2 tablespoons nonfat dry milk
3 tablespoons brown sugar
1 teaspoon ground cinnamon
1 teaspoon salt
2½ teaspoons yeast
½ cup chopped walnuts (optional)

Place all the ingredients except the walnuts in the machine, program for Raisin Bread, Basic, Basic Bread, White, Basic Wheat, White/Whole Grain, or Sweet, and press Start or On. Add the walnuts, if desired, when the beeper sounds or during the last 5 minutes of the final knead cycle.

MAXIM, SMALL OSTER, SMALL PILLSBURY, SANYO, SUNBEAM, SMALL TOASTMASTER, AND SMALL ZOJIRUSHI

2 teaspoons butter, softened

⅓ cup pitted prunes, quartered

⅔ cup warm water

1½ cups unbleached white flour

½ cup whole wheat flour

1 tablespoon nonfat dry milk

2 tablespoons brown sugar

½ teaspoon ground cinnamon

½ teaspoon salt

2 teaspoons yeast (1 teaspoon for the Small Zojirushi)

⅓ cup chopped walnuts (optional)

Place all the ingredients except the walnuts in the machine. Program for Standard, Bread, Basic, Basic Bread, White, Basic Wheat, White/Whole Grain, or Sweet, and press Start. Add the walnuts, if you wish, when the beeper sounds or during the last 5 minutes of the final knead cycle.

....

SMALL WELBILT

2 teaspoons yeast

1½ cups unbleached white flour

½ cup whole wheat flour

1 tablespoon nonfat dry milk

2 tablespoons brown sugar

½ teaspoon ground cinnamon

½ teaspoon salt

2 teaspoons butter

⅓ cup pitted prunes, quartered

⅔ cup warm water

⅓ cup chopped walnuts (optional)

Have all the ingredients at room temperature. Place all the ingredients except the walnuts in the machine, program for Medium, and press Start. Add the walnuts, if you wish, when the beeper sounds.

....

Small Panasonic/National

1½ cups unbleached white flour
½ cup whole wheat flour
1 tablespoon nonfat dry milk
2 tablespoons brown sugar
½ teaspoon ground cinnamon
½ teaspoon salt

2 teaspoons butter, softened
⅓ cup pitted prunes, quartered
⅔ cup warm water
2 teaspoons yeast
⅓ cup chopped walnuts (optional)

Place all the ingredients except the yeast and walnuts in the machine. Place the yeast in the dispenser. Program for Basic Bread and press Start. Toward the end of the last kneading, add the walnuts if desired.

COCONUT ORANGE BREAD

This moist, fragrant, sweet bread has the most deliciously mild taste and a velvety crumb. It makes perfect tea sandwiches and the most divine French toast. You can buy cans of coconut milk in most supermarkets and specialty food stores, as well as cans or bags of grated or shredded coconut. It is important to use both unsweetened coconut milk as well as unsweetened shredded coconut so as not to shock the yeast into inactivity with excess sugar.

DAK/WELBILT

1 tablespoon yeast

2 tablespoons sugar

3 cups unbleached white flour

½ teaspoon salt

½ cup shredded unsweetened coconut

½ cup unsweetened coconut milk, very well mixed

¼ cup orange liqueur, such as Grand Marnier

¼ cup orange juice

¼ teaspoon orange oil

1 extra-large egg

Grated zest of 1 orange

Have all the ingredients at room temperature. Place all the ingredients in the machine, program for White Bread, and press Start.

BLACK & DECKER, BETTY CROCKER, HITACHI, LARGE TOASTMASTER, AND WILLIAMS-SONOMA

½ cup unsweetened coconut milk, very well mixed

¼ cup orange liqueur, such as Grand Marnier

¼ cup orange juice

¼ teaspoon orange oil

1 extra-large egg

Grated zest of 1 orange

½ teaspoon salt

2 tablespoons sugar

3 cups plus 1 tablespoon unbleached white flour

½ cup shredded unsweetened coconut

2 teaspoons yeast

Continued

271

Place all the ingredients in the machine, program for Bread, Basic, Basic Bread, White, Basic Wheat, White/Whole Grain, or Sweet, and press Start.

PANASONIC/NATIONAL

2 tablespoons sugar

3 cups unbleached white flour

½ teaspoon salt

½ cup shredded unsweetened coconut

½ cup unsweetened coconut milk, very well mixed

¼ cup orange liqueur, such as Grand Marnier

¼ cup orange juice

¼ teaspoon orange oil

1 extra-large egg

Grated zest of 1 orange

1 tablespoon yeast

Place all the ingredients except the yeast in the machine. Place the yeast in the dispenser. Program for Basic Bread and press Start.

REGAL, LARGE OSTER, WEST BEND, LARGE PILLSBURY, LARGE ZOJIRUSHI, AND BREADMAN/TRILLIUM

½ cup shredded unsweetened coconut

½ cup unsweetened coconut milk, very well mixed

¼ cup orange liqueur, such as Grand Marnier

¼ cup orange juice

¼ teaspoon orange oil

1 extra-large egg

Grated zest of 1 orange

2 tablespoons sugar

3 cups unbleached white flour

½ teaspoon salt

1 tablespoon yeast

Place all the ingredients in the machine, program for Bread, Basic, Basic Bread, White, Basic Wheat, White/Whole Grain, Sweet, or Basic White Bread, and press Start or On.

MAXIM, SMALL OSTER, SMALL PILLSBURY, SANYO, SUNBEAM, SMALL TOASTMASTER, AND SMALL ZOJIRUSHI

⅓ cup unsweetened coconut milk, very well mixed

2 tablespoons orange liqueur, such as Grand Marnier

2 tablespoons orange juice

¼ teaspoon orange oil

1 large egg

Grated zest of 1 orange

1½ tablespoons sugar

2 cups plus 1 tablespoon unbleached white flour

¼ teaspoon salt

⅓ cup shredded unsweetened coconut

2 teaspoons yeast (1 teaspoon for the Small Zojirushi)

Have all the ingredients at room temperature. Place all the ingredients in the machine, program for Standard, Bread, Basic, Basic Bread, White, or Sweet, and press Start.

....

SMALL WELBILT

2 teaspoons yeast

1½ tablespoons sugar

2 cups unbleached white flour

¼ teaspoon salt

⅓ cup shredded unsweetened coconut

⅓ cup unsweetened coconut milk, very well mixed

2 tablespoons orange liqueur, such as Grand Marnier

2 tablespoons orange juice

¼ teaspoon orange oil

1 large egg

Grated zest of 1 orange

Have all the ingredients at room temperature. Place all the ingredients in the machine, program for Dark, and press Start.

....

273

Small Panasonic/National

1½ tablespoons sugar

2 cups plus 1 tablespoon unbleached
  white flour

¼ teaspoon salt

⅓ cup shredded unsweetened coconut

⅓ cup unsweetened coconut milk, very
  well mixed

2 tablespoons orange liqueur, such as
  Grand Marnier

2 tablespoons orange juice

¼ teaspoon orange oil

1 large egg

Grated zest of 1 orange

2 teaspoons yeast

Place all the ingredients except the yeast in the machine. Place the yeast in the
dispenser. Program for Basic Bread and press Start.

MANGO CHUTNEY CASHEW BREAD

When fresh mangoes are available, give yourself a treat and make this picture-perfect, sweet and spicy braid. It's a fabulous centerpiece for brunch, a tea, or even a light dessert. Did you know that mangoes and cashews come from the same family? Mango chutney is available in the specialty foods section of the supermarket.

....

DAK/Welbilt

1 tablespoon yeast

3 cups unbleached white flour

4 tablespoons nonfat dry milk

1 teaspoon salt

½ teaspoon ground cinnamon

½ teaspoon ground ginger

2 tablespoons butter

2 tablespoons honey

1 extra-large egg

¼ cup plus 1 tablespoon water

About 1 cup peeled and coarsely
    chopped ripe mango

Have all the ingredients at room temperature. Place all the ingredients in the machine, program for Manual, and press Start. Remove the dough at the end of the cycle and place it in an oiled bowl. Cover and refrigerate for at least 2 hours or as long as overnight. Follow the Baking Instructions on page 278.

....

Betty Crocker, Black & Decker, Hitachi, Large Toastmaster, and Williams-Sonoma

About 1 cup peeled and coarsely
    chopped ripe mango

2 tablespoons butter

2 tablespoons honey

1 extra-large egg

¼ cup plus 1 tablespoon water

3 cups unbleached white flour

4 tablespoons nonfat dry milk

1 teaspoon salt

½ teaspoon ground cinnamon

½ teaspoon ground ginger

2½ teaspoons yeast (2 teaspoons for
    the Black & Decker and Large
    Toastmaster)

Continued

Place all the ingredients in the machine, set the cycle for Dough or Knead and First Rise, and press Start. Remove the dough at the end of the cycle and place it in an oiled bowl. Cover and refrigerate for at least 2 hours or as long as overnight. Follow the Baking Instructions on page 278.

PANASONIC/NATIONAL

3 cups unbleached white flour

4 tablespoons nonfat dry milk

1 teaspoon salt

½ teaspoon ground cinnamon

½ teaspoon ground ginger

About 1 cup peeled and coarsely chopped ripe mango

2 tablespoons butter

2 tablespoons honey

1 extra-large egg

¼ cup plus 1 tablespoon water

1 tablespoon yeast

Place all the ingredients except the yeast in the machine. Place the yeast in the dispenser. Program for Dough or Manual and press Start. Remove the dough at the end of the cycle and place it in an oiled bowl. Cover and refrigerate for at least 2 hours or as long as overnight. Follow the Baking Instructions on page 278.

BREADMAN/TRILLIUM, LARGE OSTER, REGAL, LARGE PILLSBURY, WEST BEND, AND LARGE ZOJIRUSHI

About 1 cup peeled and coarsely chopped ripe mango

2 tablespoons butter

2 tablespoons honey

1 extra-large egg

¼ cup plus 1 tablespoon water

3 cups unbleached white flour

4 tablespoons nonfat dry milk

1 teaspoon salt

½ teaspoon ground cinnamon

½ teaspoon ground ginger

1 tablespoon yeast (2 teaspoons for the Breadman/Trillium)

Place all the ingredients in the machine, program for Dough or Manual, and press Start or On. Remove the dough at the end of the cycle and place it in an oiled bowl. Cover and refrigerate for at least 2 hours or as long as overnight. Follow the Baking Instructions on page 278.

....

Maxim, Small Oster, Small Pillsbury, Sanyo, Sunbeam, Small Toastmaster, and Small Zojirushi

About ⅔ cup peeled and coarsely
   chopped ripe mango
1½ tablespoons butter
1½ tablespoons honey
1 medium egg
3 tablespoons water
2 cups unbleached white flour

3 tablespoons nonfat dry milk
½ teaspoon salt
¼ teaspoon ground cinnamon
¼ teaspoon ground ginger
2 teaspoons yeast (1½ teaspoons for
   the Small Zojirushi)

Place all the ingredients in the machine, program for Dough or Manual, and press Start. Remove the dough at the end of the cycle and place it in an oiled bowl. Cover and refrigerate for at least 2 hours or as long as overnight. Follow the Baking Instructions on page 279.

....

Small Welbilt

2 teaspoons yeast
2 cups unbleached white flour
3 tablespoons nonfat dry milk
½ teaspoon salt
¼ teaspoon ground cinnamon
¼ teaspoon ground ginger

About ⅔ cup peeled and coarsely
   chopped ripe mango
1½ tablespoons butter
1½ tablespoons honey
1 medium egg
3 tablespoons water

Have all the ingredients at room temperature. Place all the ingredients in the machine, program for Manual, and press Start. Remove the dough at the end of the cycle and place it in an oiled bowl. Cover and refrigerate for at least 2 hours or as long as overnight. Follow the Baking Instructions on page 279.

....

SMALL PANASONIC/NATIONAL

2 cups unbleached white flour

3 tablespoons nonfat dry milk

½ teaspoon salt

¼ teaspoon ground cinnamon

¼ teaspoon ground ginger

About ⅔ cup peeled and coarsely chopped ripe mango

1½ tablespoons butter

1½ tablespoons honey

1 medium egg

3 tablespoons water

2 teaspoons yeast

Place all the ingredients except the yeast in the machine. Place the yeast in the dispenser. Program for Basic Bread and press Start. Remove the dough at the end of the cycle and place it in an oiled bowl. Cover and refrigerate for at least 2 hours or as long as overnight. Follow the Baking Instructions on page 279.

BAKING INSTRUCTIONS (LARGE MACHINES)

⅔ cup mango chutney

½ cup coarsely chopped unsalted cashews

1 egg combined with 1 tablespoon water

Line a heavy-duty cookie sheet with foil and lightly oil the foil. On a lightly floured board, pat the cold dough into a fat log and then cut the log into 3 equal pieces. Form each piece into a 12- to 14-inch length. Pinch 3 of the ends together and make a fairly tight braid, pinching the other ends together. Place on the prepared cookie sheet.

      Spoon the mango chutney onto the top of the braid, letting it seep into the spaces between the braid. Sprinkle on the cashews. Let the braid rise, uncovered, in a warm, draft-free place for about 1 hour, or until almost doubled in size.

      Preheat the oven to 350° F with the rack in the lower third, not the bottom, position. Paint the braid with the egg glaze. Bake for 50 to 60 minutes, or until deep golden brown and the inside is done (check by inserting a small sharp knife between the braids to make sure the bread is cooked throughout).

B<small>AKING</small> I<small>NSTRUCTIONS</small> (<small>SMALL MACHINES</small>)

½ cup mango chutney   1 egg combined with 1 tablespoon water
⅓ cup coarsely chopped unsalted
  cashews

Line a heavy-duty cookie sheet with foil and lightly oil the foil. On a lightly floured board, pat the cold dough into a fat log and then cut the log into 3 equal pieces. Form each piece into an 8- to 10-inch length. Pinch 3 of the ends together and make a fairly tight braid, pinching the other ends together. Place on the prepared cookie sheet.

Spoon the mango chutney onto the top of the braid, letting it seep into the spaces between the braid. Sprinkle on the cashews. Let the braid rise, uncovered, in a warm, draft-free place for about 1 hour, or until almost doubled in size.

Preheat the oven to 350°F with the rack in the lower third, not the bottom, position. Paint the braid with the egg glaze. Bake for 50 to 60 minutes, or until deep golden brown and the bread has an internal temperature of 190° to 200°F.

LEMON MINT BREAD

And now for something completely different. This bread was inspired by some of the flavors of Morocco. If you can find fresh mint, use it in place of dried.

This is a majestically high, tawny-colored loaf that comes out picture-perfect. It's great for sandwiches made with meat or cheese, then layered with slices of fruits such as fresh apples or pears.

DAK/Welbilt

1 tablespoon yeast

½ teaspoon salt

½ cup whole wheat flour

2½ cups plus 1 tablespoon unbleached
   white flour

½ cup quick-cooking oatmeal

¼ teaspoon baking soda

1 cup (8 ounces) lemon yogurt
   (low-fat, nonfat, or regular)

1 extra-large egg

3 tablespoons honey

2 tablespoons butter

⅓ cup fresh mint, tightly packed, OR 1
   tablespoon dried mint

Grated zest of 2 lemons

2 tablespoons lemon juice

Have all the ingredients at room temperature. Place all the ingredients in the machine, program for White Bread, and press Start.

Betty Crocker, Black & Decker, Hitachi, Regal, Large Toastmaster, and Williams-Sonoma

1 cup (8 ounces) lemon yogurt (low-fat, nonfat, or regular), at room temperature

1 extra-large egg

3 tablespoons honey

2 tablespoons butter

⅓ cup fresh mint, tightly packed OR 1 tablespoon dried mint

Grated zest of 2 lemons

2 tablespoons lemon juice

½ teaspoon salt

½ cup whole wheat flour

2½ cups plus 1 tablespoon unbleached white flour

½ cup quick-cooking oatmeal

¼ teaspoon baking soda

2½ teaspoons yeast (2 teaspoons for the Black & Decker and Large Toastmaster)

Place all the ingredients in the machine, program for Bread, Basic Bread, White, Basic Wheat, or Sweet, and press Start.

Panasonic/National

½ teaspoon salt

½ cup whole wheat flour

2½ cups plus 1 tablespoon unbleached white flour

½ cup quick-cooking oatmeal

¼ teaspoon baking soda

1 cup (8 ounces) lemon yogurt (low-fat, nonfat, or regular), at room temperature

1 extra-large egg

3 tablespoons honey

2 tablespoons butter

⅓ cup fresh mint, tightly packed OR 1 tablespoon dried mint

Grated zest of 2 lemons

2 tablespoons lemon juice

1 tablespoon yeast

Place all the ingredients except the yeast in the machine. Place the yeast in the dispenser. Program for Basic Bread and press Start.

Breadman/Trillium, Large Oster, Regal, Large Pillsbury, West Bend, and Large Zojirushi

1 cup (8 ounces) lemon yogurt (low-fat, nonfat, or regular), at room temperature

1 extra-large egg

3 tablespoons honey

2 tablespoons butter

⅓ cup fresh mint, tightly packed OR 1 tablespoon dried mint

Grated zest of 2 lemons

2 tablespoons lemon juice

½ teaspoon salt

½ cup whole wheat flour

2½ cups plus 3 tablespoons unbleached white flour

½ cup quick-cooking oatmeal

1 tablespoon yeast (2 teaspoons for the Breadman/Trillium)

¼ teaspoon baking soda

Place all the ingredients in the machine, program for Basic White Bread, Basic, Basic Bread, White, Basic Wheat, White/Whole Grain, or Sweet, and press Start or On.

Maxim, Small Oster, Small Pillsbury, Sanyo, Sunbeam, Small Toastmaster, and Small Zojirushi

⅔ cup (6 ounces) lemon yogurt (low-fat, nonfat, or regular), at room temperature

1 medium egg

2 tablespoons honey

1 tablespoon butter

¼ cup fresh mint, tightly packed OR 2 teaspoons dried mint

Grated zest of 1 lemon

1 tablespoon plus 1 teaspoon lemon juice

½ teaspoon salt

½ cup whole wheat flour

1½ cups plus 1 tablespoon unbleached white flour

⅓ cup quick-cooking oatmeal

¼ teaspoon baking soda

2 teaspoons yeast (1½ teaspoons for the Small Zojirushi)

Place all the ingredients in the machine, program for Standard, Bread, Basic Bread, White, Basic Wheat, or Sweet, and press Start.

Small Welbilt

2 teaspoons yeast
½ teaspoon salt
½ cup whole wheat flour
1½ cups plus 1 tablespoon unbleached white flour
⅓ cup quick-cooking oatmeal
¼ teaspoon baking soda
⅔ cup (6 ounces) lemon yogurt (low-fat, nonfat, or regular)

1 medium egg
2 tablespoons honey
1 tablespoon butter
¼ cup fresh mint, tightly packed OR 2 teaspoons dried mint
Grated zest of 1 lemon
1 tablespoon plus 1 teaspoon lemon juice

Have all the ingredients at room temperature. Place all the ingredients in the machine, program for Medium, and press Start.

Small Panasonic/National

½ teaspoon salt
½ cup whole wheat flour
1½ cups plus 1 tablespoon unbleached white flour
⅓ cup quick-cooking oatmeal
¼ teaspoon baking soda
⅔ cup (6 ounces) lemon yogurt (low-fat, nonfat, or regular), at room temperature

1 medium egg
2 tablespoons honey
1 tablespoon butter
¼ cup fresh mint, tightly packed OR 2 teaspoons dried mint
Grated zest of 1 lemon
1 tablespoon plus 1 teaspoon lemon juice
2 teaspoons yeast

Place all the ingredients except the yeast in the machine. Place the yeast in the dispenser. Program for Basic Bread and press Start.

GRANOLA CRANBERRY BREAD

This recipe calls for dried cranberries; however, you may substitute currants or any other pieces of dried fruit such as cherries, blueberries, apples, pears, peaches, apricots, figs, or prunes. Please refer to page 14 in the front of the book which describes the best way to add dried fruits to dough.

DAK/WELBILT

2½ teaspoons yeast

¾ cup granola

2¼ cups unbleached white flour

⅓ cup oat flour (see Note)

⅓ cup whole wheat flour

1 teaspoon salt

3 tablespoons powdered buttermilk

¼ cup plus 1 tablespoon orange juice

¾ cup plus 2 tablespoons water

¼ teaspoon orange oil

2 tablespoons honey

1 tablespoon plus 1 teaspoon vegetable oil, almond oil, OR walnut oil

½ cup dried cranberries

½ cup chopped walnuts (optional)

Have all the ingredients except the cranberries at room temperature. Place all the ingredients except the cranberries and walnuts in the machine, program for White Bread, and press Start. Add the cranberries and walnuts when the beeper sounds during the end of the second kneading.

Betty Crocker, Black & Decker, Hitachi, Large Toastmaster, and Williams-Sonoma

¼ cup plus 1 tablespoon orange juice

¾ cup plus 2 tablespoons water

¼ teaspoon orange oil

2 tablespoons honey

1 tablespoon plus 1 teaspoon vegetable oil, almond oil, OR walnut oil

¾ cup granola

2¼ cups unbleached white flour

⅓ cup oat flour (see Note)

⅓ cup whole wheat flour

1 teaspoon salt

3 tablespoons powdered buttermilk

2½ teaspoons yeast (2 teaspoons for the Black & Decker and Large Toastmaster)

½ cup dried cranberries

½ cup chopped walnuts (optional)

Place all the ingredients except the cranberries and walnuts in the machine, program for Mix Bread, Raisin Bread, Fruit and Nut, Basic, Basic Bread, White, Basic Wheat, White/Whole Grain, or Sweet, and press Start. Add the cranberries when the beeper sounds or during the last 5 minutes of the final knead cycle.

....

Panasonic/National

¾ cup granola

2¼ cups unbleached white flour

⅓ cup oat flour (see Note)

⅓ cup whole wheat flour

1 teaspoon salt

3 tablespoons powdered buttermilk

¼ cup plus 1 tablespoon orange juice

¾ cup plus 2 tablespoons water

¼ teaspoon orange oil

2 tablespoons honey

1 tablespoon plus 1 teaspoon vegetable oil, almond oil, OR walnut oil

2½ teaspoons yeast

½ cup dried cranberries

½ cup chopped walnuts (optional)

Place all the ingredients except the yeast, cranberries, and walnuts in the machine. Place the yeast in the dispenser. Program for Basic Bread and press Start. Add the cranberries and walnuts after 20 minutes.

Breadman/Trillium, Large Oster, Regal, Large Pillsbury, West Bend, and Large Zojirushi

⅓ cup orange juice

1 cup water

¼ teaspoon orange oil

2 tablespoons honey

2 tablespoons vegetable oil, almond oil, OR walnut oil

1 cup granola

2½ cups unbleached white flour

½ cup oat flour (see Note)

½ cup whole wheat flour

1 teaspoon salt

4 tablespoons powdered buttermilk

1 tablespoon yeast (2 teaspoons for the Breadman/Trillium)

½ cup dried cranberries

½ cup chopped walnuts (optional)

Place all the ingredients except the cranberries and walnuts in the machine, program for Raisin Bread, Basic, Basic Bread, White, Basic Wheat, White/Whole Grain, or Sweet, and press Start or On. Add the cranberries and walnuts when the beeper sounds or during the last 5 minutes of the final knead cycle.

....

Maxim, Small Oster, Small Pillsbury, Sanyo, Sunbeam, Small Toastmaster, and Small Zojirushi

½ cup orange juice

¼ cup water

⅛ teaspoon orange oil

1½ tablespoons honey

2 teaspoons vegetable oil, almond oil, OR walnut oil

⅔ cup granola

1⅓ cups unbleached white flour

⅓ cup oat flour (see Note)

⅓ cup whole wheat flour

½ teaspoon salt

3 tablespoons powdered buttermilk

2 teaspoons yeast (1½ teaspoons for the Small Zojirushi)

⅓ cup dried cranberries

⅓ cup chopped walnuts (optional)

Place all the ingredients except the cranberries and walnuts in the machine, program for Standard, Bread, Basic, Basic Bread, White, Basic Wheat, White/Whole Grain, or Sweet, and press Start. Add the cranberries and walnuts when the beeper sounds or during the last 5 minutes of the final knead cycle.

SMALL WELBILT

2 teaspoons yeast

⅔ cup granola

1⅓ cups unbleached white flour

⅓ cup oat flour (see Note)

⅓ cup whole wheat flour

½ teaspoon salt

3 tablespoons powdered buttermilk

½ cup orange juice

¼ cup water

⅛ teaspoon orange oil

1½ tablespoons honey

2 teaspoons vegetable oil, almond oil,
   OR walnut oil

⅓ cup dried cranberries

⅓ cup chopped walnuts (optional)

Have all the ingredients except the cranberries at room temperature. Place all the ingredients except the cranberries and walnuts in the machine, program for Medium, and press Start. Add the cranberries and walnuts when the beeper sounds.

SMALL PANASONIC/NATIONAL

⅔ cup granola

1⅓ cups unbleached white flour

⅓ cup oat flour (see Note)

⅓ cup whole wheat flour

½ teaspoon salt

3 tablespoons powdered buttermilk

½ cup orange juice

¼ cup water

⅛ teaspoon orange oil

1½ tablespoons honey

2 teaspoons vegetable oil, almond oil,
   OR walnut oil

2 teaspoons yeast

⅓ cup dried cranberries

⅓ cup chopped walnuts (optional)

Place all the ingredients except the yeast, cranberries, and walnuts in the machine. Place the yeast in the dispenser. Program for Basic Bread and press Start. Add the cranberries and walnuts after 20 minutes.

NOTE: You can buy oat flour at a health food store or mail-order it (page 337), or you can make your own by simply pulverizing oatmeal (quick or regular) in a food processor or blender until it is powdered. Measure after blending.

CANDIED GINGER PEAR BREAD

Pardon the lack of humility, but this bread is one of the best forms of carbohydrates that has ever passed our lips. Sweet pears, both dried and puréed (we used junior baby food, although you can make your own puréed fresh fruit), are complemented with a spark of candied ginger. You'll get raves and shouts for more.

DAK/WELBILT

1 tablespoon yeast
1 cup whole wheat flour
2 cups unbleached white flour
1 teaspoon salt
1 tablespoon dark brown sugar
½ cup dried pears, cut into 1-inch pieces (see Note)

⅓ cup candied ginger, cut into strips ¼ inch thick
Grated zest of 1 lemon
1 6-ounce jar junior strained pears
2 extra-large eggs
2 tablespoons water
4 tablespoons nonfat dry milk
3 tablespoons butter

Have all the ingredients at room temperature. Place all the ingredients in the machine, program for White Bread, and press Start.

BETTY CROCKER, BLACK & DECKER, HITACHI, LARGE TOASTMASTER, AND WILLIAMS-SONOMA

⅓ cup dried pears, cut into 1-inch pieces (see Note)
¼ cup candied ginger, cut into strips ¼ inch thick
Grated zest of 1 lemon
4 ounces (½ cup) junior strained pears
2 medium eggs
1 tablespoon water
1 tablespoon butter

½ teaspoon salt
3 tablespoons nonfat dry milk
2 tablespoons dark brown sugar
⅔ cup whole wheat flour
1⅓ cups plus 2 tablespoons unbleached white flour
2½ teaspoons yeast (2 teaspoons for the Black & Decker and Large Toastmaster)

Place all the ingredients in the machine, program for Bread, Basic, Basic Bread, White, Basic Wheat, White/Whole Grain, or Sweet, and press Start.

PANASONIC/NATIONAL

2 cups plus 2 tablespoons unbleached
   white flour

1 cup whole wheat flour

1 teaspoon salt

1 tablespoon dark brown sugar

½ cup dried pears, cut into 1-inch pieces
   (see Note)

⅓ cup candied ginger, cut into strips ¼
   inch thick

Grated zest of 1 lemon

1 6-ounce jar junior strained pears

2 extra-large eggs

2 tablespoons water

4 tablespoons nonfat dry milk

3 tablespoons butter

1 tablespoon yeast

Place all the ingredients except the yeast in the machine. Place the yeast in the dispenser. Program for Basic Bread and press Start.

BREADMAN/TRILLIUM, LARGE OSTER, REGAL, LARGE PILLSBURY, WEST BEND, AND LARGE ZOJIRUSHI

½ cup dried pears, cut into 1-inch
   pieces (see Note)

⅓ cup candied ginger, cut into strips ¼
   inch thick

Grated zest of 1 lemon

1 6-ounce jar of junior strained pears

2 extra-large eggs

2 tablespoons water

3 tablespoons butter

4 tablespoons nonfat dry milk

1 cup whole wheat flour

2 cups unbleached white flour

1 teaspoon salt

1 tablespoon dark brown sugar

1 tablespoon yeast (2 teaspoons for the
   Breadman/Trillium)

Have all the ingredients at room temperature. Place all the ingredients in the machine, program for Basic White Bread, Basic, Basic Bread, White, Basic Wheat, White/Whole Grain, or Sweet, and press Start or On.

Maxim, Small Oster, Small Pillsbury, Sanyo, Sunbeam, Small Toastmaster, and Small Zojirushi

⅓ cup dried pears, cut into 1-inch pieces (see Note)

¼ cup candied ginger, cut into strips ¼ inch thick

Grated zest of 1 lemon

4 ounces (½ cup) junior strained pears

2 medium eggs

1 tablespoon water

3 tablespoons nonfat dry milk

2 tablespoons butter

⅔ cup whole wheat flour

1⅓ cups plus 2 tablespoons unbleached white flour

½ teaspoon salt

2 teaspoons dark brown sugar

2 teaspoons yeast (1½ teaspoons for the Small Zojirushi)

Place all the ingredients in the machine, program for Standard, Basic, Basic Bread, White, or Sweet, and press Start.

....

Small Welbilt

2 teaspoons yeast

⅔ cup whole wheat flour

1⅓ cups plus 2 tablespoons unbleached white flour

½ teaspoon salt

2 teaspoons dark brown sugar

⅓ cup dried pears, cut into 1-inch pieces (see Note)

¼ cup candied ginger, cut into strips ¼ inch thick

Grated zest of 1 lemon

4 ounces (½ cup) junior strained pears

2 medium eggs

1 tablespoon water

3 tablespoons nonfat dry milk

2 tablespoons butter

Have all the ingredients at room temperature. Place all the ingredients in the machine, program for Medium, and press Start.

....

SMALL PANASONIC/NATIONAL

⅔ cup whole wheat flour

1⅓ cups plus 2 tablespoons unbleached white flour

½ teaspoon salt

2 teaspoons dark brown sugar

3 tablespoons nonfat dry milk

⅓ cup dried pears, cut into 1-inch pieces

¼ cup candied ginger, cut into strips ¼ inch thick

Grated zest of 1 lemon

4 ounces (½ cup) junior strained pears

2 medium eggs

1 tablespoon water

2 tablespoons butter

2 teaspoons yeast

Place all the ingredients except the yeast in the machine. Place the yeast in the dispenser. Program for Basic Bread and press Start.

NOTE: Use a sharp pair of scissors to cut the pears and ginger.

Variation: Instead of pears, you can use dried peaches and junior strained peaches, dried apricots and junior strained apricots, or dried apples and junior strained applesauce.

ALSATIAN APRICOT SPICE BREAD

A small, compact loaf with a flat top that doesn't rise very high, but is studded with explosions of apricots. Slice thinly and spread with cream cheese or butter.

We used a California Gewürztraminer for this recipe since it was far less expensive than the imported variety. Ask your wine merchant to recommend a less sweet variety of this particular kind of wine. The high sugar content of a very sweet wine will retard or even kill the yeast.

DAK/Welbilt

1 tablespoon yeast

1 teaspoon salt

4 tablespoons nonfat dry milk

2 cups whole wheat flour

1 cup unbleached white flour

2 teaspoons gluten

½ teaspoon ground ginger

½ teaspoon ground cloves

½ teaspoon ground cinnamon

½ teaspoon ground mace

½ teaspoon ground nutmeg

1 cup Gewürztraminer

1 tablespoon vanilla extract

2 tablespoons vegetable oil OR almond oil

⅔ cup dried apricots, coarsely chopped

Have all the ingredients at room temperature. Place all the ingredients except the apricots in the machine, program for White Bread, and press Start. When the beeper sounds at the end of the second kneading, add the apricots.

BLACK & DECKER, BETTY CROCKER, BREADMAN/TRILLIUM, HITACHI, LARGE TOASTMASTER, REGAL, AND WILLIAMS-SONOMA

1 cup Gewürztraminer
1 tablespoon vanilla extract
2 tablespoons vegetable oil OR almond
   oil
1 teaspoon salt
4 tablespoons nonfat dry milk
2 cups whole wheat flour
1 cup unbleached white flour
2 teaspoons gluten

½ teaspoon ground ginger
½ teaspoon ground cloves
½ teaspoon ground cinnamon
½ teaspoon ground mace
½ teaspoon ground nutmeg
2½ teaspoons yeast (2 teaspoons for
   the Black & Decker and Large
   Toastmaster)
⅔ cup dried apricots, coarsely chopped

Place all the ingredients except the apricots in the machine, program for Mix Bread, Fruit and Nut, Raisin Bread, Bread, Basic Bread, White, Basic Wheat, or Sweet, and press Start. Add the apricots when the beeper sounds or during the last 5 minutes of the final knead cycle.

PANASONIC/NATIONAL

1 teaspoon salt
4 tablespoons nonfat dry milk
2 cups whole wheat flour
1 cup unbleached white flour
2 teaspoons gluten
½ teaspoon ground ginger
½ teaspoon ground cloves
½ teaspoon ground cinnamon
½ teaspoon ground mace

½ teaspoon ground nutmeg
1 cup Gewürztraminer
3 tablespoons water
1 tablespoon vanilla extract
3 tablespoons vegetable oil OR almond
   oil
1 tablespoon yeast
⅔ cup dried apricots, coarsely chopped

Place all the ingredients except the yeast and apricots in the machine. Place the yeast in the dispenser. Program for Basic Bread and press Start. Twenty minutes into the second knead, add the apricots.

Large Oster, Large Pillsbury, West Bend, and Large Zojirushi

1 cup Gewürztraminer

1 tablespoon vanilla extract

2 tablespoons vegetable oil or almond oil

1 teaspoon salt

4 tablespoons nonfat dry milk

2 cups whole wheat flour

1 cup unbleached white flour

2 teaspoons gluten

½ teaspoon ground ginger

½ teaspoon ground cloves

½ teaspoon ground cinnamon

½ teaspoon ground mace

½ teaspoon ground nutmeg

1 tablespoon yeast

⅔ cup dried apricots, coarsely chopped

Place all the ingredients except the apricots in the machine, program for Raisin Bread, Basic, Basic Bread, White, Basic Wheat, White/Whole Grain, or Sweet, and press Start or On. Add the apricots when the beeper sounds or during the last 5 minutes of the final knead cycle.

Maxim, Small Oster, Small Pillsbury, Sanyo, Sunbeam, Small Toastmaster, and Small Zojirushi

⅔ cup plus 2 tablespoons Gewürztraminer

2 teaspoons vanilla extract

1 tablespoon vegetable oil or almond oil

½ teaspoon salt

2 tablespoons nonfat dry milk

1⅓ cups whole wheat flour

⅔ cup unbleached white flour

1 teaspoon gluten

¼ teaspoon ground ginger

¼ teaspoon ground cloves

¼ teaspoon ground cinnamon

¼ teaspoon ground mace

¼ teaspoon ground nutmeg

2 teaspoons yeast

½ cup dried apricots, coarsely chopped

Place all the ingredients except the apricots in the machine, program for Standard, Basic, Basic Bread, White, or Sweet, and press Start. Add the apricots when the beeper sounds or during the last 5 minutes of the final knead cycle.

SMALL WELBILT

2 teaspoons yeast

½ teaspoon salt

2 tablespoons nonfat dry milk

1⅓ cups whole wheat flour

⅔ cup unbleached white flour

1 teaspoon gluten

¼ teaspoon ground ginger

¼ teaspoon ground cloves

¼ teaspoon ground cinnamon

¼ teaspoon ground mace

¼ teaspoon ground nutmeg

⅔ cup plus 2 tablespoons
  Gewürztraminer

2 teaspoons vanilla extract

1 tablespoon vegetable oil OR almond
  oil

½ cup dried apricots, coarsely chopped

Have all the ingredients at room temperature. Place all the ingredients except the apricots in the machine, program for Medium, and press Start. When the beeper sounds, add the apricots.

SMALL PANASONIC/NATIONAL

⅔ cup plus 2 tablespoons
  Gewürztraminer

2 teaspoons vanilla extract

1 tablespoon vegetable oil OR almond
  oil

½ teaspoon salt

2 tablespoons nonfat dry milk

1⅓ cups whole wheat flour

⅔ cup unbleached white flour

1 teaspoon gluten

¼ teaspoon ground ginger

¼ teaspoon ground cloves

¼ teaspoon ground cinnamon

¼ teaspoon ground mace

¼ teaspoon ground nutmeg

2 teaspoons yeast

½ cup dried apricots, coarsely chopped

Place all the ingredients except the yeast and apricots in the machine. Place the yeast in the dispenser. Program for Basic Bread and press Start. Add the apricots 5 minutes before the end of the kneading cycle.

SWEET
BREADS AND
CAKES

TOBLERONE CANDY BREAD

A cross between dessert and heaven—not overly sweet, moist, and chocolaty. Serve this plain, with butter, or a thin coating of Nutella spread. It makes fabulous French toast.

Nutella spread, Ghirardelli Ground Chocolate, and Toblerone bars are available in many supermarkets and most gourmet food shops.

DAK/Welbilt

1 tablespoon yeast	3 tablespoons sweet (unsalted) butter
1 teaspoon salt	2 extra-large eggs
⅓ cup sugar	⅓ cup crème de cacao
⅓ cup Ghirardelli Ground Chocolate	¾ cup water
4 tablespoons nonfat dry milk	1 3½-ounce Toblerone bar (milk or
3 cups unbleached white flour	dark chocolate), coarsely chopped

Have all the ingredients at room temperature. Place all the ingredients except the Toblerone in the machine, program for White Bread, and press Start. When the beeper sounds at the end of the second kneading, add the Toblerone.

Betty Crocker, Black & Decker, Hitachi, Large Toastmaster, and Williams-Sonoma

2 tablespoons sweet (unsalted) butter	4 tablespoons nonfat dry milk
1 extra-large egg	3¼ cups unbleached white flour
¼ cup crème de cacao	¼ cup sugar
½ cup water	2½ teaspoons yeast
¼ teaspoon salt	1 3½-ounce Toblerone bar (milk or
¼ cup Ghirardelli Ground Chocolate	dark chocolate), coarsely chopped

Place all the ingredients except the Toblerone in the machine, program for Mix Bread, Raisin Bread, Fruit and Nut, Basic, Basic Bread, White, Basic Wheat, or Sweet, and press Start. Add the Toblerone slowly when the beeper sounds or during the last 5 minutes of the final knead cycle.

....

PANASONIC/NATIONAL

3 cups unbleached white flour

¼ cup sugar

1 teaspoon salt

⅓ cup Ghirardelli Ground Chocolate

4 tablespoons nonfat dry milk

3 tablespoons sweet (unsalted) butter

2 extra-large eggs

⅓ cup crème de cacao

¾ cup water

2½ teaspoons yeast

1 3½-ounce Toblerone bar (milk or dark chocolate), coarsely chopped

Place all the ingredients except the yeast and Toblerone in the machine. Place the yeast in the dispenser. Program for Basic Bread and press Start. After 20 minutes into the processing, add the Toblerone.

....

BREADMAN/TRILLIUM, LARGE OSTER, AND REGAL

⅓ cup Ghirardelli Ground Chocolate

4 tablespoons nonfat dry milk

¼ cup sugar

3 cups unbleached white flour

3 tablespoons sweet (unsalted) butter

2 extra-large eggs

⅓ cup crème de cacao

¾ cup water

1 teaspoon salt

2¾ teaspoons yeast

1 3½-ounce Toblerone bar (milk or dark chocolate), coarsely chopped

Place all the ingredients except the yeast and Toblerone in the machine. Place the yeast in the dispenser. Program for Raisin Bread, White, Basic Wheat, or Sweet, and press Start. Add the Toblerone when the beeper sounds or during the last 5 minutes of the final knead cycle.

....

Large Pillsbury, West Bend, and Large Zojirushi

3 tablespoons sweet (unsalted) butter

2 extra-large eggs

⅓ cup crème de cacao

¾ cup water

1 teaspoon salt

⅓ cup Ghirardelli Ground Chocolate

4 tablespoons nonfat dry milk

¼ cup sugar

3 cups unbleached white flour

1 tablespoon yeast

1 3½-ounce Toblerone bar (milk or dark chocolate), coarsely chopped

Place all the ingredients except the Toblerone in the machine, program for Raisin Bread, Basic, Basic Bread, White, Basic Wheat, White/Whole Grain, or Sweet, and press Start or On. Add the Toblerone when the beeper sounds or during the last 5 minutes of the final knead cycle.

Maxim, Small Pillsbury, and Small Zojirushi

2 tablespoons sweet (unsalted) butter

1 extra-large egg

¼ cup crème de cacao

½ cup water

¼ teaspoon salt

¼ cup Ghirardelli Ground Chocolate

3 tablespoons nonfat dry milk

3 tablespoons sugar

2 cups plus 2 tablespoons unbleached white flour

2 teaspoons yeast (1½ teaspoons for the Small Zojirushi)

1 3½-ounce Toblerone bar (milk or dark chocolate), coarsely chopped

Place all the ingredients except the Toblerone in the machine, program for Standard, Basic Bread, Basic, or Sweet, and press Start. Add the Toblerone when the beeper sounds or during the last 5 minutes of the final knead cycle.

Small Oster, Sanyo, Sunbeam, and Small Toastmaster

2 tablespoons sweet (unsalted) butter

1 extra-large egg

¼ cup crème de cacao

½ cup water

¼ teaspoon salt

¼ cup Ghirardelli Ground Chocolate

3 tablespoons nonfat dry milk

¼ cup sugar

2 cups plus 2 tablespoons unbleached white flour

2 teaspoons yeast

1 3½-ounce Toblerone bar (milk or dark chocolate), coarsely chopped

Place all the ingredients except the Toblerone in the machine, program for Bread, Basic, White, or Sweet, and press Start. Add the Toblerone when the beeper sounds or during the last 5 minutes of the final knead cycle.

Small Welbilt

2 teaspoons yeast

¼ teaspoon salt

¼ cup Ghirardelli Ground Chocolate

3 tablespoons nonfat dry milk

2 tablespoons sugar

2 cups unbleached white flour

2 tablespoons sweet (unsalted) butter

1 extra-large egg

¼ cup crème de cacao

½ cup water

1 3½-ounce Toblerone bar (milk or dark chocolate), coarsely chopped

Have all the ingredients at room temperature. Place all the ingredients except the Toblerone in the machine, program for Medium, and press Start. When the beeper sounds at the end of the second kneading, add the Toblerone.

SMALL PANASONIC/NATIONAL

¼ teaspoon salt

¼ cup Ghirardelli Ground Chocolate

3 tablespoons nonfat dry milk

3 tablespoons sugar

2 cups plus 2 tablespoons unbleached
white flour

2 tablespoons sweet (unsalted) butter

1 extra-large egg

¼ cup crème de cacao

½ cup water

2 teaspoons yeast

1 3½-ounce Toblerone bar (milk or
dark chocolate), coarsely chopped

Place all the ingredients except the yeast and Toblerone in the machine. Place the
yeast in the dispenser. Program for Basic Bread and press Start. After 15 minutes
into the processing, add the Toblerone.

ELLIE'S CINNAMON BREAD

"What is that heavenly smell?" I asked my recipe tester, Elinor Nelson, as I invaded her kitchen in search of something that wasn't bread. After eating my way through the second edition of this book, I was ready for a change of diet (if only temporarily). "Why, it's just a cinnamon bread I threw together," she replied, "you want to try some?" Here's a testimonial to how good this is—I overcame my vow to do without bread for one whole day (and that's not a very long time); along came Ellie and her cinnamon bread and I was a goner—and you'll be as well!

This recipe when reduced, does not yield enough dough to be viable for the small machines.

....

FOR ALL LARGE MACHINES

2½ teaspoons yeast (2 teaspoons for the Toastmaster, Breadman/Trillium, and Black & Decker)
2½ cups unbleached white flour
½ cup whole wheat pastry flour

¼ cup sugar
1 teaspoon salt
4 tablespoons powdered buttermilk
1 cup water

Place all the ingredients in the machine and program for Knead and First Rise, Manual, or Dough, and press Start or On. At the end of the final cycle, punch down the dough and remove it to a buttered bowl or plastic bag, and refrigerate it for at least 4 hours or overnight.

COMPLETE THE BREAD

1½ tablespoons butter, at room temperature
2½ teaspoons ground cinnamon

¼ cup sugar
1 egg white lightly beaten together with 1 tablespoon water

Continued

Place the butter, cinamon, and sugar in a small bowl. Mix with a fork to combine and set aside. Generously grease a heavy-duty baking sheet or line it with parchment.

On a lightly floured surface, roll the dough to a 15 x 9 rectangle. Cut the rectangle into three 9 x 3-inch strips and spoon a line of filling down the center of each one. Pinch the edges to seal over the filling so you have three 9-ropes. With the seams facing down, braid the strips together. Ellie suggests braiding from the center to one end, and then from the center to the other end. Pinch the ends together and tuck them under. Place the braid on the baking sheet, brush with the egg glaze and cover loosely with plastic wrap and place in a warm place to rise until doubled in bulk.

Preheat the oven to 375°F with the rack in the center position. Bake the braid for 30 to 35 minutes, or until the top is a deep golden brown.

ZANZIBAR BEIGNETS

A tasty treat from New Orleans, these sugar-dusted morsels of pure delight are a cinch to whip up in the bread machine. The dough should be fried as soon as the rising process is complete.

This particular recipe comes from Lynne Bail, good friend and recipe developer and tester par excellence. She made these when she lived in Africa and says that there the custom is to sprinkle granulated sugar on top. Either way, enjoy them while they're still hot.

....

FOR ALL LARGE MACHINES

2½ teaspoons yeast (for Panasonic and National, add to the dispenser) (2 teaspoons for the Black & Decker, 1 teaspoon for the Breadman/Trillium and Toastmaster)

3½ cups unbleached white flour

¼ cup sugar

¼ teaspoon ground cardamom

1 extra-large egg, at room temperature

2 tablespoons butter, softened

1 cup milk, scalded and then cooled to lukewarm

For DAK and Welbilt, have all the ingredients at room temperature. Place all the ingredients in the machine, program for Dough, Manual, or Knead and First Rise, and press Start or On. The dough will be sticky and wet until the rising process is complete.

At the end of the final cycle, remove the dough from the machine and place it on a lightly floured board. Roll it out ¼ inch thick and cut it into 2-inch squares.

TO COOK THE BEIGNETS

1 cup Crisco oil

⅓ cup confectioners' sugar OR granulated sugar

Continued

Pour the oil to a depth of 2 inches in a small saucepan. Heat the oil to 350°F (use a thermometer to check, or drop in a tiny piece of dough, which will sink and then immediately pop to the surface at the correct temperature). Don't cook more than 2 at one time.

Carefully transfer the squares to the saucepan 1 or 2 at a time and cook until they puff up with air and turn deep golden brown. Turn them once and cook until the other side is brown as well. Transfer them to paper towels to drain for a minute, sprinkle with sugar, and enjoy while they are still hot.

SWEET MARSALA PANETTONE

Panettone is a special Italian sweet bread that comes studded with raisins and looks like a tall golden chef's hat. This version is made even more delicious by the addition of marsala, a sweet Italian wine. When you buy the marsala, make sure you get a bottle that says "dry" and not "sweet."

DAK/WELBILT

½ cup dry marsala (see Note)

½ cup golden raisins

2¾ teaspoons yeast

⅓ cup sugar

½ teaspoon salt

¼ teaspoon ground cloves

¼ teaspoon anise seed

3 cups unbleached white flour (plus an additional 1 to 2 tablespoons if the dough still looks very wet after the first 10 minutes of kneading)

4 tablespoons sweet (unsalted) butter, very soft

1 tablespoon vanilla extract

¼ teaspoon orange oil

1 extra-large egg

1 extra-large egg yolk

¼ cup plus 1 tablespoon milk, heated to scalding and then cooled to room temperature

Grated zest of 1 large orange

See Note. Have all the ingredients at room temperature. Place all the ingredients except the raisins in the machine, program for Sweet Bread, and press Start. Add the raisins when the beeper sounds.

BETTY CROCKER, BLACK & DECKER, HITACHI, LARGE TOASTMASTER, AND WILLIAMS-SONOMA

½ cup dry marsala (see Note)

½ cup golden raisins

4 tablespoons sweet (unsalted) butter, very soft

1 tablespoon vanilla extract

¼ teaspoon orange oil

1 extra-large egg

1 extra-large egg yolk

¼ cup plus 1 tablespoon milk, heated to scalding and then cooled to room temperature

Grated zest of 1 large orange

⅓ cup sugar

½ teaspoon salt

¼ teaspoon ground cloves

¼ teaspoon anise seed

3 cups unbleached white flour (plus an additional 1 to 2 tablespoons if the dough still looks very wet after the first 10 minutes of kneading)

2½ teaspoons yeast (2 teaspoons for the Black & Decker and Large Toastmaster)

See Note. Place all the ingredients except the raisins in the machine, program for Mix Bread, Raisin Bread, Fruit and Nut, Basic, Basic Bread, or Sweet, and press Start. Add the raisins when the beeper sounds or during the last 5 minutes of the final knead cycle.

PANASONIC/NATIONAL

⅓ cup sugar

½ teaspoon salt

¼ teaspoon ground cloves

¼ teaspoon anise seed

3 cups unbleached white flour (plus an additional 1 to 2 tablespoons if the dough still looks very wet after the first 10 minutes of kneading)

½ cup dry marsala (see Note)

½ cup golden raisins

4 tablespoons sweet (unsalted) butter, very soft

1 tablespoon vanilla extract

¼ teaspoon orange oil

1 extra-large egg

1 extra-large egg yolk

Grated zest of 1 large orange

¼ cup plus 1 tablespoon milk, heated to scalding and then cooled to room temperature

2¾ teaspoons yeast

See Note. Place all the ingredients except the yeast and raisins in the machine. Place the yeast in the dispenser. Program for Basic Bread and press Start. Add the raisins after 20 minutes of kneading.

BREADMAN/TRILLIUM, LARGE OSTER, AND REGAL

½ cup dry marsala (see Note)

½ cup golden raisins

4 tablespoons sweet (unsalted) butter, very soft

1 tablespoon vanilla extract

¼ teaspoon orange oil

1 extra-large egg

1 extra-large egg yolk

¼ cup plus 1 tablespoon milk, heated to scalding and then cooled to room temperature

Grated zest of 1 large orange

⅓ cup sugar

½ teaspoon salt

¼ teaspoon ground cloves

¼ teaspoon anise seed

3 cups unbleached white flour (plus an additional 1 to 2 tablespoons if the dough still looks very wet after the first 10 minutes of kneading)

2½ teaspoons yeast

See Note. Place all the ingredients except the raisins in the machine, program for Raisin Bread, White, Basic Wheat, or Sweet, and press Start. Add the raisins when the beeper sounds or during the last 5 minutes of the final knead cycle.

LARGE PILLSBURY, WEST BEND, AND LARGE ZOJIRUSHI

½ cup dry marsala (see Note)

½ cup golden raisins

4 tablespoons sweet (unsalted) butter, very soft

1 tablespoon vanilla extract

¼ teaspoon orange oil

1 extra-large egg

1 extra-large egg yolk

¼ cup plus 1 tablespoon milk, heated to scalding and then cooled to room temperature

Grated zest of 1 large orange

⅓ cup sugar

½ teaspoon salt

¼ teaspoon ground cloves

¼ teaspoon anise seed

3 cups unbleached white flour (plus an additional 1 to 2 tablespoons if the dough still looks very wet after the first 10 minutes of kneading)

2½ teaspoons yeast

Continued

See Note. Place all the ingredients except the raisins in the machine, program for Raisin Bread, Basic, or White/Whole Grain, and press Start or On. Add the raisins when the beeper sounds or during the last 5 minutes of the final knead cycle.

MAXIM, SMALL OSTER, SMALL PILLSBURY, SANYO, SUNBEAM, SMALL TOASTMASTER, AND SMALL ZOJIRUSHI

⅓ cup dry marsala (see Note)

⅓ cup golden raisins

3 tablespoons sweet (unsalted) butter, very soft

2 teaspoons vanilla extract

¼ teaspoon orange oil

1 medium egg

1 medium egg yolk

3 tablespoons water

¼ cup sugar

3 tablespoons nonfat dry milk

½ teaspoon salt

¼ teaspoon ground cloves

¼ teaspoon anise seed

2 cups unbleached white flour

2 teaspoons yeast (1½ teaspoons for the Small Zojirushi)

Grated zest of 1 medium orange

See Note. Place all the ingredients except the raisins in the machine, program for Standard, Bread, Basic, Basic Bread, White, or Sweet, and press Start. Add the raisins when the beeper sounds or during the last 5 minutes of the final knead cycle.

SMALL WELBILT

⅓ cup dry marsala (see Note)

⅓ cup golden raisins

2 teaspoons yeast

¼ cup sugar

3 tablespoons nonfat dry milk

½ teaspoon salt

¼ teaspoon ground cloves

⅓ teaspoon anise seed

2 cups unbleached white flour

3 tablespoons sweet (unsalted) butter, very soft

2 teaspoons vanilla extract

¼ teaspoon orange oil

1 medium egg

1 medium egg yolk

3 tablespoons water

Grated zest of 1 medium orange

See Note. Have all the ingredients at room temperature. Place all the ingredients except the raisins in the machine, program for Medium, and press Start. Add the raisins when the beeper sounds.

SMALL PANASONIC/NATIONAL

⅓ cup dry marsala (see Note)

⅓ cup golden raisins

3 tablespoons sweet (unsalted) butter,
    very soft

2 teaspoons vanilla extract

¼ teaspoon orange oil

1 medium egg

1 medium egg yolk

3 tablespoons water

¼ cup sugar

3 tablespoons nonfat dry milk

½ teaspoon salt

¼ teaspoon ground cloves

¼ teaspoon anise seed

2 cups unbleached white flour

2 teaspoons yeast

Grated zest of 1 medium orange

See Note. Place all the ingredients except the yeast and raisins in the machine. Place the yeast in the dispenser. Program for Basic Bread and press Start. Add the raisins after 20 minutes of kneading.

NOTE: Place the marsala and raisins in a small pan or microwavable dish with a lid or covered with plastic wrap. On the stove or in the microwave, heat the liquid to a simmer and set aside until room temperature. Drain off the marsala and reserve it to use as an ingredient for the dough. There should be a total of 1 cup of liquid ingredients for the large machines and ⅔ cup of liquid ingredients for the small machines, which includes the marsala, milk, eggs, butter, and extracts. Add a little more marsala if necessary to equal the appropriate measure.

Reserve the raisins to add when appropriate for each machine.

SWEET BRIOCHE WITH DRIED CHERRIES

This is truly a wonderful loaf of bread with just the right combination of tastes and textures. Slightly sweet with the counterpoint of the tartness of the cherries, the bread is light and rich with a fine texture and is heavenly when toasted. Dried cherries are available in specialty food shops and by mail order (page 337).

DAK/WELBILT

1 tablespoon yeast

⅓ cup plus 2 tablespoons sugar

1 teaspoon salt

3¼ cups unbleached white flour

3 extra-large eggs

1 stick (4 ounces) sweet (unsalted) butter, melted and cooled to warm

½ cup water

½ cup dried cherries

Have all the ingredients at room temperature. Place all the ingredients except the cherries in the machine, program for White Bread, and press Start. When the beeper sounds, add the cherries.

BETTY CROCKER, BLACK & DECKER, HITACHI, LARGE TOASTMASTER, AND WILLIAMS-SONOMA

2 extra-large eggs

⅔ stick sweet (unsalted) butter, melted and cooled to warm

6 tablespoons water

6 tablespoons sugar

½ teaspoon salt

2⅔ cups plus 2 tablespoons unbleached white flour

2 teaspoons yeast (2 teaspoons for the Black & Decker and Large Toastmaster)

½ cup dried cherries

Place all the ingredients except the cherries in the machine, program for Mix Bread, Raisin Bread, Fruit and Nut, Bread, Basic Bread, or Sweet, and press Start. Add the cherries when the beeper sounds or during the last 5 minutes of the final knead cycle.

PANASONIC/NATIONAL

2 extra-large eggs

⅔ stick sweet (unsalted) butter, melted
  and cooled to warm

6 tablespoons water

6 tablespoons sugar

½ teaspoon salt

2⅔ cups plus 2 tablespoons unbleached
  white flour

2½ teaspoons yeast

½ cup dried cherries

Place all the ingredients except the yeast and cherries in the machine. Place the yeast in the dispenser. Program for Basic Bread and press Start. Add the cherries in 20 minutes at the end of the preknead cycle.

BREADMAN/TRILLIUM, LARGE OSTER, AND REGAL

2 extra-large eggs

⅔ stick sweet (unsalted) butter, melted
  and cooled to warm

6 tablespoons water

6 tablespoons sugar

½ teaspoon salt

2⅔ cups plus 2 tablespoons unbleached
  white flour

2½ teaspoons yeast

½ cup dried cherries

Place all the ingredients except the cherries in the machine, program for Raisin Bread, White, Basic Wheat, or Sweet, and press Start. Add the cherries when the beeper sounds or during the last 5 minutes of the final knead cycle.

LARGE PILLSBURY, WEST BEND, AND LARGE ZOJIRUSHI

3 extra-large eggs

1 stick (4 ounces) sweet (unsalted)
  butter, melted and cooled to warm

½ cup water

⅓ cup plus 2 tablespoons sugar

1 teaspoon salt

3½ cups unbleached white flour

1 tablespoon yeast

½ cup dried cherries

Continued

313

Place all the ingredients except the cherries in the machine, program for Raisin Bread, Basic, Basic Bread, White, Basic Wheat, White/Whole Grain, or Sweet, and press Start or On. Add the cherries when the beeper sounds or during the last 5 minutes of the final knead cycle.

....

Maxim, Small Oster, Small Pillsbury, Sanyo, Sunbeam, Small Toastmaster, and Small Zojirushi

2 medium eggs
½ stick (2 ounces) sweet (unsalted) butter, melted and cooled to warm
⅓ cup water
3 tablespoons plus 1 teaspoon sugar
¼ teaspoon salt

1¾ cups plus 2 tablespoons unbleached white flour
1½ teaspoons yeast (1 teaspoon for the Small Zojirushi)
½ cup dried cherries

Place all the ingredients except the cherries in the machine, program for Standard, Bread, Basic Bread, White, Basic Wheat, or Sweet, and press Start. Add the cherries when the beeper sounds or during the last 5 minutes of the final knead cycle.

....

Small Welbilt

1¾ teaspoons yeast
3 tablespoons plus 1 teaspoon sugar
¼ teaspoon salt
1¾ cups plus 2 tablespoons unbleached white flour

2 medium eggs
½ stick (2 ounces) sweet (unsalted) butter, melted and cooled to warm
⅓ cup water
½ cup dried cherries

Have all the ingredients except the butter at room temperature. Place all the ingredients except the cherries in the machine, program for Medium, and press Start. Add the cherries when the beeper sounds or during the last 5 minutes of the final knead cycle.

....

SMALL PANASONIC/NATIONAL

3 tablespoons plus 1 teaspoon sugar
¼ teaspoon salt
1¾ cups plus 2 tablespoons unbleached
   white flour
2 medium eggs

½ stick (2 ounces) sweet (unsalted)
   butter, melted and cooled to warm
⅓ cup water
1½ teaspoons yeast
½ cup dried cherries

Place all the ingredients except the yeast and cherries in the machine. Place the yeast in the dispenser. Program for Basic Bread and press Start. Add the cherries in 20 minutes at the end of the preknead cycle.

Variation: We've also made this bread using dried blueberries and cranberries. The results are just marvelous. If you want a plain brioche, leave out the fruit altogether.

STICKY BUNS

These rich, buttery coffee cakes are topped with a scrumptious, gooey brown sugar glaze, and should be eaten as soon as they are cool enough to serve but still hot enough to keep the caramel soft. As if they'll last until they're cold!

....

DAK/Welbilt

1 tablespoon yeast

3⅓ cups unbleached white flour

½ teaspoon salt

½ cup plus 2 tablespoons sugar

¾ cup water

4 tablespoons nonfat dry milk

4 tablespoons butter, softened or melted and cooled

2 extra-large eggs

1 extra-large egg yolk

Have all the ingredients at room temperature. Place all the ingredients in the machine, program for Manual, and press Start. When the cycle is completed, place the dough in a large well-oiled bowl. Cover tightly with plastic wrap and refrigerate overnight. Follow the Assembly Instructions on page 319.

....

Betty Crocker, Black & Decker, Hitachi, Large Toastmaster, and Williams-Sonoma

¾ cup water

4 tablespoons butter, softened or melted and cooled

2 extra-large eggs

½ teaspoon salt

½ cup sugar

3¼ cups unbleached white flour

3 tablespoons nonfat dry milk

2½ teaspoons yeast (2 teaspoons for the Black & Decker and Large Toastmaster)

Place all the ingredients in the machine, program for Dough or Manual, and press Start. When the cycle is completed, place the dough in a large well-oiled bowl. Cover tightly with plastic wrap and refrigerate overnight. Follow the Assembly Instructions on page 319.

PANASONIC/NATIONAL

½ teaspoon salt

½ cup sugar

3 cups unbleached white flour (plus an additional 2 tablespoons if the dough is still sticky after 10 minutes of kneading)

3 tablespoons nonfat dry milk

¾ cup water

4 tablespoons butter, softened or melted and cooled

2 extra-large eggs

1 tablespoon yeast

Place all the ingredients except the yeast in the machine. Place the yeast in the dispenser. Program for Dough or Manual and press Start. When the cycle is completed, place the dough in a large well-oiled bowl. Cover tightly with plastic wrap and refrigerate overnight. Follow the Assembly Instructions on page 319.

LARGE PILLSBURY, REGAL, LARGE OSTER, LARGE ZOJIRUSHI, WEST BEND, AND BREADMAN/TRILLIUM

¾ cup water

4 tablespoons nonfat dry milk

4 tablespoons butter, softened or melted and cooled

2 extra-large eggs

½ teaspoon salt

½ cup plus 2 tablespoons sugar

3⅓ cups unbleached white flour

1 tablespoon yeast

Place all the ingredients in the machine, program for Dough or Manual, and press Start or On. When the cycle is completed, place the dough in a large well-oiled bowl. Cover tightly with plastic wrap and refrigerate overnight. Follow the Assembly Instructions on page 319.

Maxim, Small Oster, Small Pillsbury, Sanyo, Sunbeam, Small Toastmaster, and Small Zojirushi

5 tablespoons water

2 tablespoons butter, softened or melted and cooled

2 medium eggs

1 medium egg yolk

½ teaspoon salt

5 tablespoons sugar

2⅓ cups unbleached white flour

2 tablespoons nonfat dry milk

2 teaspoons yeast (1 teaspoon for the Small Zojirushi)

Place all the ingredients in the machine, program for Dough or Manual, and press Start. When the cycle is completed, place the dough in a large well-oiled bowl. Cover tightly with plastic wrap and refrigerate overnight. Follow the Assembly Instructions on page 320.

Small Welbilt

2 teaspoons yeast

½ teaspoon salt

5 tablespoons sugar

2⅓ cups unbleached white flour

2 tablespoons nonfat dry milk

5 tablespoons water

2 tablespoons butter, softened or melted and cooled

2 medium eggs

1 medium egg yolk

Have all the ingredients at room temperature. Place all the ingredients in the machine, program for Manual, and press Start. When the cycle is completed, place the dough in a large well-oiled bowl. Cover tightly with plastic wrap and refrigerate overnight. Follow the Assembly Instructions on page 320.

Small Panasonic/National

½ teaspoon salt

5 tablespoons sugar

2⅓ cups unbleached white flour

2 tablespoons nonfat dry milk

5 tablespoons water

2 tablespoons butter, softened or melted and cooled

2 medium eggs

1 medium egg yolk

2 teaspoons yeast

Place all the ingredients except the yeast in the machine. Place the yeast in the dispenser. Program for Dough or Manual and press Start. When the cycle is completed, place the dough in a large well-oiled bowl. Cover tightly with plastic wrap and refrigerate overnight. Follow the Assembly Instructions on page 320.

Assembly Instructions (large machines)

Filling

⅔ cup dark brown sugar, firmly packed

1 teaspoon ground cinnamon

⅔ cup raisins OR ⅔ cup chopped dried apricots

½ cup chopped nuts of your choice

On a floured board, roll the dough to an approximately 18 x 10-inch rectangle. Sprinkle the combined filling ingredients evenly in a 6-inch strip down the center of the dough, leaving a margin of about 2 inches on each end. Roll the dough up the long way, ending up with a roll about 20 inches long. Place it, seam side down, on the board. Prepare the following topping.

Topping

¾ cup dark brown sugar, firmly packed

½ cup raisins

½ cup chopped walnuts

4 tablespoons butter, softened

Mix all the ingredients in a bowl. Then assemble the sticky buns.

Assembly Instructions (small machines)

Filling

½ cup dark brown sugar, firmly packed
½ teaspoon ground cinnamon

½ cup raisins OR ⅔ cup chopped apricots
⅓ cup chopped nuts of your choice

On a floured board, roll the dough to an approximately 14 x 8-inch rectangle. Sprinkle the combined filling ingredients evenly in a 6-inch strip down the center of the dough, leaving a margin of about 2 inches on each end. Roll the dough up the long way, ending up with a roll about 14 inches long. Place it, seam side down, on the board. Prepare the following topping.

Topping

½ cup dark brown sugar, firmly packed
⅓ cup raisins

⅓ cup chopped walnuts
3 tablespoons butter, softened

Mix all the ingredients in a bowl. Then assemble the sticky buns.

To Assemble the Sticky Buns

Generously butter or grease either an 11 x 5-inch rectangular baking dish (large machines) or a 9-inch square or 10-inch round cake pan (small machines). Sprinkle the topping on the bottom of the prepared pan. Slice the roll into 8 pieces (large machines) or 6 pieces (small machines) and place them, cut side up, in the pan, where they will fit right next to each other around the edge of the pan with 2 or 3 in the center.

Cover them with plastic wrap and let rise in a warm, draft-free place for 1 hour, or until approximately doubled in size. Preheat the oven to 375°F with the rack in the center position and bake for 25 to 30 minutes, or until the tops are golden brown. Immediately invert them onto a serving platter or cookie sheet. Serve them hot from the oven but be careful not to burn your mouth on the hot sugared topping.

Tips: If you don't have a warm place in your house to let the dough rise, set your oven on its lowest bake setting and leave the door ajar. Let the dough rise on an upper rack, checking it carefully to make sure the oven doesn't get hot. You don't want it warmer than 100°F.   The filling is prone to drip over the sides of the pan. To protect your oven, line a cookie sheet with foil, dull side up, and place it directly under the pan.

If the tops look like they are getting too brown, cover the pan loosely with a piece of foil, dull side up.

Variations: Add ½ cup golden raisins to the dough during the final 10 minutes of kneading.

Add ½ teaspoon powdered cardamom and the finely grated zest of 1 lemon or orange along with the other ingredients.

Just before baking, glaze the tops with 1 egg slightly beaten and dust lightly with cinnamon sugar.

Substitute 1½ cups apricot preserves for the caramel filling (easier on the teeth), then when they're finished baking, glaze the tops with a mixture of 1 cup sifted confectioners' sugar and 3 tablespoons hot water.

SHERRY TEA BREAD

This is the world's best raisin bread. The flavors are sublime, the texture is heavenly, and the aroma while it is baking will perfume your entire house. This bread rises dramatically high, forming a generous loaf with a deep brown crust and a tender, sweetly scented interior.

....

DAK/WELBILT

1 tablespoon yeast

1 cup whole wheat flour

2 cups unbleached white flour

1 teaspoon salt

½ teaspoon ground nutmeg

1 tablespoon gluten OR 2 teaspoons Lora Brody's Bread Dough Enhancer™

½ cup dry sherry

½ cup heavy cream

2 tablespoons pure maple syrup

2 tablespoons butter

⅔ cup currants

½ cup walnuts, broken into large pieces

Heat the sherry and cream together to a simmer. Cool to room temperature. Have all the other ingredients at room temperature. Place all the ingredients except the currants and walnuts in the machine, program for White Bread, and press Start. When the beeper sounds during the last kneading, add the currants and walnuts.

....

Betty Crocker, Black & Decker, Hitachi, Large Toastmaster, and Williams-Sonoma

½ cup dry sherry

½ cup heavy cream

2 tablespoons pure maple syrup

2 tablespoons butter, at room temperature

1 cup whole wheat flour

2 cups unbleached white flour

1 teaspoon salt

½ teaspoon ground nutmeg

1 tablespoon gluten OR 2 teaspoons Lora Brody's Bread Dough Enhancer™

2½ teaspoons yeast (2 teaspoons for the Black & Decker and Large Toastmaster)

⅔ cup currants

½ cup walnuts, broken into large pieces

Heat the sherry and cream together to a simmer. Cool to room temperature. Place all the ingredients except the currants and walnuts in the machine, program for Mix Bread, Raisin Bread, Fruit and Nut, Basic, Basic Bread, or Sweet, and press Start. Add the currants and walnuts when the beeper sounds or during the last 5 minutes of the final knead cycle.

Panasonic/National

1 cup whole wheat flour

2 cups unbleached white flour

1 teaspoon salt

½ teaspoon ground nutmeg

1 tablespoon gluten OR 2 teaspoons Lora Brody's Bread Dough Enhancer™

½ cup dry sherry

½ cup heavy cream

2 tablespoons pure maple syrup

2 tablespoons butter, at room temperature

1 tablespoon yeast

⅔ cup currants

½ cup walnuts, broken into large pieces

Heat the sherry and cream together to a simmer. Cool to room temperature. Place all the ingredients except the yeast, currants, and walnuts in the machine. Place the yeast in the dispenser. Program for Basic Bread and press Start. After the first kneading is completed, add the currants and walnuts.

REGAL, LARGE OSTER, WEST BEND, LARGE PILLSBURY, LARGE ZOJIRUSHI, AND BREADMAN/TRILLIUM

½ cup dry sherry

½ cup heavy cream

2 tablespoons pure maple syrup

2 tablespoons butter, at room
  temperature

1 cup whole wheat flour

2 cups unbleached white flour

1 teaspoon salt

½ teaspoon ground nutmeg

1 tablespoon gluten OR 2 teaspoons Lora
  Brody's Bread Dough Enhancer™

1 tablespoon yeast

⅔ cup currants

½ cup walnuts, broken into large pieces

Heat the sherry and cream together to a simmer. Cool to room temperature. Place all the ingredients except the currants and walnuts in the machine, program for Raisin Bread, Basic, Basic Bread, White, Basic Wheat, White/Whole Grain, or Sweet, and press Start or On. Add the currants and walnuts when the beeper sounds or during the last 5 minutes of the final knead cycle.

MAXIM, SMALL OSTER, SMALL PILLSBURY, SANYO, SUNBEAM, SMALL TOASTMASTER, AND SMALL ZOJIRUSHI

⅓ cup dry sherry

⅓ cup heavy cream

1½ tablespoons pure maple syrup

½ tablespoon butter, at room
  temperature

⅔ cup whole wheat flour

1⅓ cups unbleached white flour

½ teaspoon salt

¼ teaspoon ground nutmeg

2 teaspoons gluten OR 1½ teaspoons Lora
  Brody's Bread Dough Enhancer™

2 teaspoons yeast (1½ teaspoons for
  the Small Zojirushi)

½ cup currants

⅓ cup walnuts, broken into large pieces

Heat the sherry and cream together to a simmer. Cool to room temperature. Place all the ingredients except the currants and walnuts in the machine. Program for Mix Bread, Bread, Basic, Basic Bread, White, Basic Wheat, White/Whole Grain, or Sweet, and press Start. Add the currants and walnuts when the beeper sounds or during the last 5 minutes of the final knead cycle.

SMALL WELBILT

2 teaspoons yeast

⅔ cup whole wheat flour

1⅓ cups unbleached white flour

½ teaspoon salt

¼ teaspoon ground nutmeg

2 teaspoons gluten OR 1½ teaspoons Lora
Brody's Bread Dough Enhancer™

⅓ cup dry sherry

⅓ cup heavy cream

1½ tablespoons pure maple syrup

½ tablespoon butter

½ cup currants

⅓ cup walnuts, broken into large pieces

Heat the sherry and cream together to a simmer. Cool to room temperature. Have all the rest of the ingredients at room temperature. Place all the ingredients except the currants and walnuts in the machine, program for Medium, and press Start. Add the currants and walnuts when the beeper sounds or during the last 5 minutes of the final knead cycle.

SMALL PANASONIC/NATIONAL

⅓ cup dry sherry

⅓ cup heavy cream

1½ tablespoons pure maple syrup

½ tablespoon butter, at room
temperature

⅔ cup whole wheat flour

1⅓ cups unbleached white flour

½ teaspoon salt

¼ teaspoon ground nutmeg

2 teaspoons gluten OR 1½ teaspoons Lora
Brody's Bread Dough Enhancer™

2 teaspoons yeast

½ cup currants

⅓ cup walnuts, broken into large pieces

Heat the sherry and cream together to a simmer. Cool to room temperature. Place all the ingredients except the yeast, currants, and walnuts in the machine. Place the yeast in the dispenser. Program for Basic Bread and press Start. Add the currants and walnuts 20 minutes into the first kneading.

CHOCOLATE YEAST CAKE

To make this cake, you must have a bread machine baking pan with a solid or sealed bottom (no hole when you remove the pan from the machine) because the sponge is very thin and will leak through.

....

FOR ALL LARGE MACHINES
FOR THE SPONGE

¾ cup milk, heated to a simmer and
    then cooled to lukewarm
¼ cup warm water
1 tablespoon sugar

1½ cups unbleached white flour
1 tablespoon yeast (2 teaspoons for the
    Black & Decker, the Breadman/
    Trillium and Toastmaster)

For Hitachi, Regal, and Zojirushi, place all the ingredients in the machine. For Panasonic and National, place the yeast in the dispenser. Program for Dough or Manual and press Start or On. When it's finished, transfer the mixture to a mixing bowl.

TO COMPLETE THE CAKE BATTER

1¼ cups unbleached white flour,
    measured after sifting
1 teaspoon baking soda
½ teaspoon salt
¼ teaspoon ground nutmeg
¼ teaspoon ground cinnamon
¾ cup (1½ sticks) butter, at room
    temperature

2 cups sugar
3 extra-large eggs
⅔ cup unsweetened cocoa
½ cup hot water
1 teaspoon vanilla extract
1 cup finely chopped pecans

Generously grease a one-piece tube pan (not a pan with a removable bottom), line the bottom with waxed paper, butter the paper, and dust the pan with flour.

In a bowl, combine the flour, baking soda, salt, nutmeg, and cinnamon. In a large mixing bowl, cream the butter and sugar until light and fluffy. Add the eggs and beat well. In another bowl, combine the cocoa and hot water and mix until the cocoa is dissolved. Add the cocoa mixture to the egg mixture. Mix in the flour mixture, the vanilla, then the sponge. Either by hand or with an electric mixer, beat for an additional 5 minutes, scraping the sides and bottom of the bowl. Stir in the pecans.

Pour and scrape the batter into the prepared pan and use a rubber spatula to level the top. Place the pan, uncovered, in a warm, draft-free place for about 2½ hours, or until the batter has doubled in bulk.

Preheat the oven to 350°F with the rack in the center position. Bake for 45 minutes, checking the interior with a cake tester to make sure it is done. Cool for 10 minutes on a cake rack before unmolding. Cool completely before serving.

To serve, whip 2 cups (1 pint) heavy or whipping cream with 3 tablespoons sugar until it forms stiff peaks. Add 1 tablespoon vanilla extract. Cut the cake into small wedges (it's very rich) and serve with whipped cream.

NOTE: Your cake may not rise to double its bulk, even after 3 hours. Bake it anyway—it will rise more during the first part of the baking.

CHOCOLATE PECAN BISCOTTI

Biscotti are Italian cookies that are twice-baked, first as a loaf, then sliced into bars and baked again. In this rich, chocolaty version, the dough is baked once in the bread machine and then in the oven. Biscotti are perfect for dipping in dessert wine, cappuccino, or espresso.

Don't use Dutch-processed cocoa in this recipe, as it burns too easily. We prefer Hershey's.

DAK/Welbilt

1 tablespoon yeast
1 tablespoon instant coffee
¼ cup unsweetened cocoa
3 cups unbleached white flour
⅓ cup sugar
½ cup whole milk ricotta cheese
4 tablespoons sweet (unsalted) butter

2 extra-large eggs
⅓ cup milk, heated to a simmer and
then cooled to room temperature
¼ cup Nutella
½ cup pecans, chopped
½ cup chocolate chips

Have all the ingredients at room temperature. Place all the ingredients except the pecans and chocolate chips in the machine, program for White Bread or Manual, and press Start. When the beeper sounds at the end of the second kneading, add the pecans and chocolate chips. At the end of the kneading, remove the dough from the machine and form it into 2 thick logs approximately 12 x 3½ inches. Place the logs on a greased baking sheet. Cover with a clean dish towel and let rise in a warm, draft-free place until doubled in bulk. This will take anywhere from 2 to 4 hours. Follow the Baking Instructions on page 332.

Betty Crocker, Black & Decker, Hitachi, Large Toastmaster, Williams-Sonoma, Breadman/Trillium, Large Oster, Regal, Large Pillsbury, West Bend, and Large Zojirushi

½ cup whole milk ricotta cheese

4 tablespoons sweet (unsalted) butter

2 extra-large eggs

⅓ cup milk, heated to a simmer and then cooled to room temperature

¼ cup Nutella

1 tablespoon instant coffee

¼ cup unsweetened cocoa

3 cups unbleached white flour

⅓ cup sugar

1 tablespoon yeast (2 teaspoons for the Black & Decker and Large Toastmaster)

½ cup pecans, chopped

½ cup chocolate chips

Place all the ingredients except the pecans and chocolate chips in the machine, program for Knead and First Rise or Dough, and press Start or On. When the beeper sounds or during the last 5 minutes of the final knead cycle, add the pecans and chocolate chips. At the end of the kneading, remove the dough from the machine and form it into 2 thick logs approximately 12 x 3½ inches. Place the logs on a greased baking sheet. Cover with a clean dish towel and let rise in a warm, draft-free place until doubled in bulk. This will take anywhere from 2 to 4 hours. Follow the Baking Instructions on page 332.

Panasonic/National

1 tablespoon instant coffee

¼ cup unsweetened cocoa

3 cups unbleached white flour

⅓ cup sugar

½ cup whole milk ricotta cheese

4 tablespoons sweet (unsalted) butter

2 extra-large eggs

⅓ cup milk, heated to a simmer and then cooled to room temperature

¼ cup Nutella

1 tablespoon yeast

½ cup pecans, chopped

½ cup chocolate chips

Continued

Place all the ingredients except the yeast, pecans, and chocolate chips in the machine. Place the yeast in the dispenser. Program for Dough or Manual. Add the pecans and chocolate chips 20 minutes into the kneading. At the end of the kneading, remove the dough from the machine and form it into 2 thick logs approximately 12 x 3½ inches. Place the logs on a greased baking sheet. Cover with a clean dish towel and let rise in a warm, draft-free place until doubled in bulk. This will take anywhere from 2 to 4 hours. Follow the Baking Instructions on page 332.

Maxim, Small Oster, Small Pillsbury, Sanyo, Sunbeam, Small Toastmaster, and Small Zojirushi

¼ cup plus 1 tablespoon whole milk
 ricotta cheese
3 tablespoons sweet (unsalted) butter
2 medium eggs
¼ cup milk, heated to a simmer and
 then cooled to room temperature
¼ cup Nutella
2 teaspoons instant coffee

3 tablespoons unsweetened cocoa
2 cups plus 2 tablespoons unbleached
 white flour
¼ cup sugar
2 teaspoons yeast (1½ teaspoons for
 the Small Zojirushi)
⅓ cup pecans, chopped
⅓ cup chocolate chips

Place all the ingredients except the pecans and chocolate chips in the machine, program for Dough or Manual, and press Start. When the beeper sounds or during the last 5 minutes of the final knead cycle, add the pecans and chocolate chips. At the end of the kneading, remove the dough from the machine and form it into a thick log approximately 9 x 3 inches. Place the log on a greased baking sheet. Cover with a clean dish towel and let rise in a warm, draft-free place until doubled in bulk. This will take anywhere from 2 to 4 hours. Follow the Baking Instructions on page 332.

Small Welbilt

2 teaspoons yeast

2 teaspoons instant coffee

3 tablespoons unsweetened cocoa

2 cups plus 2 tablespoons unbleached
white flour

1/4 cup sugar

1/4 cup plus 1 tablespoon whole milk
ricotta cheese

3 tablespoons sweet (unsalted) butter

2 medium eggs

1/4 cup milk, heated to a simmer and
then cooled to room temperature

1/4 cup Nutella

1/3 cup pecans, chopped

1/3 cup chocolate chips

Have all the ingredients at room temperature. Place all the ingredients except the pecans and chocolate chips in the machine, program for Manual, and press Start. When the beeper sounds or during the last 5 minutes of the final knead cycle, add the pecans and chocolate chips. At the end of the kneading, remove the dough from the machine and form it into a thick log approximately 9 x 3 inches. Place the log on a greased baking sheet. Cover with a clean dish towel and let rise in a warm, draft-free place until doubled in bulk. This will take anywhere from 2 to 4 hours. Follow the Baking Instructions on page 332.

Small Panasonic/National

2 teaspoons instant coffee

3 tablespoons unsweetened cocoa

2 cups plus 2 tablespoons unbleached
white flour

1/4 cup sugar

1/4 cup plus 1 tablespoon whole milk
ricotta cheese

3 tablespoons sweet (unsalted) butter

2 medium eggs

1/4 cup milk, heated to a simmer and
then cooled to room temperature

1/4 cup Nutella

1/3 cup pecans, chopped

1/3 cup chocolate chips

2 teaspoons yeast

Continued

Place all the ingredients except the pecans, chocolate chips, and yeast in the machine. Place the yeast in the dispenser. Program for Dough or Manual and press Start. Five minutes before the end of the second kneading, add the pecans and chocolate chips. At the end of the kneading, remove the dough from the machine and form it into a thick log approximately 9 x 3 inches. Place the log on a greased baking sheet. Cover with a clean dish towel and let rise in a warm, draft-free place until doubled in bulk. This will take anywhere from 2 to 4 hours. Follow the Baking Instructions below.

BAKING INSTRUCTIONS

Preheat the oven to 350°F with the rack in the center position. Bake the logs for 40 to 45 minutes (cut one in half to make sure the center is done). Cool them for 10 minutes on a rack, and then cut them into 1½-inch-thick slices. Arrange the slices on their sides on the baking sheet and return the baking sheet to the oven for 5 minutes. At the end of that time, turn the cookies over and bake an additional 5 minutes. The object is to just dry the cookies a bit—not to brown them. If you want to really jazz these up, dip the ends in chocolate glaze:

¾ cup heavy cream

9 ounces best-quality semisweet or bittersweet chocolate, broken into pieces

Scald the cream in a small pan. Off the heat, add the chocolate and stir until smooth. Cool slightly before dipping the biscotti. Place the biscotti on plastic wrap or waxed paper to dry. Do not refrigerate.

Stored in an airtight container, these biscotti, both dipped and undipped, will keep for several weeks.

BRAIDED ALMOND COFFEE CAKE

Even with the bread machine, this is a time-consuming job, but the results are out of this world and well worth the effort.

....

DAK/WELBILT, PANASONIC/NATIONAL, REGAL, LARGE OSTER, WEST BEND, LARGE PILLSBURY, AND LARGE ZOJIRUSHI

¾ cup (1½ sticks) sweet (unsalted) butter, at room temperature

¼ cup milk

½ cup sour cream

1 tablespoon vanilla extract

3 extra-large egg yolks

3 cups unbleached white flour (plus up to an additional ¼ cup if necessary)

½ teaspoon salt

⅓ cup sugar

4 teaspoons yeast

....

BLACK & DECKER, BETTY CROCKER, BREADMAN/TRILLIUM, HITACHI, LARGE TOASTMASTER, AND WILLIAMS-SONOMA

¾ cup (1½ sticks) sweet (unsalted) butter, at room temperature

¼ cup milk

½ cup sour cream

1 tablespoon vanilla extract

3 extra-large egg yolks

3 cups unbleached white flour (plus up to an additional ¼ cup if necessary)

½ teaspoon salt

⅓ cup sugar

1 tablespoon yeast (2 teaspoons for the Black & Decker, 1½ teaspoons for the Toastmaster)

For DAK and Welbilt, have all the ingredients at room temperature. For all other machines, place all the ingredients in the machine. For the Panasonic and National, place the yeast in the dispenser. Program for Manual, Dough, or Knead and First Rise, and press Start or On.

If after the first 10 minutes the dough is still very wet and sticky, add

333

additional flour, 1 tablespoon at a time, up to ¼ cup. You can tell if it's too wet if there is a layer on the very bottom of the pan that is not being incorporated into the ball. Remember that as the dough is kneaded and the gluten in the flour is activated, more flour will be absorbed and the dough will become less wet. Don't rush to add flour until you are sure it is necessary.

At the end of the final cycle, remove the dough from the machine, flour it lightly (the dough will be sticky), and place in a large bowl and cover tightly with plastic wrap. Refrigerate for at least 2 hours or up to overnight.

To Form the Braid

1 egg (any size)	½ cup sugar
1 tablespoon water	½ cup sliced almonds

Line a heavy-duty baking sheet with foil, shiny side down. Lightly butter or grease the foil. In a small bowl, mix together the egg and water. Remove the dough from the refrigerator and punch it down. Lightly flour a smooth work surface and place the dough on it. Use scissors or a sharp knife to cut the dough into 3 equal pieces. Use your hands to squeeze and roll each piece to an 18-inch length.

Dip one end of each length into the egg glaze and then pinch the 3 ends together. Braid the 3 pieces together and seal the other end by painting it with the egg glaze and pinching it together.

Place the braid on the prepared sheet and brush it generously with the egg glaze. Sprinkle with half the sugar. Sprinkle the almonds on top of the sugar and then dribble the egg glaze over the almonds. Sprinkle with the remaining sugar.

Let the braid rise, uncovered, in a warm, draft-free place for 40 minutes, or until it has doubled in bulk.

Preheat the oven to 350°F with the rack in the center position. Bake the braid for 50 minutes, or until golden brown. This is best served the same day, preferably warm from the oven or reheated.

Maxim, Small Oster, Small Pillsbury, Sanyo, Sunbeam, Small Toastmaster, and Small Zojirushi

½ cup (1 stick) sweet (unsalted) butter, at room temperature

3 tablespoons milk

⅓ cup sour cream

2 teaspoons vanilla extract

2 extra-large egg yolks

2 cups unbleached white flour (plus an additional 1 to 3 tablespoons if necessary)

¼ teaspoon salt

3 tablespoons sugar

2½ teaspoons yeast (2 teaspoons for the Small Zojirushi)

Place all the ingredients in the machine, program for Dough or Manual, and press Start.

If after the first 10 minutes the dough is still very wet and sticky, add additional flour, 1 tablespoon at a time, up to 3 tablespoons. You can tell if it's too wet if there is a layer on the very bottom of the pan that is not being incorporated into the ball. Remember that as the dough is kneaded and the gluten in the flour is activated, more flour will be absorbed and the dough will become less wet. Don't rush to add flour until you are sure it is necessary.

At the end of the final cycle, remove the dough from the machine, flour it lightly (the dough will be sticky), and place in a large bowl and cover tightly with plastic wrap. Refrigerate for at least 2 hours or up to overnight.

To Form the Braid

1 egg (any size)

1 tablespoon water

⅓ cup sugar

⅓ cup sliced almonds

Line a heavy-duty baking sheet with foil, shiny side down. Lightly butter or grease the foil. In a small bowl, mix together the egg and water. Remove the dough from the refrigerator and punch it down. Lightly flour a smooth work surface and place the dough on it. Use scissors or a sharp knife to cut the dough in 3 equal pieces. Use your hands to squeeze and roll each piece into a 12- to 14-inch length.

Dip one end of each length into the egg glaze and then pinch the 3 ends

together. Braid the 3 pieces together and seal the other end by painting it with the egg glaze and pinching it together.

Place the braid on the prepared sheet and brush it generously with the egg glaze. Sprinkle with half the sugar. Sprinkle the almonds on top of the sugar and then dribble the egg glaze over the almonds. Sprinkle with the remaining sugar.

Let the braid rise, uncovered, in a warm, draft-free place for 40 minutes, or until it has doubled in bulk.

Preheat the oven to 350°F with the rack in the center position. Bake the braid for 50 minutes, until golden brown or until the bread has an internal temperature of 190° to 200°F. This is best served the same day, preferably warm from the oven or reheated.

MAIL-ORDER
GUIDE

FLOURS AND GRAINS

King Arthur Flour
RR2, P.O. Box 56
Norwich, VT 05055
800-827-6836
Send for the amazing free catalogue—full of bakers' treasures.

Birkett Mills
P.O. Box 440
Penn Yan, NY 14527
315-536-3311

Kenyon's Corn Meal Company
Usquepaugh, West Kingston, RI 02892
401-783-4054
800-753-6966

ORGANIC FLOURS, GRAINS, AND OTHER PRODUCTS

Arrowhead Mills
110 South Lawton
Hereford, TX 79045
806-364-0730
800-749-0730

Bob's Red Mill Natural Foods, Inc.
5209 SE International Way
Milwaukee, OR 97222
503-654-3215

Bouchard Family Farm
Route 1
Fort Kent, ME 04743
207-834-3237
800-239-3237

Brewster River Gristmill
Mill Street
Jeffersonville, VT 05464
802-644-2987

Deer Valley Farm
P.O. Box 173
Guilford, NY 13780–0173
607-764-8556

Eagle Organic and Natural Food
407 Church Avenue
Huntsville, AR 72740
501-738-2203

G. B. Ratto & Co.
821 Washington Street
Oakland, CA 94607
510-832-6503

Jaffe Bros., Inc.
P.O. Box 636
Valley Center, CA 92082
619-749-1133
FAX 207-785-4907

Walnut Acres
Penns Creek, PA 17862
800-433-3998

SOURDOUGH STARTERS AND MIXES

King Arthur Flour
RR2, P.O. Box 56
Norwich, VT 05055
800-827-6836

Sourdough International, Inc.
Dr. Ed Wood
P.O. Box 993
Cascade, OH 83611
800-888-9567

CHILES AND OTHER SOUTHWESTERN INGREDIENTS

Los Chileros de Nuevo Mexico
P.O. Box 6215
Santa Fe, NM 87501
505-471-6967

ORGANIC NUTS AND SEEDS

Jaffe Bros., Inc.
P.O. Box 636
Valley Center, CA 92082
619-749-1133
FAX 207-785-4907

OTHER SOURCES

American Spoon Foods
P.O. Box 566
Petoskey, MI 49770
616-347-9030
800-222-5886
Dried cherries, blueberries, and cranberries

Chukar Cherries
306 Wine Country Road
Prosser, WA 99350
800-624-9544
Dried cranberries and blueberries, sweet and tart dried cherries

Jessica's Biscuit Cookbook Catalogue
P.O. Box 301
Newtonville, MA 02160
800-878-4264
An incredibly wide selection of cookbooks on just about every subject

The Magic Bread Letter
P.O. Box 337
Moss Beach, CA 94038–0337
415-728-3502
The world's best newsletter on baking with bread machines

Magic Mill
1911 South 3850 West
Salt Lake City, UT 84014
801-467-9906
800-888-8587

SUPERIOR ELECTRIC GRAIN MILLS FOR HOUSEHOLD USE

Market Spice
P.O. Box 2935
Redmond, WA 98073
206-883-1220
Herbs, spices, seasonings, and tea

The Vermont Country Store
P.O. Box 3000
Manchester Center, VT 05255
802-362-2400
Cornmeal, cereals, and other baking ingredients

Williams-Sonoma
P.O. Box 7456
San Francisco, CA 94120-7456
800-541-2233
Boyajian garlic, chili, lemon, and orange oils

The Wooden Spoon
P.O. Box 931
Clinton, CT 06413
800-431-2207
Wide selection of useful and hard-to-find cooking supplies

If you are looking for a great place to store your loaves, consider the handsome lucite bread box from Wanda's Nature Farm Foods. You can order one by calling 800-222-3276.

INDEX

345